fighters should be
gentlemen

the story of JIMMY MCLARNIN, CANADA'S GREATEST BOXER

Des Corry

Produced by:

FriesenPress

Suite 300 – 852 Fort Street
Victoria, BC, Canada V8W 1H8

www.friesenpress.com

Distributed to the trade by The Ingram Book Company

Table of Contents

Acknowledgements

I wish very much to mention the amount of help I have had with this book about my boyhood hero, Jimmy McLarnin.

Above all, I owe my wonderful wife, Monica. She has done all the hard work on this book, making it presentable to a publisher.

Jim's family, especially his children, have contributed so much, reading the manuscript, offering suggestions, and supplying pictures, making my "sacred task" most pleasant.

I've been helped by my good friends, who have read and critiqued the manuscript, and by Jim's many friends and his club, the California Boxing and Wrestling Club.

I have taught Secondary School English and coached and played sports for over 36 years, but socializing with my hero and working on this book has topped it.

PART I
Introduction: Meeting Jimmy Mclarnin, My Boyhood Hero And BC's Only World Boxing Champion

Fighters Should Be Gentlemen

The Legend of Irish Jimmy McLarnin: Canada's greatest professional boxer, the pride of Vancouver and the Pacific West Coast, twice world welterweight champion, and the conqueror of an unequaled thirteen world pro boxing champions.

Told by Jimmy McLarnin to Des Corry

For Ernie and Pop.

"Arma virumque cano..."
"Of battles and a man I sing..."
The opening lines of Virgil's epic poem The Aeneid.

Prologue

"Well, it really all began when I was a little kid selling newspapers, The Province, on the corner of Hastings and Main -- just up from the boat, you know, at the foot of Main. It was a good corner and with our big McLarnin family I had to bring home some extra money. One day a big kid came along and tried to take over my corner. So I knew I had to fight for it, and we went at it pretty good, so good that we drew a small crowd. I caught him a couple of good ones and the big guy backed down and walked away.

I started to pick up my papers when an old man grabbed me by the wrist, bent over and said, "I like the way you handle yourself, son. How would you like to be a fighter?"

I asked, "What kind of a fighter, sir?"

He said, "The only kind worth being, son, a champion, a champion of the world."

"Everything that old man told me came true. Yes, everything!"

Jimmy McLarnin, aged 78, to the author.

Jimmy McLarnin in his study

Chapter 1
Scene: Any pub in the East End of Vancouver — How Soon They Forget

He was said to be "pound for pound, the greatest professional fighter of them all". Do you think that was written about welter and middleweight champ Sugar Ray Robinson? No, it was written by Grantland Rice, the dean of American sports writers, about Jimmy McLarnin, who was born in Ireland, raised in Vancouver, British Columbia, and who fought professionally out of Los Angeles in the 1920s and 30s.

Now let me ask you another question. Can you tell me who beat more professional champions than any other boxer, ever? Robinson again? Ali? Louis? Marciano? Leonard? No, again. Our Jimmy McLarnin beat thirteen professional world champions, yes, thirteen, in his incredible career that even we in his hometown have forgotten. No fighter can match that record or even come close. How soon we forget, even those of us who love sports and boxing. Nobody will ever beat that record, and McLarnin did it in the golden age of boxing when there was just one champion for each weight level and no "super" divisions.

However, ring historians will tell you that McLarnin held championships only twice, not thirteen times. To understand how this came about, you must understand not only the Byzantine politics of those most competitive of times in professional boxing, but also how Jim and his manager Charlie "Pop" Foster had to manoeuvre to reach their goals of winning a championship, making a fortune to last them for life, keeping Jimmy from getting seriously hurt in that dangerous process, and getting out with their money. How they did it is a story almost beyond belief, but it is time that it was told.

For boxers, "It was the best of times, it was the worst of times," as Dickens said. The boxing pool was huge. Boxing was not just the most popular sport in North America, but also the way out of poverty not only for young men of minority races, but also those of any race. During those times, a strong young man might have to fight or else half starve. Every neighbourhood in a large city had its boxing club where professional fights were staged every week. The competition was incredible. Fighters became amazingly good. Even more important, there grew up a class of coaches and managers with wonderful expertise. This class of teacher no longer exists. Only a few men still carry this arcane knowledge. "Pop" Foster was one of those men, and he and Jim McLarnin came out of our land in this era, confronted its staggering challenges, and won.

Despite all that competition, and with all the odds against them, Jimmy and Pop won the championship that Pop had promised Jim and his dad, and came home rich. Incredibly, Jimmy still had his front teeth, an unbroken nose, not a scar on his face, and, as they say, "all his marbles". He had money in the bank and married his boyhood sweetheart, Lillian, from his home town. "I met her on the tennis court," said Jim. They raised a family, sent all their kids to college, and lived happily ever after. They really did. Oh, I know that fighters are supposed to get into trouble, but let me tell you a story of trust, dedication, and honesty.

Let me take you back through the mists of time to Jim's childhood. Why Jimmy McLarnin was not champion of an unprecedented six boxing divisions, flyweight, bantamweight, lightweight, junior welterweight, welterweight, and middleweight – that is a story. So, once upon a time, in the town of Vancouver, on the shores of the Pacific Ocean, a long time ago and only yesterday...

Chapter 2
Nostalgia: When I was a Boy and McLarnin Ruled the World

"Backward, turn backward, O Time, in your flight,
Make me a child again just for tonight!"
Elizabeth Akers Allen

On a summer's day in May 1933, at the height of the Great Depression, Irish Jimmy McLarnin, from Vancouver, Canada, won the world's welterweight championship with a sensational one round knockout of cagey, defensive champion Young Corbett III from Fresno, California. It was a stunning upset. Although McLarnin had long been the leading contender for the lightweight, junior welter, and welterweight championships (for Jim was really a small welterweight), he was considered too small for the tough, rangy, strong Italian American, Ralph Giordano, whose "nom de guerre" was Young Corbett. Corbett could handle much bigger men, and good ones, too. He had beaten middleweight champions Fred Apostoli, Ceferino Garcia, and the amazing Mickey Walker, "the toy bulldog," the same Walker who, at 165 pounds, had fought a draw with 210 pound heavyweight champion Jack Sharkey, and beaten the awesome solid 280 pounds of black muscle, Bearcat Wright. (Mick's manager, Doc Kearns, advised, "Just don't look at him, Mick.") Corbett had also beaten two light heavyweight champs, Gus Lesnevich and Billy Conn, both of whom came close to taking the heavyweight championship. In short, Corbett was one of those tough, awkward fighters who are notoriously difficult to deal with. He was especially good at dealing with classy boxer punchers like McLarnin.

Like a thunderbolt, McLarnin took out Corbett with a lightning left hook while Corbett was watching Jimmy fake his famed right cross.

"I got to know Corbett later," Jim told me. "He was a nice fellow; gave me a carload of grapes to take home. I like the Italians. They have a great culture and fine family values." Jimmy is also a family man. Then he continued, with his green eyes twinkling, "But he took me for a pigeon." The headline on the front page of the Vancouver Province on May 30, 1933, was "McLarnin Brings World Ring Title to Vancouver by Knockout in the First". Underneath is a photo of Jimmy and Pop Foster. Vancouver went wild! We were all part of Jimmy's victory. One of our boys had made it. Our world was larger.

In 1934, on a hot Okanagan summer evening, I listened to the radio, as we sat in a circle in camp, along with my dad and his engineering work crew, when our Jimmy McLarnin lost a tough, disputed 15 round decision and his championship to boxing's master spoiler of brilliant fighters, Jewish American Barney Ross of Chicago. I was four years old. It is still the first clear and coherent memory of my life, and I see the group of men, and my young athletic father, full of life and Irish song and jokes, and I hear the ring announcer's decision against our Jimmy. Jim had finished strongly and most, including all of us, thought he had retained his title. "Son-of-a-bitch," said my father softly, and I looked at him, for I had never heard him swear. I see Dad's face before me now so clearly, as if this had happened last night. I see them all, as if they had just walked away from the clearing in the grove of jack pines. Then my father took my hand in his strong, calloused hand. "Come on, Des, old fellow, me lad," he said, and we walked away from the tents and the men, through the grove of dry, aromatic grey and green pine needles near the big moss-covered rock where I played during the day, by the Okanagan River falls, to our tent where Mother was waiting.

"Well, how did it go, Ernie?" said Mom.

"Not so well, Coral," said Dad. "Jimmy lost."

"Oh, lost and by the wind grieved, ghost, come back again." Come back again for a day, Dad, from the dark, silent land of shadows, on its lonely cold winds, for you had too much life in you to ever be completely lost and gone. I have to tell you. I met him after you died, after I saw you that last time in the hospital. Yes, I met Jimmy McLarnin, himself, our champion. I met him on a hot summer morning in Los Angeles in 1984, just half a century after that night.

"They stole my title, Des," said Jimmy as we sat and talked of those fights a half a century ago, in Jim's Spanish style house among the tall palm trees in Glendale, California. So we poured a vodka, ice, and orange juice for each other, like two old Irish friends remembering lost yesterday, and we talked boxing, and sang Irish songs, and remembered. Jimmy recalled the ghosts of all the champions he had fought. McLarnin was not only the best boxer to come out of our town but one of the best welterweights of all time. Frank Sinatra, a dedicated boxing fan, rated the greatest fighters of all time this way: Louis, Marciano, Pep, Zale, Robinson, McLarnin, Conn, Canzoneri, Ross, and Ali. McLarnin was at least that good. We've had some good boxers from our town: Mike Oladjide, Jackie Turner, Kenny Lindsey, Vic Foley, and Billy Townsend were all world class or near. We've had several others who might have made it, including Jim's own brother, Sammy, who quit just as he was about to become a serious middleweight contender, but no one has had Jimmy's complete mastery of the art of boxing. Oladjide, for instance, had speed and offensive skills but, as a New York writer remarked, "He reminds me of the 7-11 Store, always open."

Finally, McLarnin's record shows that he was one of the ten greatest boxers of any time.

Sometimes the greatest of fighters have to wait for years for a legitimate shot at a title. Nobody wants any part of them. When a champion thinks he may lose his title to a challenger, it takes a lot of money to get him into the ring, and Jimmy, although he was a great "draw" at the gate, didn't have a great deal of money or "the mob" behind him. Archie Moore was a perfect example of the kind of fighter that champions don't want to fight. So was Jimmy McLarnin. Although Jim defeated thirteen champions, he was allowed to fight for the title only three times. All the other times, Jim's manager, Pop Foster, had to agree that Jim would show up at the weigh-in a pound or two over the weight limit so that if the champion lost, he would retain his title. Thus the champ would have a good payday and take no chances, and it was no disgrace to lose to Jimmy McLarnin. Jimmy was too good and Pop was too independent and they were both too honest. McLarnin swept all the lighter weights absolutely clean. At age seventeen, McLarnin decisioned flyweight champion Pancho Villa. Then he won on a foul from bantamweight champion Bud Taylor. He knocked out feather-weight champ "Kid" Kaplan. At age twenty, he lost a decision to light-weight champ Sammy Mandell, but came back to beat Mandell twice, more decisively each time. He knocked out junior welterweight champ Sammy Fuller. McLarnin won the welterweight title in the shortest recorded time for that division. Finally, he lost, to middleweight champ Lou Brouillard, in a rain-soaked ring in which he couldn't move.

Incidentally, Art Lasky, a top ranked heavyweight of the day, sparred briefly with McLarnin and is recorded to have remarked after, "I can't believe it. He hits as hard as a heavyweight." Along the way, McLarnin defeated a list of greats that sounds like a hall of fame roll call.

"Well, Jim," I said, "it's a glorious record!"

"Yes, but it's a tough business!" he said. "If you don't know your business or aren't in shape, you can end up a ward of the state!" A ward of the state was a favourite term of Jim's, for he has seen many boxers in that situation and has done a considerable amount of benevolent work in this area.

"But you had luck, Jim."

"Well, you make your own luck," said Jim. "Oh, yes, I was lucky to meet Pop. He took 50% of my winnings, not the usual 30%, but he was worth every penny. You know, Pop didn't take one cent of my earnings until I had $25,000 in my own bank account. He lived on his war disability pension and expenses. Oh, he may have had something saved up. He didn't spend money. After I retired from the ring, he lived in a little apartment over in Hollywood. 'I'm saving my money for you, Jim. You did the fighting,' he told me. I told him I didn't need his money, but I couldn't shake him. He used to come over to my place and play with the kids and sweep the front path and fix the front door. When he died, he left $300,000 split between me and my family. It's in an annuity. I can't touch the principal. He was living in a Vancouver hotel when he died. I went home to Vancouver and brought him back here where we made our money. I wanted him close. He's up there in Forest Lawn now."

Jim was looking misty around the eyes, and he talked in such a way that when we heard the door bell ring, I almost expected that extraordinary man, Charlie Foster, to walk up Jim's path between the palm trees and in the front door. Instead, one of the most extraordinary characters I have ever met walked in – Billy "the Count" Varga, ex-heavyweight wrestling champ, admitted descendant of Hungarian nobility, millionaire real estate dealer, leather jacket, cobra skin boots, diamond rings on most of his fingers, cowboy belt buckle, muscles swelling his fortrel pants and T-shirt, and already telling us that he had come to visit the only other "Living Legend" comparable to himself. His long white Cadillac sat modestly outside in Jim's long driveway with "Varga 1" on the licence plate – Varga 1 because he had a fleet of Cadillacs that he drove to his houses in L.A. and his mines in Nevada.

"I heard you talking about Pop Foster as I came past the window. My dad was a heavyweight champ, and he made me a champ. Foster made you a champ. If he hadn't seen you in that fight on the street, you'd still be selling newspapers like the Irish bum you are, McLarnin." I could see that Jimmy and Billy were practised at this.

"Oh, you go on home, you old Billy goat, you round haircut, you cockroach. You've just come over here to steal my lemons for your drinks." Jim looked at me and directed a sneer toward Billy. "He steals lemons right off my tree." Jim and Billy began to punch each other.

Those of us who are sports fans remember that Jimmy McLarnin was a boy who came from Vancouver, somehow won the world championship, and had three classic fights with another world champion, Barney Ross. Those who know their boxing history may know that these fights rank with the classic encounters of Zale and Graziano, Dempsey and Tunney, Ali and Fraser, Pep and Sadler, Robinson and Lamotta, Leonard and Duran. We remember that Ross won the last one, but that they were all close.

It's time for us to remember our champion's real accomplishments, his skill and courage, his dedication and loyalty, his humanity and decency. Jimmy wanted a book about him to be called something like *The Science of Boxing* which would emphasize the values of discipline that he believes in so much. Fortunately, Jim's keen-minded wife, Lillian, overheard our talk as she passed.

"Oh, let him call it something interesting, Jim," she said.

"How about *The Killer With the Baby Face?*" I suggested.

"Yes, they used to call me that, but that's not the way I want to be remembered," said Jim. "I want boys to know that they mustn't fight unless they have mastered their trade and are in good shape, that they must get an honest manager. Fighters are made, not born. I couldn't have done it without Pop," said Jim, looking wistfully for the past, off into the corner of the room. "Pop's up there in Forest Lawn. You know, everything that old man told me came true, every bit of it."

"And did you meet him in the legendary fashion that is told around Vancouver, on that corner after a street fight with a bigger boy over a newspaper spot?"

"Not exactly, but yes, that fight happened and yes, Pop was there and that is really where my boxing career started, looking at it one way. Well, yes, I'd call it true," said Jim with his engaging Celtic grin, "And yes, he told me that he would make me a champion if I lived cleanly and did what he told me."

Many of us in Vancouver remember that story.

Chapter 3
The Coming of the Wizard

The city of Vancouver, Canada, is one of the most beautiful cities of this world. Its white towered city centre sits on a peninsula which is within a few hundred yards of being an island. The jewel of the city, a thousand acre park, crowns the end of the peninsula. It is a city of light and air where you can play outdoors most months of the year. The west side of the town thrusts out into the beautiful blue gulf toward the islands.

The east side of town, where the rail lines come in from the Prairies and Seattle, is darker. The atmosphere can be oppressive, the lots are smaller, and the iron Coast Range mountains glower over the town. It is in this section of town, in hard times, that fighters are bred.

Oh, we've had some fighters in this town. We had the incomparable heavyweight champion Jack Johnson defend against Victor McLachlan, who became an actor in *The Informer* and *The Quiet Man*. George Chuvalo went 15 tough rounds against Ali. Barney Ross fought Gordon Wallace. Mike Spinks defended against Oscar Rividenara. Jackie Turner fought Kenny Lindsey. My favourite was the fight between tough Tony Pep and Olympic medalist Dale Walters.

But the most important fight took place on the street at the foot of Main Street, near the Union Steamship Station. This portentous fight took place not between two professional fighters, but between two thirteen-year-old boys. The prize was that corner to sell papers on. "We had a big family and I needed that good corner."

McLarnin fought thirteen-year-old Mike Tomasovich, the same age as Jim, but bigger, for Jim was small for his age. "We went at it and we drew a pretty good crowd," said Jim. "Mike was no slouch, but I was smaller and the crowd began to pull for me and I got in a couple of good ones and staggered Mike, so he quit and slouched off muttering about next time."

Then, from the dark crowd, loomed the stocky form of the old magician, for he had been watching our hero, and now he knew he could really fight.

13

The wizard seized Jim's wrist and said, "I like the way you handle yourself, son. How would you like to be a fighter?"

"What kind of a fighter, sir?" was Jim's famous question.

"The only kind worth being, son, a champion, a champion of the world!" said Charlie "Pop" Foster. He had not come from Camelot, or Middle Earth, but the Midlands of old England by way of South Africa, Flanders Fields, and old New York.

Mysteriously, a true and factual story of a successful professional in a deadly blood sport turns out to be an archetypal folk tale of the wizard who comes for the young hero. He says simply, "Come with me." And they set off on the quest to win the grail and from the dark lords in the mysterious lands. They fight grim warriors and escape fatal ladies and dark lords. It begins here beneath the mountain lions of the coast range, where the thunderbird claps his tumultuous wings, across the dark blue inlet where the killer whale swims, and beneath the eerie glow of the Northern Lights. Tell me there is no magic in this story.

Chapter 4
The Search for Jimmy and Pop

Blessed are the people with a common body of legends, for they can disagree with civility. Common legends assist a democratic and civilised unity. Consider the effects of Homer's epic heroes and battles upon the classic Greek civilisation that is the foundation of our intellectual world. Such, for us, were the legends of Jimmy and Pop, as I grew up in the mid 1900s.

I began to reflect upon the dimming of the legend of the boy with the flashing fists and the old man with the limp. Remembering it from my childhood, I began to wonder just how it all did happen, for there isn't even a statue in our town to these remarkable men.

In the summer of 1982, I was sitting by the pool of my neighbour, Vic Fisher, a displaced Englishman and sports fan extraordinaire, helping him with a post-swim gin and tonic. Vic was lamenting the demise of our fine pro soccer team, the Vancouver Whitecaps, once North American champions and the biggest fan draw ever in Vancouver, more than the pro football or hockey teams.

"This darn town is a born loser," Vic groaned.

"Well, now, Vic," I replied, "we've had our share of winners. We had a splendid home grown pro basketball team, the Vancouver Hornets, and we once had a world boxing champion hero! Vic knew his sports and moved in sporting circles in Vancouver and he knew that this was Canadian B. S. He just looked at me with pity for such a blatant lie! Sic transit gloria mundi!

So I popped down to the Vancouver Library to get a book on McLarnin. Imagine my surprise when I found that there was no book on Vancouver's only world champion and favourite son. I phoned Bill Forst, who had known Jim when he was a boy, and, later, covered his fights, and he admitted he should have done it when Jim retired.

I knew a book had to be written, and I had an "in". I have most of the top fights from 1897 Corbett/Fitzsimmons to Mike Tyson, and sometimes I throw a video night to provoke discussion. Malcolm McCaw, then head of the English Department at North Surrey High, told me after a video of one of Jim's fights that he had stayed at Jim's place in Glendale. Malcolm and Jim's nephew had gone to a game together in Jim's powder blue convertible.

"Hi, Champ," the parking attendant had said at the Dodger's ball game when Jim and the boys drove up.

I seized Malcolm's hand and pumped it. "Let me shake the hand that shook the hand that shook the world," as they used to say when they shook hands with anyone who had shaken the hand of the immortal John L. Sullivan. Some wouldn't wash their hand for a month after that.

So it was that I got McLarnin's address. I surmised that, despite an article saying that McLarnin disliked talking about his boxing days, I could catch my old hero with his guard down.

Chapter 5
I meet Jimmy McLarnin, Himself,
but the Wizard has other Business.

Therefore, the following summer, my wife, Monica, and I packed the kids, Traviss and Shivaun, into the car and set off for California, where Jimmy lived. We arrived in the tall palm lined streets of Glendale where I would be going through a time warp to my childhood and my father's time when our hero, Jimmy McLarnin, was the most famous professional boxer in the world.

As Bill Kinsella said about Shoeless Joe Jackson in Field of Dreams, "I can't bring my father back but I'll try to bring back his hero." It was almost fifty years to the day since Dad and I had listened to Jim lose his title to the incomparable Barney Ross. The times were portentous.

Jim lived just around the corner from our friend Beverley's house, in Glendale, where we were staying. I dialed his number as if I were dialing back through the mists of time to King Arthur's court to ask if Sir Lancelot was available – and could he talk to Des Corry. Absurd! This is the real world, not the land of myth, or is it – because the land of myth answered in a pleasant baritone.

"Sure," said the voice from King Arthur's court, "come on over." Lord, I had talked to the greatest warrior of his time, Jimmy McLarnin himself. In ten minutes I found myself at Jim's place on North Everet Street. What Benevolent Providence had guided my steps here? I walked up the curved path and through the wrought iron gate to the porch of Jim's two-story Spanish style house among the palms. Jim answered the door. I think I would have recognised him. He looked like a retired businessman who had been athletic in his youth, which is just what he was. His mop of dark hair was thinning and white, but his face was young and lively and his eyes mirrored his grin of welcome. He stood about 5 foot 7 or 8, and weighed around 150 pounds. He was in excellent shape and his movements were quick and light as we shook hands. He wore pin-striped suit pants with a white shirt and tie. He invited me down the hall and introduced me to his wife, Lillian, still a slim and handsome woman in her 70's, and you could see Jim was proud of her. After this general impression, I noticed Jim's gnarled hands, which he had broken five times. He could have had more wins if he had not hit so hard. Had he been an average hitter, he could have worked more often, and always had his timing right on. Pop's desire to get the best deal also reduced the number of Jim's fights. A fighter needs to fight regularly to keep his timing on. Sparring is not the same. This is one of the keys to understanding Jim's career.

I asked Lillian how she got mixed up with this rascal McLarnin. She just looked at me. When they were young, he was Jimmy McLarnin, the toast of the town, and when she met him, she found, as I had, that he was not only famous, but a charmer and generally a good fellow. In the McLarnin family room were the TV and family pictures, but there were also pictures of different celebrities. There was a photo of Jim with the famous Hollywood beauty and sex queen Jean Harlow. Jim was as handsome as Jean. What a profile! What a dresser! No wonder Jim got hooked up with the Hollywood crowd, as Pop Foster disgustedly called them. Jean had a reputation. Dorothy Parker remarked, "The T is silent, like the T in Harlow." Jim said he liked Jean and that she was a really nice girl.

*Jean Harlo**w***

There were pictures of Jim with Bogart and Gable at a party. I asked Jim if Bogart was as tough in person as he was in his pictures.

"Well, I've never seen him fight but I've seen him 'restrained' a few times," said Jim grinning wryly, turning to pictures of himself with Hope and Crosby on the golf course. None of these "stars" impressed Charlie Foster. Only virtue and work impressed Foster, and yes, there was the wizard, a full size painting of him hanging on the opposite wall. "A boxer did that portrait for me," said Jim as he followed my gaze.

Foster had trained another outstanding fighter, an English featherweight named Spike Robson. Spike was the English champion and came to America and fought the greatest: Terry McGovern, George Dixon, Abe Attel, and perhaps the greatest boxer who ever lived, Joe Gans. Robson didn't win a title but he gave all those ring immortals close fights. Foster was one of the greatest teachers of boxing, partly because he had seen the greatest fighters of all time. Jim and I gazed at the painting. You could feel Pop's presence in the room. What I wouldn't give to talk to him, for I had talked to many people who had talked to him, but I couldn't get a handle on him. Had he gone backwards through time? Some wizards, like Merlin, live backwards, according to medieval scholar T. H. White. Time is like a moebious strip and bends back on itself, according to modern philosophers and physicists. Maybe he had flown away in a hot air balloon to hobnob with his fellow wizards, but he was not at home when I visited McLarnin. Damn!

Lillian had been taking radiation treatments and she was going out to have her hair done. She seemed in good health. So Jim and I sat there, under the portrait of Pop, drinking tea. This is not relaxing if you are sitting next to the man who was the hero of your youth.

Finally, I said, "Jim, do you take a drink? I just happen to have a small bottle of Canadian Club in my car which, with your permission, I'll get, and it will be an honour to share with you." So Jim got the ice and I got the bottle and then we talked boxing. Yes, I talked boxing with one of the immortals who knew almost all the immortals.

"Jim," I said, feeling much better, "I have movies of some of your fights and in your fight with Benny Leonard you carry your left low and your right wide. My college coach told me not to do that. Didn't you get caught with a right cross over that low left, especially as you drew it back from a punch as Joe Louis got caught and knocked out by Max Schmeling?"

"Well, college boy," said Jim, "you just try to catch me over my left."

"You mean it, Jim?"

So we got up to spar in Mrs. McLarnin's parlour. We put down our drinks and stood up and faced each other. I poked out a tentative left, which Jim put aside with his arm. He stood as he had for his fight with the great immortal, Benny Leonard, with a wide stance. We sparred around and I faked a few which he didn't dream of biting on, and I knew I wasn't boxing a college man. I still worked out with my high school wrestling team, and McLarnin, at 77, was as fast as any of them. Lord, what must he have been like at 25? Then I saw him bring his left back low, so I crossed my right to his chin. Jim pivoted on the ball of his left foot, making my right miss his chin by about two inches. He shifted his weight and wrapped me smartly with his low left in my now unprotected right ribs. If he had thrown his weight into it, he might have cracked one of my ribs. Everything was accomplished with a minimum of effort and with balanced precision, while he looked at me with that abstract look of concentration that I have seen in the eyes of some of the great athletes that I have been fortunate to compete against. It is the way that godlike Achilles looked at Hector before the gate of Troy. He was beautiful. Again, what must he have been like at 25? He carried his right hand wide because of his complete confidence in slipping any punch to the head, to move it sideways just enough as a punch came in. Ali did just that but he moved his head back, cutting down his ability to reply as can be done if the head is moved sideways.

Doug Jones moved in on Ali when he did that, rapped him inside hard, and actually beat Ali badly. Ali got the decision to a chorus of boos because there was more money in Ali than in Jones. Boxing is a sport but also a business. Ali usually got away with it because he was faster than men his size. Ali was intelligent enough never to fight Jones again, for he would have gotten beaten again. Fortunately, Mrs. McLarnin returned before I became Jim's 21st K.O. victim, but not before I understood more of the difference between amateur and professional boxing. "Your balance is good," said Jim as we sat down to finish our drinks. He said that perhaps he should have carried his left a little higher. His modesty overwhelmed me. Actually, I obtained movies of the first rounds of his third fight with Ross, late in his career, and his stance is much more orthodox and not nearly as open. Lillian came in with coffee and pie for us, and then quizzed me to see what kind of bird had flown in, who claimed to be an English teacher, yet a boxing nut.

As I walked away, down the front path and through the palm trees, I looked up into that hot, blue California sky and said, "Well, Dad, how about them apples? Have I shaken Jimmy McLarnin's hand? Hell, I've sparred with him!" When I got up the street and out of sight, I jumped into the air, punched the sky twice, and shouted. Dad had been dead for fifteen years but I could feel him grin. There are more things in heaven and earth than are dreamed of in your philosophy.

I had visited King Arthur's court and jousted with Lancelot, even if not in earnest.

20

Writer Al Stump, Pro Wrestler Billy Varga, with the author and Jim

Chapter 6
Lunch in L.A. with McLarnin
and his Paladins

The next morning, Jimmy phoned me. Would I like lunch with him at the Golden State Boxing and Wrestling Club? Jim picked me up and drove me to the Old Spaghetti Factory where they met weekly for business, lunch, drinks and comradeship. Ex-wrestling champ, Billy Varga, seemed to be the master of ceremonies. They were all talking about Ray Robinson, who had been there last week and hadn't looked too good. Ray was a beautiful offensive fighter, but he was not a great defensive fighter and he had taken many punches. The marks of a hundred battles were on most of their faces. I was seated next to George Latka, who had fought for the featherweight championship. Latka was a pleasant man who ran the Golden Glove bar in Huntingdon Beach. One could see that George had been hit a few times in the face. Indeed, McLarnin seemed to be the only one who had no facial scars.

Jim introduced me to Sean O'Grady, a slim, handsome 30 year old whom I had seen fight on T.V. He was trying for a part in a movie about the fabulous Harry Greb, who had been a hero of McLarnin's in his youth.

On the drive back to Glendale, Jim suggested that I might like to stop for one short drink at the Walter Scott Hotel, a pleasant Tudor style bar and restaurant. We talked about Scott and Ivanhoe, the novel from which the movie was made, and I mentioned that Scott had a publishing business that went broke and then his partner skipped out. Scott turned out novels at a great rate for the rest of his life because he felt honour bound to pay all the company's debts. "Well, I should feel right at home here," said Jim, "because I had a partner who was a crook. He was Irish, too. You can't go by race. I dropped a couple of hundred thousand. I wasn't bankrupted, but it turned out that we used Pop's money after all." Fighters should leave their money in the bank and live off the interest, frugally, and tip and bet small. The interest off Jim's half million would be comfortable. "If I'd done that, I'd have been a golf bum. I was for a few years, after I quit boxing. Win or lose, a man should work."

"Spoken like your hard-working Ulster Protestant father's son, Jim."

"Well, I had a good tool and dye business going for a while. Bought the machinery cheap, left over from the war."

"O.K., you were a reasonable businessman, but you were more than a reasonable boxer, so now tell me – I always got caught with a left hook out of no place. Not only in college, but also after. I used to spar with a teacher friend, Jack Martin, who had played football for Calgary. His left hook would go out of my peripheral vision while I watched his right. I was taught to catch them by moving my forearm out vertical."

"Amateur," said Jim with disgust, as we sat in the bar and savoured our drinks. Jim had remembered that I had brought a bottle of Canadian Club to his house, and so he ordered that for us and insisted on paying. It's hard to pick up a check in McLarnin's company. "When you see that left hook start, you go straight for the chin with your right and move in. You can use their momentum. I didn't block much. When you block, you immobilize that hand temporarily. Slipping or countering is much better." McLarnin could slip a punch coming from two feet away as fast as it could be thrown. Amateurs can't. They have to keep their hands high. "Okay, throw a left hook." Seated on the bar stool, I hooked a quick left. Before I could realise it, I found McLarnin's right fist an inch from my nose. It took my breath away and raised the hair on the back of my neck. The move had been absolute perfection. I knew instantly that that wasn't just the way you counter a hook and throw a right counter. I can't describe it. You have to see it. It was great poetry.

As Emily Dickinson said, "It is zero at the bone." When even a minor poet makes just the perfect move, it stops you dead.

Jimmy teaches the author a left hook

"They are not long, the days of wine and roses," said Ernest Dowson, of the glorious days of our youth, and you know that no one will say it better because it is perfect. I felt that I had seen Plato's "form of the good", a glimpse of infinity. I've had a few good rights come at me in the raucous bar days of my youth, but nothing near to that.

When we got to Jim's place, he took me into the room where he kept his memorabilia – pictures of Jim with movie stars, politicians, and boxers.

"That's me and Barbara Stanwyck. She used to come to all my fights here. Nice lady. She lives just over here."

Then we came to a picture of Henry Amstrong, the only real triple champ, who beat Ross so badly.

"Tell me, Jim, after you retired, you were offered a fight with Armstrong for your old title. Ross had a terrible time with him. Armstrong bobs and weaves and comes in punching all the time, like Marciano. What would you have done with him?"

"Pop said Armstrong was made for me, but we had made an agreement – no comebacks. Ross was a wonderful spoiler and boxer, but he couldn't hit hard enough to keep Armstrong off him, so Barney couldn't do his slick defensive moves and flurries that won him rounds. You had to nail Henry as he came at you." Jim was the hardest counter puncher of his day and you could see the light of battle in his eyes. Jim came at me briefly and said, "Go right after him." I saw a glimpse of the killer with the baby face.

Mrs.McLarnin gave me a coffee and invited my wife and children over the next afternoon. We all had a lovely visit. Then we drove home and I went back to read every word written about McLarnin's fights.

The McLarnins and The Corrys
Back row – Jim, Monica, Des
Front Row – Lillian, Traviss, Shivaun

Lillian McLarnin had seemed full of energy and intelligence as she questioned me. Jim was unquestioning. Weird things happened to him. Had not a magician appeared and led a newspaper boy to fame, riches, and the stars of Hollywood? Myth and fable are logic to the Celts, but not to Lillian Cupit. Only when I explained the train of events that had led me to her door did Lillian pour my tea. To Jim, she was still high romance, but to me she was logic.

But that was the year Lillian died of cancer and was put to rest in Forest Lawn, L.A., yes, the one Evelyn Waugh wrote about, where Pop Foster is buried, both looking over Jim's house in Glendale. I think she was still keeping an eye on her Jim. Jim was devastated. "I never thought my sweet Lillian would go before me," Jim said to me. It is a terrible and a wonderful thing to be so much in love with your wife after all those years. She was a fine woman, pretty and educated. Jim could easily have had some Hollywood beauty and been miserable, but he chose a college girl from his hometown.

Jim had bought his parents a new house in Grandview, looking over the lights of downtown Vancouver, after they could afford to move from Union Street on Jim's winnings. It was in this neighbourhood that I heard about Lillian's death. I was coaching my wrestling team at a BC championship meet at Britannia High. The Britannia coach walked over to me and said, "I hear you're working on a book on McLarnin. Did you know that his wife Lillian just died?"

"Dear God, no!" I thought. "Oh, Lillian. Poor Jim." I checked that month's Ring magazine and there was a note about Lillian's death. I thought of how much Jim relied on her. I wrote Jim a letter relying on the friendship of the previous summer. I wrote that I hoped that I wasn't being too personal, but I believed that a love like the love I saw between them never dies. Lillian's spirit would literally be with him until they all met again. A universe that includes anti-matter, alternate universes, quantum physics, and black holes that lead to other worlds precludes none of these beliefs. Modern physics has killed hard materialism. Francis Bacon said he would believe any fable except that this universe is without a Mind. "A little philosophy inclines a man's mind to atheism, but depth in philosophy bringeth it about to religion." If Jim listened silently in the house where they and their family lived with so much love, he would feel Lillian still with him.

When I saw Jim again the next summer, he said he had kept my letter and appreciated it. He was impressed by sharp sayings like Socrates' that nothing evil can happen to a good man in this world or the next, as he took the hemlock and as he died. Hoyle said of the universe, "It's obviously a put up job." And Rutherford, "Someone very strange has fudged all these equations."

I quoted Augustine that God has made us for Himself and we are restless until we find rest in Him. I think it all made Jim feel a bit better even though I really couldn't comment on a loss like Lillian to Jim.

In the meantime, I had contacted many people around Vancouver who had known Jim. I had a chat with Dave Brown, then B.C.'s Mr. Boxing. We talked about Jim's superior record to any other Canadian boxer. We talked about Pop Foster.

Cyril Masi, a local hotel entrepreneur who owned the Anchor Hotel on Powell Street told me to contact Earl Hilbert, who had boxed at the same time as Jim and trained with him. Jim told me he remembered Masi fighting, "He was a good hooker." Hilbert, like Jim, had gone to California to fight and told me some inside stuff, especially about the famous manager, Jack Kearns, who had wanted to manage McLarnin and ease Foster out. Jim had told me that Kearns had not been fair with his most famous fighter, Jack Dempsey, who made millions yet didn't end up rich like Jim. Hilbert had sparred with McLarnin and said that Jim was a fearsome body puncher and thought that that was Jim's strongest point. McLarnin thought speed, defence, and left jab was his strength. The press thought it was his right hand.

Chapter 7
Jim's Brother, Sister, Sparring Partner, Earl Hilbert

I bought Earl a coffee; we sat and talked in a senior's centre in downtown East Vancouver. Earl said that they all grew up boxing. If a gang of Irish boys fought a gang of Italian boys, they fought with fists, not knives, and didn't use their boots. Jim was the champion of his gang. The streets were the basic training ground for pro boxing. The rules were those of the prize ring. When Jim was a boy and you knocked a fellow down, you stepped back to see if he could get up and continue. The code of honour said that only a coward would kick a man when he was down. All Jim's brothers were good boxers. Sammy, who became a Christian minister, was an excellent middleweight prospect. Jim's youngest brother, Bob, was also a fine boxer and the only six-footer among the family. He invited me to lunch in the home where he lived, only a stone's throw from where they all grew up, just off Commercial Drive. Bob had considerable memorabilia of Jim's glory days, and I was reminded that most great athletes were usually a group production. Jim's family was behind him. Once Jim was established, Bob had gone to California. He told me that he thought Jim's best punch was a straight left. He said Jim's toughest fights were those with Billy Petrolle, and his best fight was with Kid Kaplan. He dwelt on how hard Jim trained.

Jim would train in Vancouver until a couple of weeks before the fight and then move to that area to train and get acclimatized. This was part of Jim's survival. He had no long-term effects of his fights because he was in such good shape. The same was true of Marciano, who was the best-trained heavyweight. Neither man was the slightest bit out of shape until he retired, unlike many fighters who don't worry until it's time to train for a fight. Jim said that if you were going fifteen rounds, you should be doing at least five miles a day of roadwork, on top of skipping rope, throwing a medicine ball, punching the light and the heavy bag, chopping wood, lifting weights with the teeth to strengthen the neck, exercising with dumb bells, and sparring six to twelve rounds with several sparring partners under the watchful eye of the master of boxing knowledge, Pop Foster, each day for six weeks before a fight. Without this, you would get hurt, Jim said. Fighters of the past also served a longer time before becoming headliners. It is no wonder that modern fighters can only go twelve rounds and often get hurt if they go the old standard fifteen. Now, other sports have picked up the analytic coaching and training which only boxers used to receive, and the progress has been dramatic, while boxing has almost lost it. Bob and I kicked this around and Bob remarked that he had, for a long time, a wonderful pair of jogging shoes that Jim had given him while other sports were still using tennis shoes. Bob was awed by Jim's easy familiarity with Hollywood celebrities.

Alex Lucas, ex-principal of Alpha Secondary School, remembered Jimmy coming over to his parents' place for breakfast quite often. "We all helped each other in those days," Lucas said. He also remembered the Rev. Andrew Roddan, of First United Church in East Vancouver, who helped so many people in the hard thirties that people thought of him as a saint. He probably was. Years later, his son, Sam, an outstanding journalist and fine writer, remembered how his dad had invited McLarnin, after he won his title, to come to the boys' club at the church and show the boys how it was done and how to live clean to win. The boys watched open-mouthed as McLarnin shadow boxed around masterfully, and listened as Jim told them that he couldn't have won if he hadn't lived a clean life, and reminded them always to read their Bible. The scene was indelibly etched on Sam's memory. Jim wasn't a saint, as Andrew Roddan was, but his career was a wonderful influence on the boys of his time. It's great when the hero of your childhood is clean cut and decent.

The great defence lawyer and Justice of the Supreme Court, Angelo Branca, remembered going to school with McLarnin. He remembered Jim as small but a really nice kid. "But, oh, Jimmy was a dream of a boxer. He had the most beautiful weave of any boxer I've ever seen, and an uncanny ability to anticipate a punch." Tell me about it. I couldn't touch him with a fist when he was almost 80. What the amateur boxer or street fighter is most surprised by when he spars with even an awkward looking pro is that they are almost impossible to hit. Despite what most sportswriters say, it is defence that wins pro contests, even basketball. Branca, himself, won the Canadian Amateur Middleweight Championship. "I wouldn't have missed it for worlds. We all boxed at the old Cavalry Club. George Paris was the coach, Jack Allen the promoter." Tommy Douglas, who brought Canada medicare, was an amateur lightweight champ. Among the older generation that grew up in Vancouver, McLarnin's name was still magic. Older doctors, lawyers, school principals, still consider that one of the high points of their lives was the time they saw McLarnin fight. They had seen perfection.

I met Jim's son, daughter-in-law, and granddaughter, the apple of Jim's eye. James Junior was slim, athletic, and well-mannered. He had been a farm manager, but at the time he was attending Western Washington University in Bellingham, taking education courses. He was straightforward and amiable, like all the McLarnins.

"I never saw my dad fight. I knew the Cupits better than the McLarnins. Yes, those hands bothered Dad. Sometimes Mother could beat him at golf in his last years when his hands were really bothering him. He didn't like losing, even to Mom."

"Your dad said you were a good baseball player."

"I was O.K. but I didn't have Dad's desire."

Hell, James, who did?

I had a wonderful conversation with Jim's sister, Olive Smith, in her fine home in Victoria. Despite her gracious manner, she had the fire of the McLarnins. She greeted me with, "Don't you write anything bad about my brother."

Jim told me later not to mess with Olive. "She took care of us after Mom died." So it is, with big sisters in large families. She served me tea and cookies and showed me some great photos. One was of a party at the Empress Hotel with the mayor of Victoria. Olive was a striking young woman. Jim was his usual dapper self. Jim told me that if he were to retire, he would do so in Victoria. As he was only 80 then, he didn't think of himself as retired. Olive took him to her church and introduced him to her minister, who mused that there used to be a boxer by that name. When Jim admitted his identity, the minister wanted to know where his famous "baby face" had gone. Jim had never had a "pug's" face, so scribes called him "baby face".

Olive said that Jim suffered his only K.O. hitting his head going down her basement stairs for a bottle of wine. She told me how she and her sisters couldn't listen to Jim's fights on the radio. They would go for a walk until the fight was over; it was too nerve wracking. They would hear all the radios in the district going. Her brothers would be at home with their heads stuck to the speaker.

Then she told me how they felt when James left home, aged sixteen, weighing 100 pounds and standing 5 feet tall, to be a professional fighter and take on the world. What an act of faith in the judgement of Charles Foster!

"James was so small," said Olive. "Mother pinned her last $20 bill inside his shirt, kissed him, and told him not to forget to say his prayers." Jim told me the same story later. Then we thought about the Irish boys who had left home and family, never to return.

"The Irish have had it almost as bad as the Jews," said Jim. Yes, there were 8 million people in Ireland before the potato famine of 1857. With starvation and emigration, the population fell to half.

"But Jim came home," Olive continued.

Just before next Christmas, her sister came running from the door shouting, "Jim's home, and he's grown up." Jim grew over half a foot in his late teens and eventually put on another half a hundred pounds of muscle. What a celebration the McLarnins had!

31

"I always came home for Christmas," said Jim.

"Well, he's not champion of the world, Charlie," said Jim's father, Sam, to Pop.

"No, Sam, these things take a while. But he's got $5,000 in the bank, no marks on his face, and he's gotten so that he'll throw a left as well as a right now and again. It's not pretty yet but it's getting better."

But there was to be another homecoming for Jim. Olive told me about the terrible time when Jim came home because his mother, Mary, was dying of cancer, when she was in her 40s. Olive said that Jim came in with his big coat still on and knelt beside his mother's bedside and prayed that God would take him instead. Even if you are a tough Irish kid, as Jim was, the world will still break your heart. Pictures of Jim in his late teens and early twenties show a tough looking customer with narrow hard eyes, close cropped hair, and a firm unsmiling mouth. In his late 20s, even in fights, he looks entirely different. His face is relaxed, his eyes are wide, his hair is longer and fashionably cut, and on his mouth is a slight Irish grin. Success has allowed him to relax and realise that a fighter is tough; so he, McLarnin, doesn't have to act tough. Fighters should be gentlemen more than any other men. Jim was established and humanized.

My good friend, Reni Masi, introduced me to Al Principe, who had been in Jim's gang in East Hastings when they were kids growing up. Al invited me to drop around to one of his chain of barbershops. I visited his shop in Guildford, Surrey, and there in the back, past the other barbers, cutting hair, was Al, lively and quick like McLarnin in his 80s.

He was pleased as punch that someone was writing a book about Jimmy. "And about time, too." He had a book of clippings about his friend Jim's fights. "Greatest welterweight of all time. And from right here in Vancouver, too – and a really good guy." I was very interested in a clipping of Mickey Gill, the superb little Irish Canadian fighter who had given Jim such great fights in Vancouver and who died a hero in WWII on a parachute raid in France. Al told me how he and Jim and the gang used to hustle for money on the docks and waterfront of Vancouver. Jim and Pop used to drop their luggage off at Al's dad's barbershop on Main Street when they arrived on the train from California.

Jim enjoyed hearing how Al was still working, just like old times. "Great guy!"

So Jim and I talked on the phone and decided that my family and I would spend time at Jim's place the next summer, and we would get serious. I think Jim was looking forward to talking about his salad days when he was "the greatest, pound for pound" fighter in boxing. Jim likes company. He grew up in a large family. He had been surrounded by the crowds that follow a famous fighter. They were tumultuous years. Although Jim himself was a quiet man, he was the centre of all that. Later, his house was filled with the laughter of his children and the love of his dear wife. He made numerous public appearances and rode in the St. Patrick's parade in L.A.

He played golf and partied with the famous of Hollywood and boxing in their golden age. Now, his children were grown and his dear Lil gone. I was sure when he invited us that we would not be intruding. Also, Jim had come to seem like a pal to me.

As a man of the 19th century, I write letters. As a man of the 20th, Jim phones. That Spring, Jim phoned and said, "Hi, champ, be sure to bring your children this summer. I have lots of room. I'm rattling around in this big house."

"Jim," I said, "I wouldn't come without them!"

"Did you see the Leonard/Hagler fight?" Jim asked. "Billy Goat Varga thinks Hagler won. I saw it over at my brother Joe's. Leonard fought a beautiful fight. I don't see how he could lay off so long and keep his timing. I lay off for a year after I won the championship and my timing was off when I fought Ross." Then he put Billy on the line, who did an imitation of Hagler, saying that he'd kill anyone who thought he hadn't won. I replied that I didn't care whom he killed as long as he was in L.A. I asked Jim if he thought he could beat Leonard. "Well, Ray beat the middleweight champ and I lost to the middleweight champ, so it doesn't matter what I think." Jim was impressed with Leonard.

Chapter 8
Off to see the Wizard and the Hero down the Yellow Brick Road

The next summer, Monica and I and the kids once again set off to Glendale, California. We drove past Tacoma, a tough town with beautiful scenery and tough fighters, like Freddie Steele, middleweight champ, and Greg Haugen, lightweight champ. McLarnin recently came up to Tacoma to see Haugen fight, but Greg had had a bad night, although he won.

"Happens to us all, even Louis and Dempsey," said Jim.

Then over the gentle mountains to camp in the Redwoods of Richardson Grove and down through the Napa Valley with a stop at lovely Fetzer wineries to the Coast road, and over Golden Gate Bridge, gracefully stretched across that brilliant fog and sun-filled opening to the Bay. This time, we bypassed San Francisco. It was there that modern boxing started, for it was a San Francisco bank clerk, James J. Corbett, who taught the world to box, not just fight. The old champ, Mushy Callahan, taught Errol Flynn to box with Corbett's style for the film *Gentleman Jim,* a fine movie with Ward Bond as John L. Sullivan.

"It was easy," said Mushy. "Anyone who boxes correctly boxes like Corbett." It has been a splendid art form from then until now, as well as a blood sport. Corbett loved to watch a consummate boxer so he used to come to watch McLarnin work out.

"Remember, Jimmy, a pro fighter can afford to always be a gentleman. Fighters should be gentlemen," Corbett said to McLarnin.

"I always tried to remember that," Jim told me. They should all remember that, Jim – especially people like Mike Tyson who could have saved boxing and instead ruined it by acting like a street thug.

Then there was the fight, located on the barge in the Bay so that the police couldn't stop it, between Corbett and another Frisco boy, Joe Choynski, who had beaten Jack Johnson. It went 27 rounds with skin-tight gloves until Corbett knocked out Choynski. The town is full of fistic and literary history. It was from Benicia on the Bay that America's first challenge for the world heavyweight championship came when John C. Heenan, a 190 pound Irish American, went to battle the English world bare knuckle champion in 1860. The fight ended in the 37th round in a draw, with the English champion, Tom Sayers, little bigger than a middleweight, tiring, so the crowd broke the ropes and stopped the fight. It was the first great international boxing event.

My dad went to San Francisco to see the local boy, Jimmy Britt, fight a return with the incomparable Joe Gans in 1907. Britt had taken Gans 20 rounds, but this time he only lasted 5. Britt was finally knocked out by the legendary Packey McFarland, one of Jim's early heroes, who had 140 wins and 1 early loss and never got a shot at the championship. Why fight McFarland when you know you'll lose? Jim was afraid he would end up like McFarland.

When McLarnin was fighting in Oakland, he became so popular that too many of Frisco's "finest" were finding their way there. The San Francisco police chief (the father of actor Pat O'Brien) had to make formal arrangements so that the boys on the force could see the classy little Irishman from Canada fight.

When we got to the city of the angels, I phoned Jimmy.

"Hi, champ," he said. "When are you coming over and bringing the family?"

"Tomorrow, if that's all right. Get ready to talk about your fights with Barney Ross. You know, in legends, a champ remains in a defining moment. Just as Custer remains on that dusty Montana hillside surrounded by the Sioux and the dying 7th cavalry, so you remain for boxing aficionados on that Madison Square ring for 45 incredible rounds of some of the most magnificent boxing in its history."

"Well, I'm not sure I like the comparison," said Jim, "but let's start there."

There are two ways to Glendale and McLarnin from downtown L.A. The best way is up the coast to the end of Sunset Boulevard – you know – Gloria Swansen and Bill Holden, Erich von Stroheim, and Buster Keaton, the comic genius who directed the best of all silent comedies, *The General*. McLarnin had known them all. You wind up from the beach along a pleasant, surprisingly wooded road past the big old houses until you come to Hollywood, the town, like Athens and Florence, that changed the way the world thought and felt, for, surprisingly, the better. Come back, John Garfield, and play Jimmy McLarnin in a movie! Garfield looked much like Jimmy and when Jimmy talked, he sounded like Garfield, and used that quick wise-cracking style typical of 30's movies and Hollywood's classic actors, who were his pals. They all came to his fights. Jim told me about going with "the gang" to a party at William Randolf Hearst's castle where Keaton set up a volleyball game in Hearst's ample dining room. You will find Jim in a picture in Bob Hope's book, *Confessions of a Hooker*, with Hope, Bing Crosby, and Fred Astaire, on the Lakewood course, Jim's club. Jim was partnered with Joe Louis. "Joe was a terrific golfer. Hit it a mile. Could have been a professional," said Jim. Jim tells of taking Louis to his club for a game and dinner, and having the staff set a table for them out by the pool. "How nice," thought Jim, until it hit him that they did it because they didn't want a black man eating inside the club. Jim spluttered when he told the story, for it would never occur to McLarnin that a man should be treated differently because of his colour, especially a great national hero like Joe Louis.

Lakeside Golf Course – Fred Astaire, Joe Louis, Bob Hope, Arthur Stebbings, Jimmy McLarnin

We drove out of Hollywood to Glendale, then up the hill lined with tall palm trees to quiet Everett Street, up Jim's long narrow driveway, which Jim could negotiate in any state, and there he was, the champ himself, 78 years young.

"As old as Santy Claus," as Jim grimly put it. He carried Monica's suitcase upstairs and settled us into our bedrooms. He was pleased to have children in his house again.

Jim with Des and children, in front of Jim's house in Glendale

I noticed, on his wall, a picture of the Lions, two mountains that dominate East Vancouver, where he grew up.

Then he nodded us to his spacious front room, winked, and fixed us his favourite drink – vodka, orange juice, and ice.

"Must keep up your vitamin C," Jim said, "the body doesn't make its own."

I noticed my letter on Lillian's death, open on his desk, and I was touched. I hoped I had done something for this man who had added such adventure to my boyhood. Now I would have time to observe this quiet, polite man who had been the fiercest professional fighter of his day, the man who had the 'killer instinct', the instinct, for it really can't be taught, that some fighters have so they can sense when a man weakens or is hurt, even when ringsiders can't tell, then, with incredible precision, rain blows on his opponent. Watching movies of great fighters like Marvin Hagler, who have the killer instinct, one notices that most, even Hagler, lack McLarnin's precision at such a time.

"All right, James J. McLarnin," I began, with false lack of deference to put myself at ease, "how did you lose two out of three to Barney Ross (even if he is a hall of famer) when he was lighter than you, the lightweight champ versus the welterweight champ, and most experts thought you would win easily?" The odds at fight time were 6 to 5 for McLarnin. In the ring, McLarnin looked like Roberto Duran for ferocity, and here he was!

So we began where I began to remember the world, in the summer of 1933, as my dad, his crew, and I, listened, unbelieving, while our champion lost a disputed decision to Barney Ross. I had seen my dad spar and he would spar with me. He had biceps like steel, tireless legs, and incredible hand and mind speed. He used to see how many flies he could catch with one hand while they were in flight.

"But," my dad said, "you should see Jimmy spar." He had seen Jim work out in Vancouver. Jim had never lost to any man twice, just as Ali, Louis, and Tunney and the greatest seldom do. Now I could ask McLarnin himself.

Jim told me of those three fights, reputed to be among the most artistic fistic masterpieces of all time. Jim illustrated every move. Ross won the first and McLarnin won the second, but the third is most controversial, as most sports writers said that McLarnin won easily, and bedlam followed the decision by Jack Dempsey that Ross had won.

"They stole my championship," said Jim to me that night.

Chapter 9
Belfast: the McLarnins

The legend of Jimmy McLarnin and how he became a champion begins in the grim old city of Belfast in Ulster of the Red Hand, which is its symbol. The legend of Ulster is that two heroes from the ancient heroic age were crossing the Irish Sea to claim Ulster. The first to place his hand upon Ulster's soil would own the land. One hero, as they rowed evenly approaching the land in the race, drew his sword, cut off his hand, and threw it on to the land ahead of the other boat. The land was his. Considering Ulster's recent history, a bloody hand is an appropriate symbol.

Its capital is a city of hard work and minimal pay. Samuel John McLarnin and his wife Mary Ferris were both born there. Belfast is a fine town to leave. The only songs I know about Belfast are most unlike the romantic songs of the rest of Ireland. *Windy old Weather* and *When the Shipyards go back on Full Time*. Samuel McLarnin had already been to Canada, worked on farms and ranches on the Prairies, and he knew that it, too, was a hard land. But it was a land where, if a man worked hard and hustled, he could get ahead. "And Dad was a hustler and a worker, and he didn't drink until after work." You can't ask more of any decent man.

Belfast had a high rate of emigration. It had taught Samuel and Mary to work hard, so they were good immigrants. They took their growing family and set sail for the new world by way of Liverpool, another city, like Belfast, Glasgow, or Boston, full of the working Irish.

> By the high star our course is set.
> Our end is life.
> Put out to sea.

by the fine Ulster poet Louis McNeice

Ulster, outside the big city, is beautiful, as all rural Ireland is, especially when the sun comes out on that glistening green countryside. I was standing on top of Blarney castle in the misty rain when exactly this happened.

39

I could imagine the land of legends, fairies, poets, heroes, saints: Yeats, Patrick, Chuhulan, Brian Boru.

Even Dublin, which claims its Georgian buildings are beautiful, is really only tasteful, with the Liffy River flowing through it. The pubs are full of good talk. The town is full of memories of great literature, especially of James Joyce and that greatest of modern novels, *Ulysses*.

Jim doesn't remember leaving Ireland. He was only two when Mary and Sam McLarnin took their two little boys and their little girl on the ship for Canada. Think of what those partings must have been like from the old world to the new. People could not fly back for a holiday. They might as well have been going to Mars. Letters, yes, but they would probably never see each other again in this world, their nearest and dearest gone forever.

"You'll write, Mary, Sam, and tell us how you're doing and how the dear little children are." But they knew they would never see them again.

On the first part of the trip across the Irish Sea, little Sammy took sick and died. Would Mary and Sam have cursed the day they decided to try for a better life? They named the first boy born in Canada Sammy, as was the custom of the day, and hoped that it was the soul of their little boy come back. Sam did become a Christian minister.

How must they have felt when they laid their Sammy in his lonely little grave in Liverpool and left him for the other side of the world.

"It's not the leaving of Liverpool that grieves me, but my darling when I think of thee."

Jim's earliest memories are not of Ireland, but of the Canadian prairies and the McLarnin family farm in Mortlach, Saskatchewan. That memory is as clear as an Ansel Adams photograph. It's like my memory of listening with my dad to Jimmy's first fight with Ross.

People know how the Blacks came to America, but the passage of most of the Irish was hardly better and often worse. It was good economics to keep slaves alive, but who cared about the Irish. On the sunny afternoon of May 5, 1847, the brig Midas sailed into the harbour of St. John, New Brunswick, and anchored at the Partridge Island quarantine station. An immigration officer went on board and said he saw "the most horrible, ghastly, and pitiful sight ever seen in a North American port." This was still pre-American Civil War, and black slave ships still operated, but never anything like this! Hundreds of starved families – men, women, children, and babies – were packed into the hold, and it was, as the officer said, "far worse than any slaver." Children and babies were dying in their parents' arms. They huddled, hollow-eyed, on wooden benches, surrounded by their pitiful possessions. They were too sick from Typhus to crawl onto the deck now that their prison was unlocked, for they had been locked below decks for the voyage. They had lived and died in the filth of their own excrement for weeks. Many were to die and be buried on Partridge Island in the next few days. The Midas was no isolated hell ship. She was merely the first, the forerunner of an armada that in the next seven years filled the ports of North America. Dr. Douglas, who met the ship at Quebec, said, "I never saw people so indifferent to life. They would remain in the same berth with a dead person until the seaman dragged the corpse out with a boathook." Those few years brought 350,000 Irish to Canada. 1847 was the year of the typhus epidemic, the blackest year of Ireland's sad history, the worst year of the potato famine. In ten years, Ireland's population was reduced from 9 to 6 million. It had been one of the more populous and prosperous areas of Europe for small, industrious, independent farmers. It had been little touched by the enclosure movement, which destroyed the Scottish Highlanders, or the industrial revolution, which depopulated the English countryside. Over the next few years, the population continued to drop, through bad absentee management and immigration, to 4 million, and then stabilized for a century before it began to grow again, slowly.

When the Irish sought work in the new lands of North America, they were met with signs that said, "No Irish need apply." And if they wished to use a public facility, the sign said, "No dogs or Irish." Only the forced collectivization and prison camps or Gulags of Marxist Russia under Lenin (15 million died in the Ukraine alone, in the 1920's – over double Hitler's holocaust of the Jews) was worse than what happened to the Irish. True, Cromwell had swept through Ireland with his committed army of Puritans, destroying any churches they thought too beautiful, driving the native Celtic Irish "to hell or to Connaught," Ireland's western province, and reducing the original Celtic Irish, who had repulsed the Vikings, to a mere 500,000. But in the middle of the nineteenth century, the worst of the potato famine could have been relieved by the British government. They had seen it coming. Conservative Prime Minister, Sir Robert Peel, desperately sought a solution. But the Whig administration of Liberal Lord John Russell, the ancestor of philosopher Bertrand Russell, was concerned that they were doing too much for the Irish, making them lazy, and upsetting the workings of laissez faire economics. Even Peel found that the Irish famine had become inextricably tied up with the Free Trade issue and the repeal of the "Corn Laws". Ireland even exported wheat at the height of the potato famine! The worst province was Donegal, which lost 80 % of its population, while Ulster was the best, losing only 18 %. Ulster was continually the best economic area of Ireland. During their struggle in the new land, they rose first in competitive athletics, like other races finding themselves at the bottom of the social ladder, and they dominated boxing and became "the fighting Irish".

When Sam McLarnin bought his farm outside Mortlach, Saskatchewan, he was prepared to work as hard as he had worked hard before, as a diver on the Clyde Bridge in southwestern Scotland, in the Belfast shipyards, and as a butcher. He had worked on farms in Canada, so he knew what lay ahead. I talked this over with Jim one evening. "Oh, dad was a hustler. If you were Irish, you had to be! Boxing gave me a chance to do better. My kids went to college. On the Prairie, it was a tough life. We went to school four miles away and sometimes it was 40 below."

"Dad raised wheat and got 15 cents a bushel for top hard wheat – 15 cents!" These are Jim's first memories. "I can still see the chickens, and the cow, and the waving wheat." The McLarnins farmed for seven years. They lived and broke even, but Sam McLarnin was determined to get ahead. They sold and packed up and moved on west, as most North Americans did when things didn't work out. So the McLarnins came to their home on the West Coast, where Jim grew up. "I was born in Ireland, but I'm a West Coast of America boy."

Jim and his father, Sam

Jim and his mother, Mary

Chapter 10
Vancouver "I'd have hated to have grown up rich."

When Jim was nine, the McLarnins settled in Vancouver, British Columbia, on the shores of the Pacific. Samuel McLarnin was determined to do anything to support his family. His daughter, Olive, told me he got one job in a mill by excusing himself to the front of the line. Well, he had kids to feed, and it always pays to be a gentleman. The McLarnins were tough and determined but polite, not a bad combination. So Sam moved from one job to another and saved his money and managed to buy a second-hand furniture shop in the 700 block of Hastings Street in East Vancouver. They had rented a large apartment that you walked up to from the street, close to the store, so that someone could be there at all hours. When they began to do better, Sam bought a house on Union Street, about a block away, in a decent residential area. The area, although not the tenants, has not changed much. It was full of families, mostly Irish and Italian, with plenty of kids. Jim liked it. There was action. Jim always liked lots going on.

But with the family growing to thirteen, every penny counted, so the oldest boy, Jimmy, began selling newspapers on Hastings Street when he was ten. The Province was not only Vancouver's, but also B.C.'s, leading newspaper. There used to be about 200 guys who claimed to have sold papers just across the street from the great Jimmy McLarnin. Jim found the best corner was just off Hastings and Main, where the Union steamship docked. You could sell people a paper as they came out of the station, carry their luggage if they gave you a chance, hail a taxi, and get a good tip. Jim was ideal for that job. He was quick as lightning, smart, strong, and a good-looking little kid. Jimmy became street smart, just as most future boxing greats did.

Sam McLarnin's business was prospering and he was respected. Jimmy was doing well in defending himself, but he was small. "Dad did well, but there were a lot of us to feed. When I started out working, I weighed 60 pounds. You don't know what it's like to be poor unless you were a poor youngster who went short of food," said Jim. "But I'd have hated to grow up rich." Jim meant it helped him understand life, and it made him a fighter. Many boys became fighters because they were in trouble with the law, or hated to go to school, or had no chance to get another job. Jim wasn't one of those boys. He went to a good school, Strathcona School, a few blocks from his home, and he has fond memories of it. He said the teachers were all good people and the principal was a very fine man. Jim was not a discipline problem. He took part in school activities. He played basketball, soccer, baseball, and anything else going. He was small, but he was a natural athlete.

Charlie Foster, an Irish longshoreman from Liverpool, was watching a soccer game between the school from the East End and another school when he noticed a little kid with husky legs playing well, with no fear of anything, and he asked who that kid was. Sam McLarnin's boy, Jimmy, he was told. Next time Foster dropped into Sam's shop on Hastings, he said to Sam, "That's a good boy you've got there, Sam, I like his spirit. Saw him play soccer the other day."

"Yes, he's a good boy," said McLarnin senior, "but his mother worries about him. He gets into a lot of fights."

"Does he indeed," thought Foster to himself. "Well, I'd like to see him fight, even if Mrs. McLarnin doesn't."

I asked Jimmy's old friend, Earl Hilbert, why Foster had chosen McLarnin rather than another kid in the area where a lot of kids were tough and could fight. There must have been many kids there willing to try pro fighting for a living.

Hilbert said, "Oh, Jimmy was the best of us. He could jump somersaults in the air, just like that."

McLarnin denied any special athletic excellence. "Champions are made, not born," he declared emphatically.

I believe Pop Foster knew what to tell a talented youngster. "You're not bad, son, and if you work hard we just might be able to make something of you." Pop knew that it isn't worth fighting professionally unless you could get to the top and be, at least, a contender. The only way to do that is to get a talented youngster and convince him that only hard work will do it for him, and then, with luck and good management, he might make it. All the work and average talent, or great talent and not much work, won't do it. He must have both. The kid also has to have been fighting since he could first remember. The great champion, Tony Canzoneri, said that he started late, not really having a serious fight until he was eight. You can't start late and be a champion. You can sometimes start a professional career late, as Marciano did, but you must have been fighting in the streets when you were a kid.

I learned to box in university, but you don't learn to fight there. You learn in the streets and then a professional trainer takes you and teaches you how to box well. It helps if you were small when you were a boy and were from a minority race so that when they called you derogatory names, you would fight for your life. That is what a pro boxer's job is, and to do less is unforgivable, as Max Baer and Roberto Duran found out. It is the job of their managers and the referee to see that they don't die.

Jim grew up fighting on the streets of East Vancouver. To go from there to a pro boxing ring simply meant that you would get a fair fight, with less chance of getting hurt because there's a referee and a doctor in attendance.

If you had a good corner to sell papers on and you were small, and you expected to take your money home to your mom, you had to be a fighter. Al Principe told me that if you wandered into someone else's territory, you would get your nose broken. Jim wasn't born a fighter but he was born with good reflexes and balance.

"I hated flying to a fight," Jim told me. "I used to get sick. I asked a doctor about it and he told me my sense of balance might be too good, and easily affected by flight."

Anyway, Jim's dad gave him a pair of boxing gloves and told him roughly how to use them, when Jim was about ten. After his brief lesson, Jimmy went out onto Union Street looking for a sparring partner. Down went his first opponent with his first blow – most encouraging. Jim continued down the street looking for another worthy opponent. The next pugilist knew a bit about boxing and handed the future welterweight champion of the whole world a good trimming. It does little good in most cases to win them all. Even then, Jim hated to lose and so he began to haunt the local gyms in his spare time. He was determined to master this business. He began to work out at one of the gyms – punch the bag, watch the better boys spar.

Local promoter, Charlie "Roughhouse" Burns, seeing Jim often there, encouraged him to take a fight at the bottom of the card at a small club. "You're a comer kid. You'll be all right."

"I never had an amateur fight," Jim told me. "I was a pro when I was 12, getting paid for fighting once a week or so, before I met Pop Foster." Jim always had a good right hand punch and he had guts. "I came at them," said Jim. "Mom didn't like me fighting so I called myself by another name for a while. My record says I had about 80 fights but I had well over 100 pro fights. I fought at 'smokers' and in 'free-for-alls.' I don't know how many." Smokers were part of the times. A group of well-to-do men paid to watch a few teen-aged fighters coming up to fight privately. It was growing up too soon.

Jim remembers a tough four round bout with Clarence Brown at the Cavalry club on Granville and Smythe when he was eleven and Brown was thirteen.

"I remember fighting in a club so far out that I had to walk home late at night through dark streets. I don't think I got paid, or it was so late that the streetcars weren't running, and I was scared I'd get licked when I got home after I'd got licked in the ring."

You didn't get paid off until the whole card was over, and that was how he arrived home after dark when his parents expected him well before nine.

Jim dreamed of being the lightweight champ. He would be rich and famous and life would not be so hard for the Irish boy from the East End, or for his brothers and sisters or his parents.

Burns wasn't the only promoter around. The Australian heavyweight, Jim Tracy, began to promote and Jim fought for him. If they liked the bout, people would throw extra money into the ring, so a boy could come home with a few more dollars.

Pro boxing was a widespread and pervasive activity in the first half of the 20th century. A tough young man could take a preliminary fight for a few dollars, and, if he learned a bit, he could supplement his income considerably by fighting regularly on the under card. Jim had become the leading fighter of his gang of kids, so, although he fought for money, he also fought for his gang's honour in the streets. Earl Hilbert said, "Sure we fought. The Italians against the Irish. But we both fought fair. No knives. No guns. We formed a ring and when a boy went down, we didn't kick him. That would have been considered cowardly." Boxing is an archaic hangover from a gentler age, like giving your place to a lady on a streetcar. The historian Trevelyan said that boxing had a civilising influence on the British when it became popular in the 18th century. A man could have an argument in a pub and get out alive. He could box on the street and learn and live to fight again. He even had time to take off his coat and hand it to a friend. Jim said his pal, Bill Forst, who became a successful journalist and businessman after he covered all Jim's big American fights for The Province, used to hold Jim's coat in those street fights when they were both boys.

"I remember I fought Guido Cima in an alley. He wouldn't go down or quit. It seemed to have gone on for two hours. The alley was jammed. Guido was good and tough. Couldn't have been two hours but it felt like it. Never mind Madison Square Garden in New York. I had my toughest fights on the streets of Vancouver."

The streets of the East End were damp and musty most of the year. There were guys selling pencils for a living. Over it all, towered the oppressive mountains of the Coast Range. It called for a hard people.

How did our champion become a pro? In the centre of a ring of boys in a tough neighbourhood, he fought until his opponent couldn't get up again. He was carried back on his pals' shoulders and they shouted, "You got him, Jimmy. What a fight! Jimmy won for us." Did the thousands of cheers in Madison Square Garden sound as good as those from his pals when he won for his gang?

But, along with this, Jim trained to be a boxer. He punched the bag in the gym, did roadwork like a pro, running beside the streetcar tracks along Hastings Street. Pop saw him jogging and thought, "There's that McLarnin kid. He's serious."

Once, Jim went to Nanaimo, across on Vancouver Island, for a fight. They were offering $15 and a full steak dinner for good boys to fight in the preliminary of a big fight. Jim won, got his money, but couldn't eat his steak, because he had broken his thumb and couldn't hold his knife. Damn, you didn't get steak very often at the McLarnins, maybe chicken on Sunday.

Jim was not a complete novice when Foster got him, so it was now time for the appearance of the old magician, the great white wizard, for Gandalf, himself, or Merlin. The hero was ready for the quest.

Chapter 11
The Coming of the Wizard : Pop Foster

All good fighters are basically junkyard dogs, and Jim had done his time fighting in the "junk yard." The young hero had served an apprenticeship; the wizard appeared. There lived, in that section of East Vancouver, a mysterious and watchful old man. He had recently come there, and people thought that he was only a longshoreman who worked on the waterfront, but there was more to him than that, and you could feel it when he spoke to you in his Liverpool Irish accent. Moreover, he had a quiet confidence and an inner depth that made people defer to him. He had apparently done considerable fighting someplace, but no one guessed the extent of his powers. He said his name was Charlie Foster, and he looked closely at things, with a squint, for he saw this world not too well, he said. But, being a wizard, he saw into the hearts of men and he saw into the future. He walked with a limp, but his muscular stocky build, thick hands and neck, made you never think of it as a handicap. He went for treatment to Shaughnessy Military Hospital, for his body was scarred with the wounds of battles from Africa to France and back to England. He watched the soccer and sports fields of the East End and he watched the boxing gyms and rings, and he seemed to be quietly waiting for something, with confidence that it would come. Who knows what a wizard thinks? Did the plan come to him after he saw Jim as an extraordinary prospect, or did he have it already for a lad just like Jim? The wizard knows the hero of the quest as soon as he sees him.

Foster had grown up with his father's circus, where he boxed all comers for money in what was called "the booths". It was a strange phenomenon. Each circus would have a professional fighter who was prepared to take on anyone who paid down some money. The circus would then pay back one pound for every round that the person could stay in the ring. It was the business of the pro to K.O .everybody in a round, if possible. It made for good entertainment and involved the spectators. Foster probably weighed only about 175 pounds as a young man but he had to take on anyone at

47

any weight. Nevertheless, light heavyweights, like Billy Conn, who weighed 168 when he fought the great Joe Louis, have beaten top heavyweights. Jim said Foster was middleweight champion of England, but I expect that it was more informal than that. Foster not only took care of the tough customers who thought that they could stay with him a few rounds, but he bought bottles of whiskey for his father, and took care of him when he'd had too much. Thanks to this, Foster had seen enough of liquor, and apparently never touched it himself. I believe that Foster was looking for a good prospect and in return he was going to do right by this boy and not let what happened to Spike Robson happen to this kid. Spike had made a lot of money, but was still almost penniless. Next time, there would be no mistakes. Next time, they were not going to cheat his boy.

Then Foster saw McLarnin. "I liked his spirit most," Foster said, years later. "You couldn't help but like him." Foster saw something in the young man's heart that was championship potential. Foster thought he and Jim could make money together, but I think it was mostly the joy of creating that motivated Foster, as it moves all really good coaches, the artistic satisfaction of seeing that you have created a great athlete. In return, Foster would see that this boy was financially secure for the rest of his life. He had seen young Jim play soccer in Grandview, and he had noticed him in the gyms, and then came the clincher. He saw Jim in a fight with a bigger boy, Mike Tomasovich, on Jim's newspaper corner. Jim's sister, Olive, said that she thought the other boy was the same age as Jim, but Jim was small for his age. Jim said that Mike was a good fighter and had as much right as he had to that corner, but he wasn't about to give it to him.

"Anyway, we went at it and we drew a crowd, and when Mike had had enough and left, I suddenly saw this big husky old man limp over to me and squint down at me with a penetrating look -- I can see it today -- grab my right wrist in his huge hands, and say, 'I like the way you handle yourself, son. How would you like to be a fighter?' I was a little puzzled, so I asked him what kind of a fighter he meant. 'The only kind worth bein', son, a champion."

Foster had set the goal in front of Jim. It was Merlin come for Arthur, Gandolf for Frodo. Now, Pop began to train Jim into possibly the greatest welterweight who ever lived, and yes, one of the greatest fighters of all time.

> "And down the wave and in the flame was borne
>
> A naked babe, and rode to Merlin's feet,
>
> Who stoopt and caught the babe, and cried 'The King!
>
> Here is an heir for Uther!' And the fringe
>
> Of that great breaker, sweeping up the strand,

Lashed at the wizard as he spake the word,

And all at once all round him rose in fire,

So that the child and he were clothed in fire.

And presently thereafter followed calm,

Free sky and stars"

From *The Coming of Arthur*
by Lord Alfred Tennyson

I wish I could have talked with Foster in the flesh. He was in Vancouver when I was there in university and I may have walked by him on the street.

Homer says, as he begins the epic story of Ulysses, "I sing of a man who was never at a loss." There are such men, and Foster seems to have been one. Do they ever have inner doubts? Didn't he worry that he would bring home the McLarnin's little boy, beaten and injured. Managers have done that, even well-meaning managers.

They had to talk to Jim's mom and dad, for Jim was thirteen, and most kids that age had to ask their parents even if they could go out and play. Jim stood about five feet tall and weighed just under 100 pounds, and he was going to fight the toughest and most skilful fighters in the world.

So, again, Foster dropped in to Sam McLarnin's used furniture shop. "Morning, Sam," said Charlie, "I've just seen that fine young lad of yours in a fight on Main Street."

"Have you now indeed," said Sam, "I've several young lads and they all eat considerable and get into fights and I'll thank you not to worry their mother Mary about it. Which one is it this time?"

"I mean that fine lad of yours that sells papers."

"Oh, James is at it again, is he then? He thinks he'll be lightweight champion of the whole bloody world if he can just get enough black eyes brawling in the alley. Yes, he's a good lad. Behaves himself. Respects his elders. Works hard. Goes to school every day. But he keeps fighting. Funny, because he's a friendly kid, with lots of pals. Doesn't have a mean streak in him."

"Well now, Sam, that's exactly what I've come to talk to you about. I think that he really has the makings of a boxing champion. I've just seen him in a fight in front of the station with a bigger kid and a lovely thing it was to behold. Handles himself nicely, a bit crude. Thinks he has only one hand, but if I had him for a couple of years, I could teach him a thing or two, and we could see just how good he could get. If I managed him right, we could make a lot of money, and I believe that in the long run we just might have a champion, really, Sam! In two years, I'll put $5,000 in the bank in his name, maybe more, before I take my manager's cut. Then I want 50 %. Then we'll come home and you can reconsider. We'll have to go to the States. That's where the money and the titles are, and it won't hurt that he's Irish."

"Good Lord, Charlie, you seem to have thought this out in detail."

"Well, yes, I have, Sam, I've given it thought. I've been there before, you know."

"Well, I'll have to talk it over with Mary. But you'll take the best care of him, now, Charlie."

So they spat on their hands and shook on the bargain, as good Irishmen should, and that is all the contract Foster and the McLarnins ever had, for that sealed it, and what more could a decent man want?

They called in young Jim. "Mr. Foster tells me that you're not satisfied brawling in the alley. You want to do it in public now, is it James? Mr. Foster thinks you might just make a bit of money out of it. You'll have to obey him just as you do me and your mother. You'll give your word now!"

"Sure I will, dad."

"Do you want to be a professional fighter, James?"

"Yes, dad, I do!"

"All right, Charlie, if it's all right with Mary, he's yours. My store does all right, but I've too many mouths to feed. If Jim can feed himself, more power to him. But you'll bring him home safe? That boxing for money is a chancy business, and I've seen some as ended up badly. Mary would never forgive us if anything happened to Jim. We lost one poor little fellow you know. But all right, James, shake hands with your manager and promise you'll do as he says for I know he's an honourable man."

So the old man with the limp and the boy with the flashing fists, the wizard of secret boxing knowledge and the young athlete with lightning reflexes, shook hands on the bargain. Foster was Pop to Jim ever after that handshake. Only once did either threaten to break it, and that was when McLarnin was taking a terrible beating from that high plains assassin, hard-hitting Billy Petrolle, who caught Jim with a hard right to the temple and stunned him. Pop wanted to throw in the towel, but Jim said that he would never fight for him again if he did. Jim never quit. Pop knew Jim meant it.

"The only time I regretted it was when he kept feeding me Brussels sprouts. Maybe we couldn't afford better at the time, but they're a third class vegetable. Pop made me promise to stay away from wine and women until we finished. Heck, I was thirteen. I was a virgin until I was 21. Isn't that terrible? Well, maybe it isn't."

"No, Jim, I don't think it is."

McLarnin had heard that about wine and women from his Methodist mother. And so the wizard began training the young hero for the quest.

Pop supervises Jim's left hand

PART II
California: Jim's Early Boxing Career

Chapter 12
Forging the magic sword: a Great Left

Pop, I suspect, could hardly wait to get his protégé to the big time in the States. Nevertheless, he knew better than to rush a good prospect and certainly such a young one, and in those days there were other good little fighters in Vancouver. They set up a gym in the McLarnin back yard. They worked on speed and the left hand. It's the left which is your best defence, and which prepares any sophisticated offence. In that home-made gym, Pop turned Jim into a complete fighter. Jim worked on the heavy bag, which builds muscle in the back, arms and shoulders. Look how broad McLarnin's shoulders are, even in early pictures. I think that leverage is where Jim's power came from. He definitely had a great right and a strong left hook. McLarnin constantly complained of punching the bag until his arms felt as if they would drop off. Pop worked on Jim's balance until he could throw any punch and then counter it with a combination and remain in balance. Then the light bag. Pop said this produced speed, the most important thing in boxing. Watch Ali, with his speed, completely humiliate the awesome Liston, one of the hardest hitters and toughest boxers who ever lived.

McLarnin was faster than almost all the men he fought. The average fan has no idea how fast a young athlete can be.

"Pop kept me punching the light bag with my left hand until I couldn't hold it up any longer. You can get along without your right if you can left jab and move, but you can't get along without your left." McLarnin thought of his left jab as his best punch. I think he was most proud of it because he and Pop created it. Billy Petrolle, for example, would have killed McLarnin, perhaps literally, after he caught Jim with a hard right to the temple, if Jim had not spent all those hours in the gym working on his left jab, speed, and footwork.

Down on East Hastings, in the 20s and 30s, the neighbours would lean over the fence and watch Jim punch the light bag. Pop made him shadowbox with a book on top of his head so he could move around without any jerky head movements, and not lose sight, even momentarily, of his opponent's eyes or hands. Pop had Jim jog, jump hedges, exercise with weighted Indian clubs, use his teeth to swing a 12 pound weight held by a rope to strengthen his neck and do surprisingly advanced series of exercises. But, always, they worked on speed and Jim's left hand. The kids in the district would hear the light bag start, rat a ta, rat a ta, rat a ta, and they would run to look over and through the fence to see Jim train. Later, when he was a headliner in New York, Chicago, and L.A., he would come home, go out into the back yard, punch the bag. All the kids would shout, "Jimmy's home!" and run to see their champ. It was a thrill they never forgot.

Jim had told me about Mickey Gill, his closest competitor in Canada. A newspaper article referred to his three great fights with McLarnin, but the headline was that Mickey had been killed in France in the Second World War, while serving in the paratroops. There was a picture of Gill in a fighting pose, looking like McLarnin.

Mickey and Jim fought a four rounder and then a six rounder for the city championship. Jim won both but they were close. They fought a third fight, ten rounds in Oakland, when Jim was on his way to the championship, and it was a good fight, but not as close as the Vancouver ones, for Jim had learned a lot. Jim learned every time he fought. Some fighters do, but not all. That's how Jim got as good as he did. Before he began taking lay offs, Lord, he was good. They didn't see him when he took out Kaplan and Terris and completely dominated Petrolle and the great Canzoneri in the second fights. Jimmy said that you have to be pretty stupid not to learn a lot about a fighter when you had fought him for 15 rounds. Unfortunately, there are some pro fighters who are not as smart as McLarnin was.

He had to fight the best to improve. Pop knew how to match Jim. Besides, Pop was put off with the promoters and matchmakers in Canada. They were making great money every time Jim fought, and paying him peanuts. He didn't owe the Canadian promoters anything. No fighter in Canada could give Jim competition by that time. Mickey Gill got pretty good and fought semis at Madison Square Garden in New York, but Jim fought the headline fights there. Maybe Pop put their money in a bank he trusted. He didn't trust many things. Pop wouldn't take cheques, even for a big fight. He wanted cash. He would stay at the Cobalt or the Ivanhoe or the Abbotsford, far from the expensive hotels in town. He lived all his life in hotels. Jim would go home to William Street in Grandview and the McLarnins would celebrate. It was a good community. The kids all sold newspapers down on the docks; wharf rats they were called – Al Principe and Jim and Guido Cima and Nodge Megro, Scotty Lermond, Mike Thomas, Don Christian, and Harold Hudson. These were the kids Jim didn't get to hang around with when Pop took him to California. They were pals but they fought.

One of the fights between Jim and Guido was over giving a kid with an English accent a hard time. An English accent would get you despised and beaten up. The colour of your skin meant nothing. They'd lend dockworkers change when they needed it. They had change from the papers. Then, on payday, they'd get paid back with a big tip. They trusted each other.

My dad said that when you went into a bar, they passed you the bottle and you poured your own drink. Nobody would cheat on it. You bought a beer and you could fix yourself a sandwich from the sideboard. Dempsey said he lived on that for a while – tough times, but good times. There were jobs and you worked long and hard, but there were opportunities.

Jim had some good fights in Vancouver, not only with his rival, Mickey Gill. He had ten fights, 4 rounds each, in 1923, won them all from good boys, Ainsworth, Frye, Peterson, Wallace and Hector McDonald, with a final 6 rounds with Gill. However, with Pop, Jim had gone beyond them, and so the wizard led Jim to the next stage, to the fight clubs of Oakland, California -- a tough town then and a tough town now, and a hotbed of boxing.

How do you become a champion? You need to have a wizard, as Jim had, to point you in the right direction for the quest. Tolkien will tell you about wizards and heroes and how they accomplish their tasks despite, 'the dark lord on his dark throne in the land of Mordar where the shadows lie'.

"That's how it all started," said Jim. "Pop taught me how to box, not just fight, before we went to the States, so I could handle myself with just about anybody. Well, maybe not Bud Taylor. I wish I could have fought him later. By the time we went to California on that boat, I could tie a guy up if he stung me, slip punches – there are headliners today that can't really slip punches. No wonder they get hurt!" He looked off into the corner of his front room as if he were waiting for Pop to appear again, as he did on Main Street in Vancouver many years ago, and Jim would jump up and shout, "Pop!" But the wizard has gone ahead and we will follow him to that "undiscovered country from whose bourn no traveller returns".

"Jim," I said, "it sounds as if it all came from a storybook."

"It does indeed. I can hardly believe it all happened to me," said Jim, shaking his head, and I remembered how a sports writer had said that McLarnin sometimes had the look, not of a fighter, but of a kid who suddenly found the candy store unlocked. "Jesus loves me," Jim said.

I thought of what Sir William Temple said about heroes, "A hero must not only be brave but also fortunate."

"Yes," said Jim, "I was very lucky to have Pop as manager. Pop's up there in Forest Lawn. Looking down over Glendale. He can see our house from there. Pop died in a hotel in Vancouver. I went and got him. I wanted him here. I think he would have liked that." Jim was Pop's boy to the end.

"Then it turned out that he had left his money to us, to me and Lil – and the kids – in trust. I can't touch the principal. He was a careful old guy. Left nothing to chance. He'd spent hardly a cent of what we'd made. He lived in a single little room in North Hollywood. He bought an old used car, but he could hardly drive it; he was half blind. Probably, he lived on his war pension as we did when we went to San Francisco. He was a canny old character. He used to come over for Sunday dinner and play with the kids, sweep the front walk, fix the door, and say grace at dinner. I used to go to see him in his little room and ask him what he was saving his money for and he'd say, 'For you, Jimmy.' Damn it, I had lots of money, but I must admit that his money came in handy later. I'd tell him to get himself a nice place, but he'd say, 'What does a man really need, Jim?' But he seemed to see the future. What a man! He made me. Greatest manager in the world."

"Jim, he knew you and he knew fighters; he knew the fight game and he understood human nature. Fighters must take chances with their health in the ring, so they often take chances with their money out of the ring. Wizards sometimes live their lives backwards." Jim looked at me funny.

Charlie Foster came from Liverpool, Liverpool Irish, and so probably had an accent something like the Beatles, but with a touch of Irish lilt in it. Liverpool is a tough town. I've never seen a town with so much graffiti on walls and litter on streets, and a beautiful new cathedral looking it all over from a hill, full of life and people whistling Beatles' tunes.

Foster's dad ran a circus and his grandfather ran the boxing booths. Foster wasn't that big but he was thick of build. People remember his thick neck and big hands and wrists. The McLarnin and Cupit children remember his big strong hands. He was about 5 foot 10 and 165 pounds as a young man, but 180 pounds without much fat as an older man – an ideal warrior size – not too big to feed or get tired on a fast march – just the size the Roman legions liked. He went partly bald early, so he cut his hair close. In the booths, he would fight six days a week but not on Sunday. That is work but it kept his father in whiskey. "I took them all on, bare knuckles or gloves, big or small. Heavyweight? Didn't matter. Hit 'em right and they all sit down." In war and peace, Foster was a warrior.

As well as that incredible training, Foster had the opportunity to see, train, and fight the most original genius of the entire boxing ring in history, the Swafham Gypsy, Jem Mace, from county Norwich. The turf rings of England, based in Liverpool, were dominated by the world's heavyweight champion, Mace. This was the man who, more than any other, invented the science of boxing, as Jim calls it. At Newcastle, when Foster saw the fading shadow of this immortal, his analytic mind took flame. This man knew exactly how to fight. Foster hung on every move that Mace made. Charlie could try each move, for every day he had toughs to practise on.

I wrestled at college and trained high school wrestlers in all the standard moves, but I had a chance to watch and work with Canada's silver medallist from the Pan Am games, Mimo Marello, who helped me train some of my best prospects. He didn't just do the move right. He did it exactly right to the inch with perfect timing. Wow! I'm sure that Foster felt like that when he watched Mace.

Mace was an extraordinary man. He always dressed like a dandy. He stood just over 5 foot 10 and weighed around 170 pounds, about Billy Conn's size, when he demolished the previous heavyweight champ, Sam Hurst, "the Stalybridge Infant," who stood 6 foot 3 and weighed 215, just Ali's size. The difference was that Mace could box like Conn and Ali, and Hurst slugged like Liston. Mace retained his title until the age of 59. Yes, 59! Bare knuckle fighting was a combination of boxing and wrestling. In a clinch, for example, you could throw your man with a head and arm (my own favourite throw) and that counted as a knock down. You could use your feet as a judo expert does, sweeping the feet from under your opponent. However, time catches even the greatest, and Mace was knocked senseless by Charlie Mitchell in four rounds, just before Mace turned 60. "Jolly Cholly" was famous for knocking down the great John L. Sullivan, and then retreating for the remainder of the fight, making sarcastic remarks about Sully. The great John L. hated Mitchell and despised him as a 'sprinter', as they used to shout at a man who wouldn't stand still and punch toe to toe. However, he must have had a punch to put down Sullivan, who was thick and tough at just over 6 feet and 215 pounds. Sully had won his championship in New Orleans, from Paddy Ryan, who was bigger than John L., with Oscar Wilde and Jesse James watching. Sully was not only the fighting champion of the world but also the drinking champion of the world, and as proud of one record as the other. After he had come into a bar and said that he could lick any man in the house, he would demand, "What's the record of this establishment?" In his book *Heavyweight Champions*, Stanley Weston claims that it is authenticated that over one evening Sully put away 60 two-ounce shots of whisky, and then said, "Now bring me a bottle. I'll drink for me own pleasure."

Sullivan used to do his roadwork with his girlfriend, Anne Livingston, the burlesque queen. Rocky Marciano, who came from John L.'s area and was a similar type, once used his line in a speech in London, where he said, "I don't know what I'm doing up here. I can't sing or dance or make a good speech, but, just to be sociable, I'll fight the best man in the house."

Jimmy told me that famous old champ James J. Corbett, who defeated Sullivan, used to come around to his camp.

But back to Mace. Mace put on boxing exhibitions into his 60's with leading active English boxers. When he was in Liverpool, he gave an exhibition for the Prince of Wales, who was a sporting gentleman in many ways, and I have been told that Charles Foster appeared in one of the preliminary bouts.

At any rate, Foster fought as a middleweight until he enlisted in the army and went to South Africa to see action in the Boer War.

Corbett, despite being "Gentleman Jim", had a superior attitude that made other fighters dislike him. He was an astute businessman, a member of the posh Olympic Club in San Francisco, an actor, and a classy dresser with a classic profile, who got along with intelligent fighters like Tunney and McLarnin, but often wouldn't speak to brawlers. McLarnin doesn't make this distinction, I noticed, as I met his old boxing pals at the Golden State boxing and wrestling club.

Foster, who served in the Scots Guards, was wounded three times in the Boer War. Jim didn't know a lot about Pop's war experiences in South Africa because Pop didn't talk much about himself, but he was present one time when Pop ran into one of his army buddies from that distant war. He was down on his luck. Jimmy says he saw Pop give the old soldier $10,000.

The old soldier told Jimmy that Pop should have received the Victoria Cross, the award for bravery, for his absolute fearlessness under fire. Several times he retreated, carrying wounded men. Under fire, Pop's chief concern seemed not to be his own skin, but that of his buddies. In World War I, Pop re-enlisted. He was too old for active front line duty so he served with the railway construction corps, but they were close to the front and came under fire often. Jim said Pop was "blown up at Popperinge".

In between the wars, Pop began training fighters. His wounds from Africa made him too slow in a ring to continue his own career. It was at this time, in a gloomy Leeds gym, that he saw Spike Robson, aged 18. As with Jimmy, Pop taught him all the moves and took him to America. Spike fought close fights with the legendary greats of his day. I believe that Pop thought his boxing was as good as or better than Mclarnin's, but he didn't have Jimmy's punch. Robson retired with enough money that should have done him for life, if frugally used, but ended up broke. On and off all his life, Pop would send Spike money. When Pop and Jim went to England they went to see Spike, and Pop again gave him money. "God bless you, Pop," said Spike.

To be a pro fighter, you can't be a cautious person. To be a pro fighter, you must start fighting when you are a boy. It is no wonder that so many of them end up broke. Fighters are notorious soft touches. Having come from poverty in almost every case, they have a natural sympathy for anyone down on his or her luck. They tend, except for Marciano, who never picked up a check in his life, to be overly generous with their money. Joe Louis was the softest touch in history. A champion fighter also used to be so well known in those days that he was instantly recognised by most of the public.

"Hey, champ, can you spare a fiver?"

"Sure, pal, good luck!"

"God bless you, champ."

Most boxers know from the early years of their career that a few dollars, which most of us hardly miss, can be the difference between eating or starving, and that is a big difference. Pop and Jim nearly starved in their early years in Oakland and again in Chicago. I have seen McLarnin give a parking lot attendant $20 for pointing out a space. The Bible tells us that to those who ask, "Turn thou not away," and "In as much as you have done it unto one of the least of these my brethren, you have done it unto Me." Perhaps fighters will fare better than most of us on the day of judgement.

Boxers' talents are mainly physical, and few are devious. Jimmy, for example, was a great boxer, a talented Irish step dancer, a natural gymnast, and he became a fine golfer, but, despite his native intelligence, he was too trusting. One of his business partners cheated him out of thousands of dollars. Foster, for all his generosity, kept his eye closely on people. Promoters were never too keen on him, although they respected him as a man of his word. When he limped into their office bearing the wounds from the mine that had blown him up in Belgium, they knew they had to deal with a man who could not be bribed into throwing a fight.

Foster took this talented kid and showed him how to use his speed to avoid getting hit in a boxing ring. Norman Mailer said of Ali in his early years that he seemed to think it obscene to get hit. "No," said Jim, "just suicidal. The brain's a delicate thing. You don't learn from getting hit. You just get slowed down. Anybody hit me, it was a mistake. In his last years, Ali forgot this and seemed to think it was macho to take a punch. Ridiculous! You can never laugh off a punch. They tell on you. Pop told me that."

Mankind does boast a few like Charlie Foster, men of integrity and fearlessness who seem to care little for themselves and spend their lives protecting their friends from their human foibles because, although they are very human, they themselves seem to be above such things. Their own deaths seems to be beneath their notice. They ask little reward but the satisfaction of a unique job well done. A Vancouver reporter tells of sending a cab to bring Foster, then in his 70's, across town, and being told that Mr. Foster could walk across town very nicely, thank you. He drank water when he could have drunk the best liquor and he thanked his God he had good water. The wizard did what he was sent to do. O brave soul! O great heart! O indomitable warrior! Mighty wizard of arcane knowledge! In what Valhalla of the brave does your immortal soul live? Are you talking to Sullivan or Mace or Dempsey or Achilles or Roland or Bayard or El Cid or Richard Cour de Leon? Hail and farewell, great warrior. As Charlie Mitchell said when he heard that John L. Sullivan had died, "By God, he was a man and a half, that one. No, make that two and a half." So was Charlie Foster.

So Jim, with the consent of his parents, decided to become a professional boxer. He had been a very satisfactory student at Strathcona School and an eager participant in school athletics. He showed me a picture of the school baseball team, winners of the city championship, and there was Jim, at second base. Jim remembered with great affection the school and its teachers, and especially the principal, a backer of sports. Jim missed his family, his pals, and his school. He visited the school after he became world champion. What a thrill for all those kids, and the teachers, too!

When Jim talked, you would not realise that he had left school early. He made few grammatical errors and was well informed. While I was with him at his house in Glendale, he dropped over to see an old teacher from Vancouver who now lived in L.A. When I asked about leaving home at sixteen, he said that it seemed a good opportunity for a boy from a big working family in those days. He phoned home after all of his fights and told his mother he was all right. I don't think he regretted his decision to become a boxer. What he did regret was that in his teens, he didn't get to hang out with his pals, and he regretted that he didn't fight Bud Taylor when he was at his peak. I think that he wished that he could have had a fourth fight with Ross because, although he admitted Ross's talent, he was confident that he was better than Ross.

Jim worked hard at his job. "Your training must be harder than the fight." Jim constantly improved until he won the championship, and then he relaxed and lost some of his intensity. After the loss of his title, he again improved, to win it back. It is said that Irish fighters mature late, and if Jim had had reason to fight into his thirties, he would have reached his peak then. However, Jim fought professionally for nearly twenty years and he showed no signs either physically or mentally of all that pounding. Maybe not so much pounding, for Jim said to me, "If they hit me, they were lucky." Nevertheless, those fierce battles affected him noticeably. When Jim had just had a touch of "the creature", you could see the glitter in his eyes . With narrow slitted eyes, he would tell you how he would have beaten triple champ Henry Armstrong. It was Pop's idea to retire, not Jim's. Although I believe that Pop would have dearly loved to see his marvelous fighter take on the unbeatable Armstrong, they had taken an oath. No comebacks. Foster had seen even the great Jim Jeffries humiliated in a comeback. If you quit, stay quit. Ah, but just one shot at Armstrong. Pop and Jim were sure Jim had the correct style to beat him. Armstrong was simultaneously featherweight, lightweight, and welterweight champ – the greatest achievement of its kind before the proliferation of titles made a farce of multiple champs.

They planned to set out for California, which, at that time, contained almost all of the great fighters under the lightweight limit. "You'll look after him, now, Charlie," said Sam McLarnin, "His mother dotes on him and I'm somewhat partial to him myself."

"Like my own son, Sam, you can count on it."

Foster once said, after Jim had retired, that he was never quite satisfied with Jim's left jab.

"Well, maybe Pop liked to play it down. My right was supposed to be my best punch and perhaps he wanted to keep them thinking that. He was a foxy old beggar." I believe Foster was a purist. He had seen the greatest left jabs in history – Gan's, Corbett's, Leonard's, McFarlane's, Dixon's – and he would have liked McLarnin's to have been the very best of all, not just very good. I think Jim's left hook was his best punch because it was so well disguised, and almost as powerful as his right.

Jim got a dollar for his first professional fight in Nanaimo. That would have disqualified him for

the Olympics, not that anyone from the Canadian Olympic committee would have bothered about the brilliant little flyweight from Vancouver. The young men that Jim fought in California, when he became a headliner, had all boxed for the American Olympic team in 1924 and won medals for their country – Jackie Fields, Fidel LaBarba et al.

"All fighters are a bit crazy," said Jim. "I was a crazy kid when Pop got me, but I began to get $20, $50, $75 for a fight and, with Pop coaching, guys were having trouble even hitting me, so I began to think that this is not so bad. Once I got in a ring, I couldn't stand anyone beating me."

Jim picked up a few dollars fighting at smokers. "Well, it all helped the family. I liked to win in front of my friends, and at that age I liked to get out there and punch." His first bout was at the age of 12, against Clarence Robinson, at a military smoker. It was a draw. These were four rounders to begin with. "As time went by and I was fighting 10 or 15 rounds, that meant six or seven miles of roadwork in the morning before anyone else was up. Then you have breakfast and work on the light and heavy bag. In the afternoon, you work with sparring partners, going at least 150 rounds before the fight." Marciano, the hardest working of all heavyweights, used to do 250 rounds. Pop didn't let Jim use headgear during his sparring because he didn't want Jim to get used to it and get nailed in the fight.

"You should fight at least twice a year, maybe three or four times, depending on how tough or how long your fights lasted. Give yourself time to recuperate, then, six weeks before the next fight, go back to training. Watch your diet all the time. Pop believed in herbal teas, no sugar, just honey. I never had a drink of liquor until I stopped fighting professionally. Drugs? Lord, no! I wouldn't have been able to tie my shoelaces right if I'd had even a beer before a fight. To bed by nine every night and no tobacco or alcohol. Rest on Sunday. Yes, even Lil says it's good for a boy to know enough to protect himself, but we didn't have encourage our boy to be fighter. I took a couple of bad beatings. The ref will stop it and ask you what your name is and where you are. I've never been so dazed that I couldn't answer that, but some guys couldn't."

Willie Pastrano was taking a terrible beating from Jose Torres for the light-heavyweight title and, when asked, said, "My name is Willie Pastrano and I'm in Madison Square Garden getting the shit beaten out of me."

There is some sense in fighting until you drop. "Your opponent can get arm weary if he isn't superbly conditioned, or he may get overconfident and you can catch him coming in and add his momentum to your punch. I knocked out featherweight champ Kid Kaplan that way after I'd been down several times." The whole point is that the referee must be alert to the condition of each fighter.

By the beginning of 1924, Pop and Jim had decided to go to San Francisco. Pop sat down with Mary and Sam McLarnin and worked things out. "If this is what you really want," said his mother Mary.

"Was I sorry to leave Canada and home and family? Sure, but I had just gotten $65 from a big-hearted Canadian promoter for a fight where I filled the arena. Pop was disgusted. What would you do?"

Pop knew he couldn't go wrong. Jim had good legs, a natural hard right hand, and a good attitude. He would listen to instructions, and, above all, he had a fighting spirit. He didn't cut, and he had a cast iron jaw. Years later, Pop was proven correct. Jim had been knocked down only four times in twenty years of fighting and he was never knocked out – never! He was stopped once on a cut and Jim swears that his opponent, Ray Millar, had something in his glove. Millar got good mileage out of that punch, as the only man ever to stop Jimmy McLarnin, but once was refused a drink by an Irish bartender in San Francisco who said he couldn't stand to listen to how Millar had beaten the best fighter of our time. Foster did have a problem matching Jim because he started so early that he was always growing and you wouldn't know just what his weight might be by fight time. Many times, early in Jim's career, Foster was accused of getting him a small weight advantage. Jim would be fighting a full grown 25-year-old when he was 16 and Pop wanted things to be even when Jim was still growing.

California, at this time, was full of the returning victorious boxers from that great team of the Paris Olympics – the Olympics of *Chariots of Fire*, the Olympics of the great British track team of Harold Abramson and Eric Liddell. The American boxing team was equally great. Several of them became world pro champions. Two of those future champs, Jackie Fields and Fidel LaBarba, were waiting for Jim and any other rising prospect in California. The top lightweight fighters in the world were almost all, by strange coincidence, fighting in California, many of them to be hall of famers. Foster and McLarnin were really walking into the lion's den, but it may have been this competition that made McLarnin so good. LaBarba commented on Pop Foster, "He was a tough old guy, but a nice one, and he didn't care about anyone, high or low, as long as he protected his fighter."

When I mentioned to Jim what LaBarba had said, Jim said, "Even Mike Jacobs liked Pop, and he was pretty tight-fisted, but he knew Pop would keep his word."

Madison Square Garden had the money, the prestige, and the political connections, but Mike

Jacobs, a graduate of selling peanuts on the Coney Island excursion boats, had the brains. He set himself up as a rival to the entrenched Garden with his 20th century Boxing Club. He made good money promoting the sensational K.O. artist from the West Coast, Jimmy McLarnin, and he didn't forget Jim. Jim wrote to "Uncle Mike" to see if he could get some tickets for the SRO Louis Conn fight. Jacobs phoned Jim to tell him to come and there would be free tickets for the McLarnin party. "Just say how many there will be." Eventually, when Jacobs had Louis under contract, he took over the Garden as promoter. Now, however, he promoted Ross and McLarnin at the Garden Bowl.

The Bowl seemed a jinx. Champions always lost there. Primo Carnero had lost to Max Baer there, as had Baer to Jimmy Braddock. Carnero, at six foot six and 260 pounds, had been a professional strong man who had killed men in the ring. It seemed unfair to expect a 190 pound man to fight a 220 pound man. Jimmy Braddock was a workman inside the ring and outside of it, needing money to feed his young family. He had been on welfare for a couple of years. When he became champion, he paid back the government exactly the amount that he had received when he was down and out. The great movie *Cinderella Man* tells his story. He was your standard Irish 6 foot 1, 195 pound heavyweight who knew how to jab and slip and had a good right hand that even put down Joe Louis, but he wasn't a great fighter. He outboxed Baer, a better fighter, for 15 rounds, a stunning upset, at the Garden Bowl. The movie shows Baer making faces and acting the fool until the last rounds, when he realised that this journeyman was going to beat him because he had prepared and Max had not.

There was the same cry when Jess Willard knocked out Jack Johnson, for he was close to Carnero's size. But, in his first title defence, Willard was almost killed in a single round by the 185 pound Jack Dempsey, who hadn't had a decent meal for years. Dempsey was so fast that he hit Willard any time he wanted to, and Dempsey always felt like killing anyone who stepped into a ring with him.

Carnero was knocked down eleven times before the referee stopped the one-sided farce, and that was the end of the super heavyweight division. The annihilation of Willard and Carnero, the two largest heavyweight champs ever, should have settled the matter.

The greatest of heavyweight champs, Dempsey, Louis, and Marciano, were known for the ease with which they knocked out bigger men. Ali was so great because he was the fastest heavyweight of that size. Jimmy always declared that Pop said speed was the most important thing.

Concerning Baer and Braddock, Baer was a superb looking athlete with a wonderful right hand punch. He was 6 foot 4 and weighed 220 pounds. He had a physique like a Greek god. He was curly haired and handsome, with a golden smile and a great sense of humour, and he loved the ladies. They took one look at him and loved him back.

"Yeah," said Jimmy, "he was at a party in Hollywood with us -- I think it was at Clark Gable's house -- and I saw him looking at my Lilian. I'd have killed him if he had made a move."

Max died of a heart attack when he was staying at a hotel. He crawled to the phone and contacted the desk to ask for a doctor. The desk clerk asked if he wanted the house doctor. Max chuckled and said that no, he wanted a people doctor, chuckled again, and died.

One doubts that either Ross or McLarnin were concerned with the jinx at the Garden Bowl. It was sold right out that summer night, May 29, 1934, to see the two greatest boxers of their time meet. 60,000 fans paid $225,000 at the height of the Depression. They were not disappointed. Barney Ross's mother was there. Jimmy McLarnin's dad was there from Vancouver. How proud they both were when Jimmy and Barney came down the aisles, to the cheers of their fans. The event was a gala affair in New York, with all the rich and famous there in their finest clothes. Mayor Jimmy Walker was there. He never missed one of Irish McLarnin's big fights in his town, for Jim had become the toast of Broadway. Walker had a great appreciation of a classy stylist, especially if he were Irish, for the Mayor was a classy stylish Irishman himself. The Bowl was crowded with Irish and Jewish fans, as Barney and Jim were symbols of the manhood and courage of these two talented but abused and persecuted races, and when their compatriots became famous, they made the lives of all their fellows that much richer. This was not an expression of racial hatred, but of racial pride. Both Jimmy and Barney seemed completely void of racial prejudices.

The introductions took place, the whistle sounded, the seconds were out of the ring, and a hush fell as the long awaited contest began. "I was rusty and I had trained hard and that puts you on edge. I probably trained too hard. I was lighter than I had been for years. More endurance but not as strong as I should have been."

A couple of rounds were spent "feeling out the opponent". By the first round of the third fight, Jimmy and Barney still spent two minutes faking with their heads, their fists, their shoulders, and their feet, like two great chess players.

"Let's see, if I do this, will he do that, and then if I try that again, I can follow it with this, so I'll pretend to do this and watch his reaction and see if he will follow with that, so I can do this, and we'll know the sequence; he will probably follow for that."

All that time, Barney would be thinking in a similar fashion. Ross was particularly careful because of Jim's awesome reputation as an early K.O. puncher. "A fighter is easier to knock out early before he gets warmed up. He's a bit stiff and doesn't give with a punch. Then, of course, as he tires, he becomes easier again," Jim told me. Jim was probably slow because he was rusty and needed time to get loose. All the sparring you can do in training is not the same as one good fight. Barney was confident of his boxing ability, but it was a fool who took chances with a puncher like McLarnin. Through rounds 3, 4, 5, 6, 7, and 8, Barney realised what his cagey managers had hoped and probably counted on to some extent. Jim was, indeed, rusty.

Chapter 13
Golden California and the Quest Begins

What a day it was when Pop and Jimmy left Vancouver and took ship together on the adventure that was to bring both fame and fortune. What hopes, dreams and fears must have filled young Jimmy's head? If there were any doubts in the old wizard's head as he looked at the pint-sized warrior that he was going to show how to beat the world, he showed none to Jim.

Sam McLarnin talked to Pop. "Do you think he can do it, Charlie? You won't bring him back all broken up? He's pretty darn small."

"But he's fast, Sam, and they're not going to hit him much," said Pop, reassuringly. "Doesn't even matter if you're scared, as long as you're fast."

Jim said goodbye to the brothers and sisters who had been his playmates as he grew up, then shook hands goodbye with his dad. Now, grind your teeth. you cynics, and reach for your handkerchiefs, you sentimentalists, for though money was short in that big family, Mary McLarnin pinned her last twenty dollar bill inside the pocket of wee Jimmy's coat and blessed him. She kissed her boy goodbye, told him to say his prayers and write, and probably wished he wouldn't get into any fights, for it always worried her. Both Jim and his sister Olive separately told me that. Who can measure the love in a mother's heart that breaks and goes with her little boy? Jim never had been much on letters, but he said, "I'll phone you, Mom, after every fight, to tell you that I'm O.K." And he did, by God, he did, for he was a good boy. "So we waved and off we went," Jim said to me. Life is not like a well-written novel. It is melodrama. It is more like country and western songs that sing of heartbreak and lost sweethearts and lost children and dead parents and lovers. They set out with faith in their own magic, as wizards do, and walk on the dragon's breath over the dark chasms.

The worst part of the whole adventure was the trip south to San Francisco. They left from the station where Pop had seen Jim fight at the foot of Main Street. There, they bought two steerage tickets to Frisco. "Cost us 39 dollars," said Jim with a grin. "We sailed to Victoria and that was OK except that I'd never been away from home before." Then out they went, through the straits between the Olympic Mountains and Vancouver Island, which Captain Cook missed because of fog and Captain Vancouver found with his first officer Captain Bligh, to the Pacific Ocean and down the coast sailed by Francis Drake. "Pacific, my foot. I was sick all the way down to Frisco. Couldn't keep a thing down. 'Hang on Jimmy, boy,' Pop told me. 'We've only got three days and we're there, and isn't this a lovely boat, the Dorothy Alexander.' As we turned in to San Francisco Bay, the waves dropped, and did that lovely city ever look beautiful to me! But there wasn't much left of me. I didn't feel very tough!" What a pair they must have been, Pop squinting and limping and Jim almost crawling down the gangway to meet the toughest crop of small fighters ever assembled in the world. Look out world, here we come – a half blind and crippled manager with a tiny fighter who looked like a fragile choirboy. That was the first problem they had to overcome in California -- their appearance. Jim didn't really have a baby face, just a young handsome face that didn't look a bit like a pug's face. After he began to make his mark, scribes seized on this and his good manners and dynamite punch and called him "Babyface McLarnin, the killer with the baby face".

Years later, Jim liked to tell of a conversation he overheard in Vancouver. He heard a lady say to her husband, "Look over there, dear, that's Jimmy McLarnin."

"The boxer? No," said her husband.

"Yes, it is. I can tell him by his little baby face."

Pop and Jim made the rounds of the fight promoters in Frisco, some of whom Pop knew or had communicated with. They pretended Jim was 18, not 16, so he would be old enough to fight professionally in California, and you will see an incorrect date for his birthday in the Ring Record book. This is true of many fighters. Archie Moore was still fighting when the records said he was about 42 and his mother told a scribe that he was fifty.

They settled in Oakland because the rent was cheap.

The promoters said to Pop, "All right, Foster, let's see this tiger you've brought us."

> "Tiger, tiger, burning bright
> In the forests of the night.
> What immortal hand or eye
> Could frame thy fearful symmetry?"

William Blake

"Standing right here beside me," said Pop, pushing wee Jimmy forward.

Jimmy smiled behind the cap he was holding in his hand, and politely said, "How do you do?" to the gentleman, as his mother had told him to.

"Get out of here, Foster, you criminal, and put that kid back in Sunday school where he belongs. Do you want to get us arrested?" shouted Frank Schuler, who ran weekly fights in an ice rink. He told Pop to try Oakland; cops weren't so particular over there.

"We couldn't get a fight. We darn near starved to death in Oakland."
No promoter would take a chance on Jimmy. They borrowed a row boat
and lived on crabs that Pop trapped in San Francisco Bay, but Jim claims
that he lived mostly on Brussels sprouts, and he doesn't think that much
of seafood. Pop, however, was giving Jim as wholesome a diet as he could
afford. Jim was getting plenty of vitamins whether he liked or knew it.

Pop tried promoter Tommy Simpson again and was told, "Look, Foster,
what that kid needs is not a fight, but a nursemaid."

"It was a tough time. We had to hang around Frisco for three months
before I got a fight. I was homesick. I missed the family. I had no friends.
We lived in a miserable little room in the Black part of town." Then they
got the break they had been waiting for. They were in the gym in Oakland,
watching the leading California welterweight, Jimmy Duffy, 150 pounds,
work out. His manager, Al Brown, complained loudly that he couldn't get a
sparring partner fast enough for Duffy, to work on his speed. Pop spoke up
loudly, "Let Jimmy, here, work a few rounds with him. Jim`s fast." Jim, by
this time, weighed 105 pounds.

"All right, kid, stay in there if you can. It's your funeral."

Pop put his thick arm around wee Jimmy's shoulder, "Get in there
before they change their minds and if you ever boxed well, do it now. Look
good!" This, after his fight on Main Street, may have been Jimmy's most
important fight.

"We'd both been watching Duffy work," said Jim. "I sailed right into
him. I nailed him hard. I stuck and moved and jabbed and hooked and
boxed rings around him. I was fast enough that he couldn't hit me." Guys in
the gym came over to watch what was going on and just look at this kid in
with Duffy. Who is he?

"I made him look like a bum and gave away fifty pounds to him." Guys
started tossing jokes at Duffy and he didn't think it was funny. After those
rounds, the word was out. Now, Simpson wanted him and wanted to talk
to Pop. From then on, Simpson was a great help to McLarnin. I met a guy
who said that it was Simpson who made McLarnin. Jim became a favourite
on Simpson's weekly boxing cards in Oakland. Who was this little intense
Irish kid with "all the moves" as they say? Where did he come from? He
could box like Benny Leonard. How could a kid that young, box like that?
Oh, the real boxing fans like to see the sweet science done correctly. They
watch intently, and say to themselves every now and again, "Beautiful!"

As an old man once said to me in a gym we both hung around, "I don't
do much now. I just like to see a good boy work, with class, and a lovely
woman take off her clothes, with style, so I go to the fights and the burlesque." That old man was a natural art critic, for those are the most beautiful things in this world. Well, and maybe a baby's smile.

The San Francisco police force began to attend Jimmy's fights. Actor Pat
O'Brien's father, who was the Frisco police chief, said later that he had to ask the
local mobsters to lay off any night Jimmy fought because he didn't have enough

Irish cops to chase them, and the game wasn't fair. The cops took the ferry from the old terminal at the foot of Market Street to Oakland for the fight and then back in time to sign out for the shift. The cops were right to be there. The gym was crammed when Jimmy fought and he got $150 a fight and fought every couple of weeks. They were on their way. "His defence was so good that he took very few punches, so I could match him as often as Simpson wanted him," said Pop later. Pop watched from the corner and told him what to do and then in the week off, would tell him what he did wrong and how to do it right. These clubs were where great fighters learned their lessons. These training grounds are now gone and the world is the poorer. Reports of these fights were written up in the Vancouver papers of the day and you can read them there now. Jim had more fights than he needed.

In 1924, when Jim was 16, he had seventeen fights in California. On February 13, he beat Frankie Sands in 4 rounds in Oakland. On February 22, he knocked out Eddie Collins in Oakland. On March 5, he knocked out Joe Conde in San Francisco, and on March 19, he beat Sands again in Frisco. On March 26, he beat Sammy Lee in Oakland. He had six more successful fights in a row and now he was a sensation around the Bay area. Promoter Jack Doyle of Los Angeles phoned Pop and said, "Say, bring that young kid of yours that I've been hearing so much about down here for some fights."

These conversations are what I've been told, often from several sources, and if they are not the exact wording, the sense is just about right. But sometimes someone very close to McLarnin will not have heard of a certain story, and it will stop you, with a jar. Al Principe, for example, had never heard of McLarnin's fight on Main Street, where Pop is supposed to have found his fighter. I've also heard several conflicting stories of the end of the promising middleweight career of McLarnin's brother, Sammy. I rely mostly on Jim, although he is sometimes fondly remembering his boyhood.

Jim, Pop, and Sammy, Jim's brother

Jim and Pop went to Los Angeles, where Jim made his fortune, fame, and fistic career, and finally his home and most of his best friends. He began there by beating Benny Diaz at the Vernon arena and then, on October 7, he beat Frankie Dolan there. Dolan was a name fighter, ranked in the country, and his fight was written up well and reported back in Vancouver. "Local Boxer impresses LA sports writers in recent bout. In his recent bout here with Frankie Dolan, Irish Jimmy McLarnin, 'Wee Shamus' looked like a miniature Mike Gibbons." Gibbons was a superb boxing middleweight. He and his brother Tom, a small heavyweight, were considered the epitome of boxing skill at the time. Tom had just boxed 12 close rounds with heavyweight champ Jack Dempsey when it was considered a moral triumph to go two or three. The town of Shelby, Montana, put on the bout and went broke on it. Gibbons had often made Dempsey look bad. Watching the bout was Gene Tunney, who said that Gibbons had shown him how to box Dempsey. Later, Tunney saw Dempsey staggered by French war hero Georges Carpentier with a straight right as Dempsey bored in, bobbing and weaving, before Jack knocked Georges out. Tunney later said that what surprised him was not that Dempsey was hard to hit, he wasn't, but that he was hard to hit squarely. The same was true of Marciano.

The account of the fight with Dolan continues. "McLarnin had no trouble winning all four rounds with the highly touted Dolan. Jim knows how to feint and step in immediately -- how to duck and use the opponent's punch for his reply. He has better control of his body than any fighter I have seen." -- high praise for a boy of 16. Jim was also putting on a little muscle and beginning to look more like a fighter. On October 14, in the Vernon arena, Jim beat Young Nationalista, a fighter ranked in the top ten in the flyweight division.

"McLarnin moved in early, raining blows on Nationalista, and simply overwhelmed him for the six rounds of the fight," said the LA report.

"I forget how much we got for that one but it was big money at the time." Pop banked the money for Jim and they continued living in a poor part of LA. Jim phoned home after every fight to tell his mom that he was OK. Pop knew that Jim was ready for anyone in his division. Surprisingly, McLarnin at 17 was already one of the best defensive fighters in boxing. Pop had seen to it that Jim could take care of himself. It seems hard to credit, but it was true, for shrewd old Foster matched Jim from now on against the best in the flyweight division, a division that was reaching an all time high and was full of future hall of famers, all just reaching their peak and all fighting in the Los Angeles area -- Pal Moore, Fidel LaBarba, Jackie Fields, and the great little Phillipino who boxed under the nom de guerre of the famous Mexican outlaw, Pancho Villa. All these fighters were young and on their way up. On December 9, 1924, Jim fought the unorthodox Memphis Pal Moore at the Vernon arena in LA for Jack Davis. It was a wild fight.

"I'll never forget it," Jim told me. "Moore fought with his hands down around his hips the way Ali sometimes did." Moore had fought Jimmy Wilde, "The Mighty Atom", the greatest little fighter of all time, and given him a good fight. Jim sailed into Moore and won the first two rounds with his hard punching. However, Moore's jumping tactics with his hands low began to confuse McLarnin. Moore could dodge and slip and duck punches like nobody Jim had met before. Jim was unable to land solidly and Moore took the last rounds and earned a draw. Jim was now ranked in the top ten in the flyweight division. Pop could ask for good opponents and good purses. They were established, and Jim was only seventeen.

Chapter 14
Top Challenger in the Flyweight
Division, Aged 17

Foster knew that there is no point in taking the risks involved with pro boxing unless you are going to the top, "the only kind worth bein' son, a champion."

Mohammed Ali said to Peter Heller, "Speaking of champions of the past, there ain't but one way to train. Running is the same. Going to camp, resting, following the dietary laws. Clean living is the same. They must have felt it the way I felt it. It's rough, it's agony, it's grueling, the training. Only for those who are good does it provide a way. Most should stay in school. Don't be no boxers. Stay educated and use your brains. Be doctor, be lawyer, carry a briefcase. Forget about it."

Jimmy would agree 100%. A champion is the goal, but a top contender can earn enough money and then live on it if he is careful. Otherwise, learn how to box and have a few amateur fights to get the hang of it, and then quit. Then walk with some confidence, and go to watch a good pro, and you will enjoy it all the more when you have the chance, and thank the good Lord that you're not in there with him. And don't think you can beat up everybody you meet because you never know what you've got until it's too late. With twenty years of fighting, hitting a good street fighter is, as Billy Conn said, 'like hitting your sister' but it's not worth it, unless you've made a small fortune at it.

So Pop decided that Jim should go for the best. On his way to the crown was another great young fighter, Fidel LaBarba. LaBarba was to become flyweight champ, defeat bantamweight champ Bushy Graham twice in non-title fights, and lose in a challenge for Bat Battalino's featherweight crown. Fidel was smart. He retired as undefeated champ and went to Stanford University, an excellent academic school. LaBarba is always considered one of the top five flyweights of all time. McLarnin fought this great little fighter three times. LaBarba was Olympic champ already. At the time, he figured that he could beat any Canadian wetback who had had some fights in clubs in the Northwest. What did it ever do in Seattle or Vancouver but rain anyway? For the first fight, Pop saw to it that Jim had a slight weight advantage. Pop figured every angle. The fight took place on October 28, at the Vernon arena, where all the movie stars came when there was a good card. Mushy Callaghan, the old champ who trained all the movie actors for movie fights, said, "All great actors want to be fighters, and all great fighters want to be actors. I can help the actors but God help the fighters." Callaghan trained Kirk Douglas for *Champion*, Monty Cliff for *From Here to Eternity*, Errol Flynn for *Gentleman Jim,* and Elvis Presley for *Kid Galahad.* Flynn had done a little boxing, but had a physical condition that wouldn't allow him to exercise hard for very long. Douglas was athletic, and Cliff was a really nice guy. Presley had had some karate and was unassuming.

McLarnin won the first and last of their fights and the middle one was a draw. Fidel claims he won that one but that his brother kept shouting "LaBarba" as the ref was marking his score card and the referee turned to him and said, "F--k LaBarba" and wrote down "Draw".

But, as Fidel said, "What did it matter?" The fans loved it. It was a hell of a fight. Jack Doyle loved it. Same boys again and more money for everyone and the LA papers wrote it up. What does LaBarba think of McLarnin? "Well, he got the decisions and maybe rightly so. We have always been friends. He lives in Glendale and I live in Redondo Beach. We see each other now and again."

What does McLarnin think of LaBarba? "Fidel's left hook was beautiful and deadly."

Champ Jack Britton saw them fight and told newsmen, "Those boys were marvelous. They box as well as anybody today."

LaBarba was born in New York in 1905. His father, who was born in Italy, got work in Bakersfield, California, and the family moved to L.A. Fidel worked as a newspaper boy for the LA Express, a tough paper to sell, so they had to pay you to hustle it. He learned to fight at smokers. If this all sounds familiar, it should. However, he continued to go to school, for he was a fine student, and to box amateur. When told he might make the Olympic team and go to the 1924 Olympics in Paris, he didn't know what the Olympics were. He learned what they were! "Oh, God, when I won the gold," he said, "and they played The Star Spangled Banner 'o'er the land of the free, and the home of the brave,' I thought of all the kids back home and my girlfriend and my parents and the athletic club and Coach Blake, and the whole damn country, I just started to cry like a baby as I stood there on the winners' platform with the tears running down my face. But it was from my heart. We won the team championship for America, especially the boys from California, me and Jackie Fields and Ray Fee and Joe Salas."

All these boys became successful professionals, but you will notice that Canada did not send McLarnin from B.C. Pro wrestler, John Tenta, whom I trained at North Surrey Secondary School, beat Canada's silver medallist,

Bob Molle, and was invited to the Olympic trials in Ontario, then told he could hitchhike there. Then there was Doug Hepburn, the world's greatest weightlifter. Hepburn was never considered for the Olympics, probably because he was from the West Coast and no one in Toronto would believe his totals. A group of Vancouver businessmen "passed the hat" and sent him to the world championships in Helsinki, where he easily defeated the Americans and the Russians. He could probably have had three golds for Canada in the Olympics. Percy Williams and his coach had to hitchhike to the East the year he won gold medals for Canada in the 100 and 220 runs.

Losing to McLarnin, however, did not ruin LaBarba's career. On August 22, 1925, LaBarba won the world flyweight title. Then he retired as champ and went to University. LaBarba also coached the Stanford boxing team. None of the big heavyweights from the football team could ever lay a glove on their coach. He said what amazed him was that he had professors come up to him and ask why he quit boxing just to get a degree from Stanford. Then he began to realise its importance. When you become a Ph.D. in your profession, you realise that it's a lot more significant for a man to be featherweight champion of the world than a top scholar or artist.

Fidel was a fine intelligent man and a great fighter. He lost $250,000 in a brokerage business in the crash of 29, but survived and came back to make a reasonable living and retire, with a house on the California beach.

The man who is considered to be the best flyweight of all time is the legendary Welshman, Jimmy Wilde. Wilde had over 100 K.O.s in his career, many over men much bigger than he. He won 132 fights. He was a slim, little man out of the Welsh coalmines, and nobody could understand where his tremendous punching power came from, so he was known as the "Mighty Atom". Of course it is timing, speed, leverage, style and weight shift as well as total weight that determines power. Boxers fight for a million dollars now, and guys say that for that they'd get in for a few minutes themselves. No, they wouldn't, unless they'd like to go out in a box. One punch could break your neck.

Tex Rickard lured Wilde to New York to defend his flyweight title at age 32 against the newest American sensation, Francisco Guilledo, who fought under the name of the famous Mexican guerrilla leader, Pancho Villa, for he looked a bit like him. Villa, at 22 and just reaching his prime, charged at Wilde like a miniature Dempsey, and was simply too strong for Wilde, bulled Wilde around, and knocked him out in the 7th round. Villa is usually ranked second among all time flyweights. Shortly after his triumph over Wilde, he signed to meet the new young sensation in California, Irish Jimmy McLarnin. The odds were on Villa 10 to 1. "I think Villa underrated me. Villa was a heck of a fighter. He beat Jimmy Wilde."

Now Pop and Jim ran into the peculiar situation that kept a world title out of their grasp for years. Promoters and managers loved matching their champions against McLarnin because they could make so much money. Fans flocked to see the classy handsome Irish boy with dynamite in his right hand. However, they didn't want to lose their championship to this Canadian with an independent manager. Who knows, Foster might stage fights in Vancouver or London or Liverpool or Belfast and there would be no way to get Jimmy to throw the fight when the odds were right. Waste of a good championship. Again, we see the over-the-weight trick. Even if Jim knocked out the champion, he would just remain number one challenger and the writers could call him the uncrowned champion if they liked, as they did, and that just drew more people to his fights.

I asked Jim if he could have made the flyweight limit for that fight and what about all the other non-title fights he had in which he showed up a couple of pounds too heavy to take the title. "Heck, yes, I came in only a pound and a half or so over the limit. One time we almost goofed and I was only a quarter of a pound over. I could have sweated that off in a few hours. Usually I had to eat to get up over." To make the situation more galling, Foster always got Jim a small weight advantage for many of his fights so Jim could be stronger than his opponents. Some advantage! Win and you don't get the title. I quote *The Encyclopaedia of Boxing*, by Gilbert Odd, Hamlyn Publications, N.Y., 1983. "It was years before McLarnin got a real title shot, mainly because of the boxing politics of the day which were so dubious."

So Jim signed for the fight with the champion, with no chance to win the championship. The hometown newspapers, nevertheless, were ecstatic. Jim told them that although no one else thought so, he thought he could beat the great champion, the man who beat Jimmy Wilde, Pancho Villa. The fight took place at the Oakland Ball Park, July 4th, 1925. Jim came in at 122 pounds, over the flyweight limit, as Pop had agreed he would, and then Pancho Villa showed up knowing he would not lose his championship. Sadly, poor Villa lost far more than his championship. He lost his life. It was a fierce fight. Mclarnin was in top shape for the fight, and so, apparently, was Villa. "Listen," said Jim, "Villa was a classy fighter, and tough. He came at me -- Gangbusters. He was a great infighter. On the inside he kept hooking to the side of my head. I've had black eyes before, but never black ears, two of them, and did they hurt the next day." McLarnin gave Villa a sound licking. It was an upset.

Age 18, Jim's first shot at the title. Jim beats Pancho Villa, 1925

"Attaboy Jimmy" was the headline in the Vancouver Province. Jim had hit a fistic pinnacle and became the most talked about fighter in boxing. Grinning all through the fight, McLarnin outfought the great Villa that Saturday afternoon in Oakland. "I had the reach on him so I stood up and speared him with the left and then nailed him with a straight right as he came charging in -- just what Pop told me to do. It was just what Tunney did to Dempsey."

"News of our Irishman's triumph was flashed to all corners of the civilised world," said the Sun. It was literally true, for boxing matches involving champions were world news in that golden age of boxing. Who knows who the flyweight champ is today?

"Jimmy's clear head, crafty ring brain, and two sturdy fists have carried him from the pug obscurity of Hastings Street Clubs to elite matches. The days of crab fishing are over, but acclaim hasn't gone to his modest Celtic head," wrote Andy Lytle. "McLarnin has advertised Vancouver to two hemispheres." Vancouver knew they had a champion to be, but they had to wait much longer than anyone could realise.

"Jim will be home in a few days," said the Vancouver World, "but he's going back to ringside in Oakland on July 17 when Villa fights Vancouver's other fine fighter, Vic Foley." Villa had been overconfident and signed to fight two Canadians within a couple of weeks, thinking that they would give him no problem. Tragically, it was not to be. Villa had looked in superb condition when he entered the ring. Unknown to the McLarnin camp, however, Villa was suffering from a toothache the day before the bout and had had a wisdom tooth removed. It should have been no big deal. However, he took severe punishment and his jaw was badly swollen the day after the fight. He had another tooth extracted, but failed to follow his dentist's advice to have more teeth removed, then developed an abscess that required an operation. He died on the operating table at the age of 23. Nobody blamed McLarnin, but it was a terrible lesson that even the best can die if everything is not right.

McLarnin was now a headliner. He had become a sensation in California. Every promoter wanted him, even if he did look like a choir-boy, indeed, partly because he did. The fans flocked to see this kid with the classic boxing style who had a face like a movie star and a deadly punch. He had made $3,000 for his last fight with LaBarba. In 1925, Irish Jimmy was the most talked about fighter in boxing. Newspapers were in love with this modest, polite, articulate young man and his colourful old war hero manager with the squint and the limp. Jim appeared to be unaf-fected. Newspapers spoke of his approachability. He came from a decent, hard working, God-fearing family. His sisters played classical piano. The McLarnins even had good books in the house. Jim had a Bible with him in training camp and had actually been seen with a copy of Byron's poems. His favourite opera singers were John McCormick and Nellie Melba. This kid was no ordinary pug. He was no intellectual, but he was bright and knowledgeable -- an ideal hero for the kids of North America.

Even though Villa's death was not Jim's fault, the newspapers pointed out that the last man he fought had died after the fight. So the papers had a new hero, the deadly little killer with the baby face, Irish Jimmy McLarnin – a gentleman outside the ring and a killer inside it. Hold the presses!

Unfortunately, not everybody loved Pop Foster. "They're not going to get your money, Jim." You couldn't buy Foster with a drink or a fancy woman, and toughs did not frighten him. He had looked at death in two wars.

One evening, I asked him, "When you got so popular, weren't you approached by 'the mob' or whatever that means, or somebody with 'real' money or 'real' connections, to accept other management that would be easier for the 'powers' in boxing to deal with?"

In the archetypal boxing movie of our cynical times, the successful young fighter is overwhelmed by his success and under the persuasion of smooth operators, dumps his hometown manager and his hometown sweet-heart, falls for a movie starlet, and gets managed by crooks who ease "Pop" out, perhaps even keeps him on as a trainer, and cuts his "take". Now, well connected, he wins the crown, fame and fortune, but they turn to ashes. He loses a fixed fight, becomes alcoholic, punch drunk, and ends in the gutter. That's the kind of fight story that sells because it pretends to be realistic. It has happened, but often it hasn't.

But this is a true story of faith and trust. Jimmy stuck with his manager, married his hometown sweetheart, despite all the starlets he met, kept his money and his brains, sent his children to college, and lived happily ever after. But not quite. He paid for his decency with his reputation as a boxer. If he had been managed by an insider, he could probably have been succes-sively flyweight, bantamweight, featherweight, lightweight, junior welter-weight, welterweight, and probably middleweight champ. And broke. He would have been considered the greatest pound for pound boxer of all time. Maybe he was. But at what cost to his personal life? Which will you have -- glory or a good life?

"Oh, they sent Jack Dempsey around to see me, or I assume they did. Jack told me to dump the old guy from Canada and get a new manager so I would get better fights. Dempsey was my idol. Dempsey was tougher and faster than Joe Frazier and much harder to hit. Ali got away with mistakes because most of the men he fought were slower. Dempsey had done me some favours. He told the big boys back East about me and said they should be booking me into New York. Besides, Jack didn't have that much money. His manager, Jack Kearns, made more money out of his fights than Jack did. Kearns was no Pop Foster. Jack didn't own that restaurant in New York. He just ran it and fronted for it." Jim felt he had said enough about it for this time. I make several possibilities out of this situation. First, I suspect that Dempsey thought that McLarnin would actually get further with a mob manager with connections. Jim was not getting the shots he should have. After all, Dempsey had made out all right, and they saw to it that he never went very short of ready cash. It's a tough business and a manager has to walk a tightrope to protect his boy and not offend the powers that set up good fights. Pop erred on the side of protection and went a touch too light on the side of power. To this point, Pop had managed to match Jim perfectly. But now Jim met one of the toughest fighters who ever entered the squared circle, Charles "Bud" Taylor, the cold, blond, blue-eyed "Terre Haute Terror." He looked like a western gunslinger. Whip-cord lean, he fought about once a month on average, and fouled whenever he found it useful. Taylor had won the bantamweight championship from Tony Canzoneri. McLarnin was 17 and Taylor was 23. "I wish I had met him later," said Jim. Jim had grown into a bantamweight, and Taylor was a popular fighter, so it seemed like a good thing. Pictures show him thin lipped and unsmiling, with narrow eyes. Bud Taylor was, in the language of the ring, "a nanimal, a nanimal". The ultimate ring compliment! As McLarnin said to me, "Taylor was the toughest man I ever fought." This, from Jimmy, who never cut, whose nose you could break without him blinking, who had a cast iron jaw, and who was never knocked out in 100 pro fights. Taylor didn't simply beat other fighters. He beat them up. He had 104 recorded fights. Some fighters don't fight just for money and prestige, but just because they love to punch people, and don't much mind being punched themselves. Lou Ambers said, " Oh, sweet Jesus, I loved to fight. But all good things come to an end. God, I miss it! I just loved to get in there. I had 238 fights altogether. I was lucky. Them was the good old days!"

Jim, who knew Lou well, said, "Lou said that, did he? Well, I suppose Lou might. I liked it for a while, but the novelty of getting punched in the head wore off," said Jim, grinning wryly. But Taylor liked it as long as he could hurt somebody. Rocky Graziano, another "nanimal", liked a good fight so much that he often went over to his opponent after a real pier six brawl and kissed him on the top of the head for giving him so much fun.

Bud Taylor, the Terre Haute Terror, literally beat up the Killer with the Baby Face. Taylor handed Jim his first real professional loss. He hit Jim low, again and again, in the first two rounds. Jimmy complained to the referee in the second round, something he never did in any other fight. The referee asked him why he had signed to fight Taylor if he didn't expect to get fouled. It was a terrible fight. Jimmy got slaughtered. He had never taken a beating like this, even in the alleys of East Vancouver. At the end of the 8th round, Foster wanted to throw in the towel and quit. Jimmy told him not to. So Jim stayed in and Taylor beat the hell out of him. "I'll say," said Jim, as I went over the report of the fight, "but I wasn't going to let him stop me. It went ten rounds." Taylor didn't destroy Jim's spirit.

Pop knew the thing to do if Jim was to be the fighter he could be, was to turn right around, after sufficient rest, and go right back in with "the Terre Haute Terror". Pop thought Jim could do it. Back in camp, they figured out Taylor. Pop and Jim became famous for this, and they never failed against a single boxer, even Barney Ross. This strategy failed only against Ross, Dempsey, Commissioner Phelan, and a cabal of gamblers working together. "Thinking back over a fight, you see parts of it in your mind, like a movie." Joyce Carol Oates says that sometimes a fighter seems as if he's fought this fight before. Exactly, Miss Oates.

On December 8th of the same year, 1925, Jimmy went back into the ring with the same man who had beaten him so terribly, and decisively out-boxed Taylor in the Vernon arena. Of course, he was required to be over the weight. "I moved," said Jim, "it's a silly pair of legs that sit there and let their face get battered." When Jim wanted to move, he could move with the best. He fought Taylor again, and when Bud could see that it was a different McLarnin, and that he wasn't going to catch him, he fouled Jim so badly that the referee had to award the fight to Jim, on a foul. But they were all tough fights. At the age of 77, McLarnin said to me, "You know what I'd like? Just one more fight with Bud Taylor. I was too young when I fought him." Well, a real fighter is born not made and never really gets over it. "Oh, no," says Jim, "fighters are made. Pop made me a fighter." No, Jim, you were born a fighter and Pop made you a boxer, artist, and champion.

Jim learned a lot from fighting Taylor. To learn how to handle a man who is your physical superior is a great and satisfying lesson. Jim improved his slipping, blocking, rolling and footwork. An undefeated fighter is never quite as good as he should be. He's never really been stretched. Pop matched Jim well in the long run, but I doubt that he figured on the beating that Jim took from Taylor in that first fight. I think that he thought it was time for Jim to have a tough fight. Pop must have known that Taylor had killed two men on his way to the championship. That must have been why he was ready to throw in the towel in the 8th round of the first fight. Perhaps, after Jim's great victory over Villa, Pop was a bit overconfident. Robert E. Lee, a great general, sent in Pickett's charge at Gettysburg to slaughter, probably because after their great victory at Chancellorsville, they seemed unbeatable. Foster had taken a chance on Taylor and got away with it, but just. Young fighters have been rushed this way and ruined. This biography should have been written before Foster left us, in 1959, aged 83. What did Foster think of life? The "talk on the street" at the time was that McLarnin would never get a real shot until Foster cooperated or somebody shot that old bastard. Oh, he was a man, take him for all and all, and one manager in a million.

"Among the faithless, faithful only hee;

Among innumerable false, unmov'd,

Unshak'n, unseduc'd, unterrifi'd

His Loyaltie he kept, his Love, his Zeale;

Nor number, nor example with him wrought

To swerve from truth, or change his constant mind

Though single. From amidst them forth he passd,

Long way through hostile scorn, which he susteind

Superior, nor of violence fear'd aught;

And with retorted scorn his back he turn'd

On those proud Towrs to swift destruction doom'd."

John Milton, from *Paradise Lost*

Coming back to beat Taylor did a great deal for Jim's confidence. People in boxing knew that as Villa was as good as they come, so Taylor was as tough as they come, and Jim had come through three fights with him and was not seriously hurt.

"Did Taylor hurt you in those fights?" I asked Jim.

"You're darn right he hurt me. I was so sick inside I thought I'd throw up. I could hardly stand. We had protective cups but they weren't very good then, not like the ones today. They cut down the injury. I was just a kid. I wish I could have got him later," said Jim, grinding his teeth. So Pop got Jim an easier fight next, shrewdly chosen to show how far Jim had come. They went to Oakland, familiar territory. They fought a man who could give Jim a tough fight and not foul, Jim's old rival from Vancouver, Mickey Gill. Gill had been fighting around the Bay area and doing well. McLarnin beat Gill a lot easier than he ever had in Vancouver, for he had learned a lot, but Gill did okay with Jim, and that is something.

The end of the first stage of McLarnin's career, the stage of the brilliant boxing teenager from Canada, who fought in California and beat the fly-weight and bantamweight world champs, was coming to a close. It was a remarkable chapter, hardly mentioned in boxing histories. There was to be one more great victory before the disastrous year of 1926, when Jim was sick. His victory, a two round K.O. of Jackie Fields, Olympic champ and future welterweight world champ, capped Jim's career among the light-est weights, and filed his claim to have been one of the best ever in those divisions. During all those fierce battles and strict training, young Jim was growing up without the company of his pals or girl friends. Of course, there were "groupies" who wanted to meet the handsome, rich, famous boxing sensation from Canada. A few young starlets and one famous star were interested in meeting young Jim, but Pop shewed them all away. Pop said marry a nice girl and don't hang around dames. It was a tough life for lively young Jim, for Jim always liked a party and company and had an apprecia-tive eye for the ladies. I told him about Chief Justice Oliver Holmes who, in his nineties, would turn happily on a Boston street to admire a handsome woman, and mutter, "Oh, to be 80 again!" By now, Jim had his $25,000 in the bank and Pop began to take his 50 % cut. Foster had now accomplished most of what he had promised Sam McLarnin, so Pop decided it was time for a break.

"Well, Jim," said Pop one day, "let's go on the train to Vancouver, not the boat, sit in the diner, and sleep in a berth."

"Wow! Let's go, Pop!" Jim could hardly wait.

When they got to Vancouver on the Great Northern, Jim raced up Hastings Street to his parents' home on Union and knocked on the door. His sister answered, took a second look before she knew who it was, and raced back into the house shouting, "Mom, Dad, it's Jim. He's come home and he's different. He's grown up!" He had, indeed. He had gone away standing 4 foot 10 weighing 95 pounds. He came back at 5 foot 7 weighing 125lbs. He had confidence, a new suit of clothes, and more money than the hard working McLarnins had ever seen. He gave his mom $300 to replace the $20 she had pinned to his shirt when he left.

So the young hero went home. How proud he must have been. If he had done nothing else, he would have been a success. How pleased Mary and Sam must have been, for he was looking fine.

"Well," said Sam to Pop, "I don't see any championship belt."

"No, Sam, but Jim's got a nice bit of money in the bank, and you don't see any scars on his face do you? He's got a reputation and we're in a good position for a shot at the title. These things take a little time." Foster was a man who could wait, but even the wizard couldn't have known that it would take seven divisions and thirteen champions before Jim could call himself "champ". Later in life, when he got to know and accept you, he called you champ.

Right after his great win, Jim sent a telegraph home, and then phoned his mother to tell her that he was all right. He spoke to his mother and dad, and some of his brothers and sisters. There were no celebrations until he had talked to his family.

So Jim went home, as he did after each major fight, to see now not only his family, and they were a close family, as most immigrant families were, but also because he was in love. Most old time fight managers claimed that being in love took the edge off a fighter, and perhaps that may help to account for the loss of intensity that could be sensed in McLarnin's ring work.

Lillian was always referred to in the Vancouver newspapers very coyly as "a certain young person who had news of Jim." Her privacy was respected. The media has changed! By this time, Jim and Lillian were engaged. Now they could report that Miss Lillian Cupit, Jim's affianced, said that Mr. McLarnin would be returning, by way of California, that he would fly from New York to Los Angeles, and then he and his manager, Mr. Charles Foster, would motor to Vancouver, and James was expecting to arrive in two weeks.

Theirs is a life long love story. This is not to say that it was all perfectly smooth sailing. Jim loved a good party, and while Jim always retained his dignity, Lillian was more reserved. Lillian had her bridge club, and Jim had his business, and they both played golf, and had their family, and Jim considered Lillian's wishes. Jim's failings are good-hearted human failings, and he was full of affection and good humour. Jim liked celebrity parties in Hollywood and Los Angeles, where he was always welcome as a famous professional athlete who was very socially presentable, good looking, well mannered, well dressed, and well spoken. Jim loved to take Lillian to parties with his Hollywood friends.

Chapter 15
The Deadliest Puncher in Boxing,
and the K.O. of Jackie Fields.

From this point on, until he won his championship and became mellow, McLarnin was known for his lightning knockouts of top ranked fighters. Jimmy told me that the best time to knock a man out was early, while he was still cold. His record is now studded with quick early knockouts.

The California papers began to print statements like, "Fields cannot duck McLarnin any longer." This was Jackie Fields, the premier small boxer of the West, who had led the American boxing team to a brilliant victory in the 1924 Olympics in Paris. It had been as brilliant, in its way, as that of the British track team led by Harold Abrahamson and Eric Liddell at the same time. Fields had been born Jacob Finkelstein in the Jewish ghetto of Chicago in 1907. But those were the days when people got out of the ghetto in a generation or so, instead of staying there. Field's father was a butcher, so they weren't destitute, but, as Jackie said, "We lived in the Ghetto, so you had to fight."

Fields was a superb boxer with a mean right hand. He retired in 1933 with 70 wins and 28 K.O.s. He was knocked out only once, and that was by McLarnin. Jimmy's hands were sound and he could use his power. Fields eventually went blind in one eye and quit fighting. He became a film editor for MGM, and part owner of the Tropicana Hotel in Las Vegas. He and McLarnin remained friends, and the summer I visited Jim, he went over to Jackie's birthday party, especially as Fields was ailing. At the party, the photographers wanted Jackie to put his hands in boxing stance, and Jackie, in a wheel chair, had trouble. The picture shows McLarnin helping Fields. Some say there are no pals like those who have given each other a good fight. "I caught him early. Got lucky. Jackie was a little cold."

As I've journeyed around the areas of the veterans of boxing, I've run into strong opinions about some of its famous pioneers, particularly Jack Kearns. Kearns was a cagey character who lived on the edge of society's rules. I was told that he had run several houses of ill repute in Vancouver. He managed many good fighters, but it was his management of the sensational punching Dempsey in the 1920s that made boxing into the financial gold mine that it became during its golden age. Kearns could publicize an ordinary fight like the Dempsey/ Carpentier fight into the fight of the century so that no sports fan would want to miss it, but would be ready to pay top prices for the first million dollar sports event. Carpentier was a good light-heavyweight champ. He was also handsome, built like a Greek statue, and a French war hero. Unfortunately, Dempsey's left hook was faster than Carpentier's. The fight was no contest.

Kearns teamed with flamboyant promoter Tex Rickard, and boxing went big time. Promoters and managers and a few boxers got rich. Kearns would have liked to have Jimmy McLarnin, but they couldn't pry him away from Foster.

Fields was managed for a while by Kearns. Fields said, "Never mind Kearn's methods. He made modern boxing. I think he was a great guy." He could have gotten all sorts of legitimate championship shots for McLarnin. Fields talks about fighting the superbly awkward welterweight champ Young Corbett, really an Italian from Fresno who fought out of San Francisco. "You couldn't beat Corbett in San Francisco, not if you were Jewish or Irish. But I'll always be grateful that I got to be a fighter. Where else could a kid like me from the ghetto have a chance in life and meet the friends that I have? But people forget old boxers today."

But let us remember Jackie Fields. He was a sweet guy. Joyce Carol Oates remarks how sweet some old boxers are when you meet them. I suspect they are among the few males who have beaten all their aggressions, looked violence in the face, mastered their fears, and attained peace. Fields said he had a good offer to fight McLarnin.

"Jackie was a great jabber, but Pop and I studied him out, well, not quite." After McLarnin had whipped Spec Rames, Taylor, Villa, and Gill in effortless succession, California scribes and promoter Jack Root thought Jimmy was ready for the brilliant boxing Fields.

Fields says, "We took the McLarnin fight because I was offered $5,000 clear. I could pay off the home I bought for my mother in Boyle Heights. I remember it like yesterday. The first round I outboxed him. The second round I walked out there, started my jab, and then I was on the floor and the ref was counting. When I got up, it looked like McLarnin was coming at me in slow motion. Then I was on the floor again. He knocked me down five times.

Analysing the fight, the experts said that Fields had brought his hands back a couple of inches too low, and McLarnin, sensing this, stepped in and caught him. A great pro picks up mistakes and acts on them instantaneously. An uppercut put Fields down. He clambered to his feet only to be floored with a right. The fact that old time fighters were better conditioned than moderns probably accounts for the fact that all these knockdowns didn't kill them. Jackie was out for five minutes before his doctor could revive him. Fields had not been knocked out in 56 fights until the "Belfast Spider" hit him with that terrific right.

Sometimes, everything seems in slow motion. Oddly, Field's knockout by McLarnin put him into some fine matches, while McLarnin's sensational knockout of Fields led to the lowest point in McLarnin's career.

PART III
The East: Jimmy's K.O.s Make Him Top Contender

Chapter 16
The Bad Year: Jaundice, Chicago, McLarnin's Greatest Fight

On December 8, 1925, McLarnin had smartly outboxed Bud Taylor. As he grew, he should have been on his way to the lightweight championship, as he had dreamed. He was just 18 and he had beaten the best. He was growing fast, and I suspect that he had pushed himself a bit too hard, for in 1926 he came down with the debilitating and lingering disease, jaundice. He felt lethargic and apathetic. On January 12, 1926, he lost to his rival, Taylor. It wasn't a disaster, like the first fight, but it was the first fight in which he didn't show improvement.

Pop was now undermatching Jim, to allow for his lethargy. He began having trouble getting the fights he wanted, and the scribes said that Jim was being mismanaged. They wrote that McLarnin was finished, and blamed Foster. Pop decided it was time for a big move. He had been frustrated with the promoters in Canada, and now he became frustrated with promoters in L.A.

Jimmy had money in the bank and was homesick. He wanted to go back to Vancouver. Pop was bitter. "To hell with them, Jimmy, we'll show them," said Pop and told Jim what he had planned. I think that the wizard looked into his crystal ball and saw Madison Square Garden, the Mecca of world boxing. The next day, Pop arrived, squinting through the windshield of an old Buick, driving so slowly that drivers honked. "Get packed, Jimmy," he shouted over the motor, "We're going to drive this crate to Chicago and hit the big time." Jim could have a much-needed rest on the way.

"It was some trip," says Jim. "Sometimes we slept in the car and sometimes in a hay field and sometimes in a hotel. There was no Route 66 in those days. You drove local roads from one town to another. We really saw America and the people and had our adventures. The sky seemed so big. I had a lot of fun, but it was a long way from Mom and Dad and the gang, and when I arrived in Chicago, my mouth dropped open. I had never seen buildings so tall."

As in San Francisco, they had trouble getting a decent fight. Two offers fell through, and then they got an offer to fight the tough and dangerous reigning featherweight champ, Louis "Kid" Kaplan. Kaplan was outgrowing this division, and had just run off a string of eleven straight wins against lightweights. The promoters took the usual precaution of stipulating that the new arrival from the West Coast come in weighing over the feather-weight limit. Jim was now healthy again, and had grown into a lightweight, so it was no problem. Both boys weighed in as lightweights, although it was advertised as being a challenge for the featherweight championship. Nevertheless, no title was at stake. Kaplan was the biggest man Jim had fought. Nat Fleischer rates Kaplan as the 10th best featherweight of all time. Pop turned down the first offer for Jim to fight Kaplan. He accepted when he couldn't get another decent fight.

"We were desperate. We had to eat. We were alone in Chicago and needed ready cash." Also, Jim needed a solid win over some name fighter to establish himself in the East. So, with misgivings, they accepted the fight.

The fight was sensational. Pop always said it was Jim's best fight. Jim's brother Bob told me the same thing. I can see how they felt, but I would say that the second Petrolle and the second Canzoneri, and Jim's last fight, were Mclarnin at his best. Undoubtedly, it was one of those classic pier six brawls like the Zale/Graziano fights or the Dempsey/Firpo fight or the Hearns/Hagler fights where one fighter drops the other and then gets dropped himself and this goes on until the crowd is in a state of frenzy. The excitement comes, I believe, from the feeling that these young men are super human and almost indestructible. We all know how fragile our bodies are. These young men seem to defy the limits of humanity. The downed fighter seems to arise like an ancient god from apparent death. He couldn't possibly get up after taking that punch. Watching, we feel that we are participants in defying death, as in a religious ceremony. The ring becomes an altar. John Ralston Saul says about bullfighting that it is not a sport, but a religious ceremony. One witnesses death, revival, and transfiguration, and one leaves with the feeling, as Aristotle would say, of catharsis. Our young god of artistic violence, McLarnin, went through one of these nights on October 18, 1927, in Chicago, and the riches of the East opened to him and Pop. His popularity after this was incredible because, as Chicago sports writers put it, nobody had seen anything like this since Lazarus came back from the tomb.

"Well, I felt like a god when they raised my hand."

I remember a Viet Nam vet saying that despite the horror, he felt more alive during combat than at any time in his life. Steinbeck said that it is the pity and the glory of mankind that it can only keep its soul pure and full through violence. We must realise this and formalise and ritualise and contain our violence. The wine as blood in the mass is a variation of this. The fighters themselves can hardly believe what is happening to them.

Graziano, after seeing the movie of his fight with Tony Zale, said, "If I'd a known dat was goin on, I'd a left." Jim can still hardly believe his fight with Kaplan.

Kaplan's first punch broke Jim's jaw, and Jim went down in a ring for the first time in his life. In his pain and bewilderment, Jim lurched upright at the count of four, with his gloves up, ready to fight. Pop's heart sank. Should he throw in the towel? Neither Jim nor Pop knew just how badly he was hurt until Jim went to a dentist, who said, "I see you've had your jaw broken."

Jim said, "Kaplan was the wrong man for our opener in the East. I told Pop that if Kaplan stunned me, I'd start running and he'd have a heck of a time catching me. I didn't get time to run. He came charging out and nailed me with his first punch. I'd never been knocked down, so I got to my feet as fast as I did in East Vancouver. Of course, he nails me as soon as I get up, and down I go again. I'm like a yo-yo. He keeps knocking me down and I keep getting up." Through three rounds, Kaplan kept following McLarnin along the ropes, sinking his fists into this human punching bag.

Pop remembered, "Kaplan just couldn't keep Jimmy down. Jimmy was really hurt, but he had the heart of a lion. When he came back to the corner, I talked to him, and I could see that he still had his wits." After round three, both of them noticed that Kaplan was getting a bit arm weary. Kaplan was born in Russia and grew up in the slums of Chicago, but he'd never hit anyone this hard and had him keep getting up. Pop was a sober man in a sober world, but he had a wry sense of humour. "Why don't you start knocking him down, Jimmy?" Pop said. "The next time he starts that hook, step inside and nail him with your right."

"So out I went and in came Kaplan. Left jab. I slipped right. Hard right swing. I slid back. Big left hook and I stepped in and nailed him on the jaw with a right all the way from my right toes. Over he goes flat on his back. Boy, do I get confidence! This is better. I must have knocked him down ten times. Boy, was he tough." And that knock down, by the way, was the same move Jim put on me in the bar of the Walter Scott in L.A. Actually, Kaplan went down six times, but how could Jim be expected to remember?

Just before round 8, Pop could see that Jim was almost done. "You've got to finish him now, Jim," said Pop. "Go get him, before he gets out of his corner." He pushed Jim off his stool. Across the ring sailed Jim and hit the "Kid" with a left and two rights to the jaw. Finally, Kaplan's eyes glazed. Jim measured him and gave him one more perfect right on the front corner of the chin. His head snapped around and back and down he went and out, lying on his side.

"I prayed that he wouldn't get up. I don't think that God cares who wins a pro boxing match, but I prayed." Pop leaped into the ring, forgetting his war wounds. Jimmy did his handspring. The crowd went crazy! What a fight. The Chicago sports writers hammered their typewriters and a new hero was born in Carl Sandburg's windy city of the big shoulders, a tough town, but this was something else. Today, this fight would have been stopped after Jim went down for the third time, maybe earlier. Which is better? Can we risk a young man's life for glory? Should we reach for infinity and risk death? No more of this, but oh, you poets, weep for the passing of the heroes and the death of the gods – and remember Jimmy McLarnin from Vancouver, Canada, and Ireland.

Chapter 17
Leaving Chicago and the Mob for New York and Madison Square Garden – Boxing's Ultimate Success

McLarnin had now beaten the world flyweight, the world bantamweight, and the world featherweight champions, but received no offers of a legitimate title fight. Hell, you could lose your title to this guy.

But Jim did get the attention of Eastern promoters, especially the legendary Tex Rickard. Rickard could smell money as a shark smells blood. He came looking for this young killer, McLarnin. His last primal tiger, Jack Dempsey, had just retired, and this was the time when the most mechanically perfect of heavyweight champs, Gene Tunney, was on the throne. Gene could knock out people, but he did it in a cool mechanical way, taking no more chances than necessary. Aficionados appreciated it, but did not go wild about it. Will Rogers said, "We need champs with more punch and less Shakespeare." Dempsey had just "gone animal" when he smelled blood, about the same as Rickard when he smelled money. Dempsey, not an especially big man at 6 foot 1 and 190 pounds, was incredible to watch, given a big 6 foot 5, 240 pound tough. He would tear him to pieces in minutes, and once the big fellow started to bleed, Jack could hardly be stopped from killing him. "Kill him, Jack, kill him!" The fans missed Jack and so did the promoters. Tunney, however, had seen that Dempsey could be outboxed by a smaller man with a good left jab (as indeed could Ray Robinson), plus a move to the side, and a hard right as Jack bulled in. Gene hit Dempsey so often this way that Jack's wife, the beautiful Estelle Taylor, was shocked when she saw Jack and asked what had happened to him. "Honey, I forgot to duck," said Jack. President Reagan used this line to his wife Nancy after he had been nearly killed by an assassin's bullet close to his heart. Reagan wasn't a great actor but quite a man and a president who knew how to use the legends of America. Reagan had the killer instinct, like Dempsey, and went for the Marxist weak point, economics. He played the Star Wars card, and broke them into pieces, ending the cold war. Dempsey was also a surprisingly intelligent man outside the ring, but Tunney was not only intelligent, but also well read; while not a great scholar, he enjoyed a Shakespeare play and was knowledgeable on the subject. Tunney actually gave some guest lectures on the bard. Before his first fight with Dempsey, a reporter noticed Gene passing some spare time in camp reading serious stuff. He took the first train to New York and told his newspaper mates, "Boys, put all your money on Dempsey. That big sap Tunney is up there reading Shakespeare." Tunney eventually gave the media and Dempsey a boxing lesson. But people missed Dempsey when he was gone.

This Kaplan/McLarnin fight seemed the closest thing to the Dempsy/Firpo fight, where those two titans knocked each other down and sometimes right out of the ring until Jack finally put the Wild Bull of the Pampas, 6 foot 3 and 220 pounds, down for the count. Rickard saw a smaller Dempsey in this Irish Canadian kid from the West Coast, so he contacted Foster and they began to discuss a debut for Jim, in Madison Square Garden. For the moment, however, they were in the Mid West, so Pop lined up some fights there and in nearby Detroit. This was the age of gangsters in Chicago: Al Capone, Legs Diamond, Dillinger, and Baby Face Nelson, the real killer where the scribes had gotten the name for McLarnin. Prohibition had made liquor the best business around. Neither Jim nor Pop drank much, but they were around town, and pleasant, intelligent, young Jim was always welcome in anybody's company. Many of these notorious characters would seize Jim's hand, slap him on the back, and say, "Great fight, Jimmy."

"Thanks pal," Jim would respond, like Dempsey. It was some time for Jimmy, but it made Pop nervous. It was time for a move. One afternoon, Pop dropped in to a restaurant, Dinty Moore's, where Jimmy often went for his favourite lemon pie. Pop saw him sitting, eating his pie, with a congenial group of well dressed gentlemen with bulges around their pockets, engaged in conversation. Pop began making signals and funny faces at Jim until he got up and went over to the door.

"Jim," said Pop, "do you know who you're talking to?"

"No," said Jim, "they seem like nice fellows and wanted to sit and talk with me."

"Nice, my eye," said Pop. "That's Legs Diamond and his gang and they're loaded to kill. He's killed more men than you've knocked out. Let's get out of here before someone drives past with a sub machine gun and we're in the middle of a massacre."

While we were speaking of those famous gangsters, Jim dropped a bit of fascinating underground information. Every fighter who came from the West to fight in the East, where the big money was, was expected to get himself an "Eastern representative" who had good mob and high official boxing connections. Every fighter from the West had this useful person take 10% off the top of his purse, before he got any money or more fights. It was a form of protection and assured that everyone was "one of us." I have no idea if this practise now is honoured in the breach or the observance. The leading figure among the dark lords who ran this particular scam was an Irishman named Owen Vincent Madden. He controlled liquor in Chicago and New York. Like many gangsters, he liked boxing and had an admiration for how tough you have to be to be a pro fighter. By a fortunate coincidence, Madden was not only Irish but had been born in Liverpool, like Foster. When the Italian mob of Luciano and Costello moved in, Madden took his million and retired to Hot Springs.

Charlie Foster was not going to put up with being "handled", so he went to see Owney Madden. He marched into his office, past Madden's "boys" with sub machine guns etc. and put his argument to Madden like this.

"Owney, we're from the same town and the same blood. I've brought this boy along all by myself, and I'd like to keep it that way. I promised his parents that I'd see that nobody else got his money, and that he wouldn't get hurt if I could help it."

"Well, Mr. Foster, I hear he's a fine boy, but it's most irregular and wouldn't look good."

"Besides that, Owney, he was born in Ireland itself and there's not many of those around at the top now."

"Well, Mr. Foster, since we're both from Liverpool, I think it's about time some people see how a real Irishman can fight. I'll see you won't have to worry."

So it was that McLarnin was the only fighter from the West who didn't have an Eastern representative getting 10 %.

"Gee, ain't it great to meet a guy from your home town?" as the old song goes. Sometimes it pays to be stubborn and fearless.

It was Jim's friend, Mayor Jimmy Walker, who legalized boxing again in New York, with the "Walker Law". Boxing has often been outlawed because, while it doesn't kill as many people as football or hockey, it upsets the fastidious. Jim doesn't say much about the gangster element in boxing except to say, "It's a tough business -- a hard way to make an easy dollar."

In a large family, if one boy is a great fighter, you can assume that the other boys are pretty good, and it was about this time that Jim's brother, Sammy, joined them, as did Jim's youngest brother, Bob. Both would work out with Jim. Jim wasn't alone. Jim's sister Olive told me that he was often lonely in his life. You could see a bit of this in Jim's eyes and his liking for company. Jim related quickly to people and it was easy to like him. Moreover, with this donnybrook with Kaplan, Jim had won the hearts of boxing fans. He had been a boxing phenom when he was a boy on the West Coast but now they knew they had the real "fighting Irishman". This kid McLarnin was the kind of Mick you could take to your heart.

Financially, they never looked back from this point. The next month, on November 24, they took a fight with tough Billy Wallace in Detroit. They also got a fight for young Sammy McLarnin against Paul Pullman of Windsor.

Sammy came through with a T.K.O. When it came Jim's turn in the feature, he started slowly, perhaps thinking of Sammy's fight. In the final rounds, Jim shook Wallace with a succession of right hooks. Wallace was popular around Detroit, with a solid reputation and was paid more, $10,000 to Jim's $8,000.

So it was that McLarnin went to New York, to Madison Square Garden, the sacred temple of boxing. For his next fight, they matched this brash Westerner against the newest sensation in the East, the fastest left jab in history, the expected next lightweight champion, Sid Terris, "the Ghost of the Ghetto", a Jewish boy whose boxing style and speed sent Eastern aficionados into trances. It was the sensation of the East against the sensation of the West. Fans, especially Jewish and Irish, of whom there were several living in New York the last time promoters Mike Jacobs and Tex Rickard counted, were fighting for tickets and the Garden was Sold Right Out.

The Garden is holy ground. When Rocky Graziano talked about his first fight there, he talked about that holy feeling. He says he was awed by the ghosts of all the great boxers who had fought there, and mentioned the names of the greats who came to his mind. He names the legendary Jimmy McLarnin among the heroic warriors of boxing Valhalla.

The night of February 24, 1928, Jimmy's opening night, was pure lightning. His opponent, Terris, was the finest young boxer who had been seen in New York since the great Benny Leonard.

Jim jogged down the aisle, with Pop limping behind him. Jim's robe was wrapped around him and a towel circled his head to keep him warm. Jimmy had sparred in the dressing room to break a sweat, because he wanted to come out fast, in keeping with the decision that the easiest time to knock a man out is early. They were not going to give the "Ghost of the Ghetto" a chance to disappear behind his smooth boxing. The writers were already hammering their typewriters. The radio announcers were working. The promoters were counting the till. These multicultural events had much to be said for them financially.

Terris was supremely confident of his artistry as he entered the ring. McLarnin looked determined.

Back in Vancouver, the Province Newspaper was confident and felt that morality would help him. "Jimmy is a clean cut, clean living boy, and a credit to the terminal city (of the C. P. Railway)."

But all other papers expected him to lose. "Young McLarnin has bitten off more than he can chew," and "The independence of his manager has led young James to complete folly," were two typical headlines.

Both boys weighed 134 pounds at the weigh-in. That was considered the only equal thing. Terris was a 2 to 1 favourite.

"Terris will completely bewilder the West Coast boy. He hasn't a chance!" The New York Times said. This almost matches Jersey Joe Walcott's comment just before he was knocked out by probably the hardest punch ever thrown -- by Marciano, "If I can't beat this bum, take my name out of the record book."

Jim was only twenty and he hadn't fought anyone from New York and where the hell was Vancouver, B.C.? Terris and the Eastern writers could not have been more wrong.

"Sid was another guy who took me for a pigeon," said Jim, when I read these comments to him.

The great fight lasted one minute and 36 seconds. To the tumultuous cheers of the packed Garden crowd, Terris slid smoothly out of his corner and put out a beautiful lightning-fast jab. "Then," says Jim, "I simply took one step outside of that jab and threw a fast overhand right." This caught Sid about an inch from the point of the chin where a small blood vessel crosses the bone. Jim's fist looped just over Terris's left as he brought it back from the jab. His head snapped around just past his right shoulder and, says Jim, "He fell on his head." The Ghost of the Ghetto, the smoothest thing seen in the East in years, was lying on the floor.

There was dead silence. Then there was bedlam. It was the upset of the decade, and was written up as such. Some fans, who'd come all the way from Vancouver, hadn't sat down. Jim told me that years later, a man came up to him in Vancouver on Granville Street and said, "Hey, McLarnin, you owe me twenty dollars."

"I didn't know him, but he had paid for that fight and flown to New York. I gave him a pat on the back and called him Pal and that seemed to make him happy."

But the Irish fans descended on the ring and seized McLarnin. That right hand would have done credit to the great John L. himself, and gave Jim a reputation as a great right hand puncher. Remember that. They put Jimmy on their shoulders and carried him to his dressing room, and then they surged out into the street to every Irish cop, and into the taverns to every Irish drinker, to declare that a new hero was born and there hadn't been such a fight since Finn McCool, Brian Boru, and Chuhulan. They were not the only ones grinning, for the boxing promoters of New York were counting the number of Irish in the city. Not only that, the Irish would come in droves, and there was another interested race rising from humiliation and poverty which would like to see this Irish kid get his comeuppance. That was Sid Terris's race, the Jews, for their heroes had been Samson, Joshua, and the Maccabees, but now the most outstanding fighters in Jim's divisions were of that great and brilliant race. The greatest of these had been undefeated, just retired, lightweight champ Benny Leonard. Young McLarnin's hero had been this same man. Young Jim's other hero had been Packey McFarlane, a boxer out of Chicago who had won 149 fights and lost one, early in his career, and never got a shot at a championship. No champion would get into the ring with him, for they were sure to lose. Jim was afraid that would happen to him. On the West Coast, he had showed them he could box. In Chicago, he had shown he had guts. In New York, he had shown a hell of a right hand. No champion was getting into a ring with that kid from Vancouver without a lot of guarantees and the taking of certain precautions.

Chapter 18
The Fight with Mandell for the Lightweight Championship

Far be it from promoters like Tex Rickard or Mike Jacobs to stir up racial rivalry unless there was money to be made by it. When Irish Jimmy McLarnin was fighting one of the outstanding Jewish American fighters, there was a great deal of money to be made. The arena was packed with Irishmen who had come to see Jim win and Jews who had come to see McLarnin lose. McLarnin seemed completely free of racial feelings. In his day, the ring was full of good boys of many races: Jewish, Irish, Italian, Black; it made no difference to Jim. But Jim was now twenty and reaching his full growth and punching power, and as Jim knocked out one leading Jewish fighter after another, the press began to take note of just that fact. They began to write of him as not only the killer with the baby face but also as the Jew Killer, for the press was very racially conscious. It would refer in headlines on the sports page to an Italian knocking out a Jew as "Wop blasts Kike" without the slightest embarrassment. It sold papers. And it brought fans into the arena for Mike Jacobs, even though he, of course, was Jewish. Business is business. Jacob's other favourite was the black, Joe Louis. Jacobs had financial control of Louis. Louis was a great friend of McLarnin's, and one of his golfing partners. Jim often told me what a great golfer Joe was, how long a ball he hit, as one would expect, and how he should have been on the pro golfing circuit.

Unfortunately, the regularity with which McLarnin knocked off good Jewish American boxers began to get under the skin of the great Benny Leonard. He took to coaching Jewish fighters on how to beat McLarnin. When none were successful, Leonard, himself, came out of retirement "to redeem the honour of the Jewish race."

"Damn foolishness," snorted McLarnin, puzzled by it all. "Maybe it was all part of the hype. Benny had lost a lot of money in the crash of 29." Leonard had been Jim's idol, for Benny was such a classy, skilful boxer.

Benny wore his hair long and slicked back and took pride in getting through a 15 round fight without having his hair mussed.

Jim told a story of an early meeting with Leonard that becomes ironic in the light of future developments. Leonard was on the Orpheum circuit in San Francisco in 1925 and Pop suggested to Jim that they might be able to get Leonard to box a few rounds with him on the stage. They went to see Leonard, but he said, "Well, Mr. Foster, we already have our programme."

Now, Leonard could not get enough of McLarnin. He came around to Jim's camp to watch him work out. Pretending friendship, Benny had even read Lilian's letters to Jim. Jim was still shocked, but Leonard was famous for trying to understand his opponent before boxing him, and this must have been what he was trying to do.

One of the few times Leonard had been really stunned in the ring was by Lew Tendler, an eminently fair man. Leonard remarked, "Keep them up, Lew," implying that Tendler, also Jewish, by the way, was fighting foul. Lew, because he was shocked, hesitated, allowing Leonard to get his senses back, and continue, to win. Nat Fleischer, in *History of Boxing*, calls McLarnin a perfect ringman, but even the best have some weakness. Leonard looked long and hard and found one. Jim sometimes had a habit of leaning in and under to avoid a right hand punch, and so was briefly vulnerable to a second quick right if it were thrown low and hard. Leonard filed that away in his mind.

Now, at age twenty, McLarnin was the number one challenger for the lightweight title, the dream of his life. Newspapers were all calling for the fight. "Mandell can no longer duck the murderous Mick," one of the sports pages said. Rickard always billed Jim as an Irish Catholic, rather than the Irish Methodist that he was. The forces that ran boxing could no longer deny McLarnin a legitimate shot. So it was that Jimmy McLarnin signed to fight slick Sammy Mandel, for the lightweight championship of the world -- and, for the first time, there were no strings attached. If Mandel lost, he lost his championship. Mandel was the first man to take that chance with the fearsome McLarnin. The reaction in Vancouver, at the McLarnin household, was excitement! Anticipation! New York! The Garden! A title shot for our boy Jimmy! Wow!

The dark lords of boxing had noticed something that the media had not. McLarnin had grown into a welterweight, and would have difficulty making the lightweight limit. Pop realised this, but it was Jim's big chance. Still growing, Jim weighed about 145 pounds when not ready for a fight. Now, Jim had to take off ten pounds just to make the lightweight limit. And that was to be the problem. It's all right for an older fighter who can trim off a bit of beer fat from around his waist, but it isn't for a young twenty year old who is lean muscle already. The young athlete doesn't burn off fat; he burns off muscle. McLarnin stood just under 5 foot 7, reach 68 inches, neck 16 inches, chest 40 inches, thigh 19, calf 15, forearm 12, bicep 15, waist 30, fist 11. Pictures show him broad in the shoulders, slim and tapering of body, husky in the upper arms, and long in the arm for his height. You can see where his punching power came from -- the shoulder area. Jim had grown to be a small welterweight, not a big lightweight. Jim set in to train off over ten pounds in six weeks, and not to grow in the meantime. Jim had to be ready for the opportunity of his life on May 21st, 1927 and Sammy Mandel was no cheese champ.

The Garden is more than a sports venue. It is a symbol of excellence. Originally a New York, New Haven, and Hartford freight yard and depot, the structure had been converted in 1874 by P. T. Barnum into a magnificent hall called Barnum's Monster Classical and Geological Hippodrome. In 1890, William Vanderbilt put together a syndicate, including J. P. Morgan, to raise 1.5 million to build a new pleasure palace on the spot of Madison Square. Opened in June of 1890 with a concert and a ballet, it was described by the New York Times as "one of the great institutions of the town, with Central Park and the Brooklyn Bridge". Twenty-five years later, it was refurbished for championship boxing matches. By Jimmy's time it was already an institution.

Jim's opponent, Mandel, was a good looking, smooth boxer and smart dresser, with a solid punch. The press called him "the Rockford Sheik". He was an outstanding champion. Nevertheless, the wise boys were so impressed with what McLarnin had done to Kaplan and Terris that they felt that "McLarnin will take Mandel". They didn't know the trouble that McLarnin was having in training to make the lightweight limit. Pop and Jim thought he could beat Mandel, and indeed he did beat Mandel twice later, but Jim would have to be in top form. Mandel held the title for nearly five years, won 168 bouts, and lost only 12 times. However, he was knocked out 5 times, and McLarnin was the premier knock-out artist of his time. By training hard, McLarnin came to the weigh-in at exactly 135 lbs, but he didn't feel good. He had weakened his ability to knock out Mandel. Jim's hometown knew nothing of this, however, and was wild with enthusiasm for Jimmy's first real chance at a championship. Hadn't he beaten every other champ he had met? Was Mandel better than Pancho Villa? No. Was he better than Taylor? Was he better than Kaplan? Our Jimmy would finally be the champion he should be. Pop had outfoxed them and Jimmy will be champ for a decade. What a day it will be! Fight fans up and down the Coast from Vancouver to Los Angeles were confident. You should have seen the newspapers just before the match. Jim's childhood friend, Bill Forst, who used to hold Jim's coat while he fought in the alley, would be covering the fight for the best paper, The Province. But only insiders knew what trouble Jimmy was having, and that with his loss of strength, it was unlikely that he could knock out Mandel. There was another reason. Mandel was trained for this fight by Jack Blackburn, who later trained Louis. Blackburn had been an outstanding fighter himself, but colour had restricted his own chances, so he turned to training. You like to bet? To put money on a fighter? Instead, put money on the trainers -- Whitey Bimstein, Angelo Dundee, and Jack Blackburn. "Blackburn," said Jim, "boy, was he tough. He knew the game. He'd killed men. I'd rather have fought Louis than Blackburn. He taught Joe that great left jab and those lovely combinations. But he was cold as ice. You just had to look into his eyes."

The bout was twice postponed on technicalities, making it even more difficult and draining for McLarnin to maintain his weight. Terris was supposed to be better than Mandel. McLarnin congratulated Mandel in the ring just after the decision. Jim didn't even look like himself. His ribs stuck out. His face looked skeletal from the prolonged weight drain. Was McLarnin nervous? "Sure I was, until the first guy got hit, and then I could relax and concentrate."

It was an excellent fight. Jimmy hit harder but Sammy hit more often. Years later, Foster explained the fight to a local newspaper scribe. "Mandel won by slapping and flipping, tactics that are illegal today. He would just slap and back away with my boy after him. Jim was brilliant in the last five rounds and really tagged Mandel in the 14th, but it was too late then." Slapping is a short cuff with the front of the glove and flipping is the same with the back of the glove. Neither is a punch, but they all counted for the number of times Mandel had hit McLarnin. I have had this done to me by a pro sparring partner. It's confusing but it doesn't amount to much. He would push my shoulder when I was about to punch. A good referee would stop most of this. Ali got away with a lot it.

Both Pop and Jim were frustrated. Jim was the aggressor, but perhaps he was outmanoeuvered. Mandell kept his left in Jim's face, "and his thumb in my eye," said Jim. It was enough to retain Mandell's championship. When Jim caught him solidly in the 14th, Mandell hung on and then retreated. He had fought a shrewd fight. So leather-lunged Joe Humphries announced the decision – Winner, and still champion. Jim wasn't satisfied with the result.

Oddly, the Vancouver papers took it as if it were the end of McLarnin's career. He had fallen just short, but had done better than any Vancouver boy had done before, was their attitude. Nobody seemed to remember that Jim was only twenty years old. The Province said, "Nice try, Jim. You've done us proud." McLarnin was to come back and beat Mandel twice, decisively. The fights for which McLarnin is remembered were mostly ahead of him. McLarnin was paid $50,000 and Mandell $75,000. Jim's comments to me were that Sammy was a very competent fighter who knew how to protect himself at all times, that he felt weak for the fight, and that anybody looks awkward with somebody's thumb in his eye. Eastern USA and Canadian papers said that McLarnin was a much overrated fighter who had probably reached his limits. Pop had learned that Jim was a welterweight or junior welterweight and not a lightweight and would never be again, and never had him fight so light again. So Jim was a welterweight, and at the centre of the boxing world for the next eight years, fighting the contests that boxing historians rate among the greatest performances in ring annals.

He was given the key to the city of Vancouver, and was inducted into the Halls of Fame of both Canada and B.C. You can see the gloves with which he finally won the welterweight title in the B.C.Hall of Fame. Of course, Jim is in the World Boxing Hall of Fame as well, and had a ring from that hallowed institution. People alive now still remember the excitement in this young steamship and railway town when our Jimmy fought for a championship.

Chapter 19
The Toast of Broadway: the Glory Years, Millar, Mandel, Goldstein, Thompson, Singer, Petrolle, Brouillard, and Benny Leonard

Thus it was that Jim had to abandon his quest for the lightweight title, but Providence had better things in store for our hero, as often happens when we think our prayers have not been answered; if we keep the faith, better things are given us. Jim now had his full growth, and they never took another match where Jim had to lose weight and weaken his punch, although, by mistake, Jim trained too hard after an almost two year lay off, and came in weak on the first Ross fight. After their retirement, Foster complained of the difficulty of matching Jim right, since he was growing and his weight was constantly changing. But from now until he won his championship, McLarnin fought at the same weight and was unbeatable. It was then that Grantland Rice called him "the greatest fighter pound for pound of them all." Scribes referred to Jim as "the uncrowned champion" and "the awesome McLarnin". He fought each of the next three months. A month after the Mandell fight, he K.O.ed Phil McGraw in New York. Jim weighed 146, not the 134 that he had weighed for the Mandell fight, and he looked and felt strong. A month after that, he fought an exhibition with the colourful Packey O'Gattey in Detroit. Then on August 2, in Detroit, Jim knocked out the South American, Stanislaus Laozola. This put McLarnin back in the active picture, for Laozola was considered the number one contender for the lightweight title after Mandell had defeated Jim. Now, Jim reappears in the ranking as number one contender.

However, on November 30,1928, the boxing world was surprised. McLarnin was stopped on cuts and, for the only time in his career, did not finish a fight. The man who accomplished this was a very good but not great fighter. Today, Ray Millar would be a champ, but wasn't, in those salad days of boxing. Everybody knew he was a dangerous fighter. He had a superb left hook which had brought many K.O.s, but he is always remembered in boxing as the only man to stop Jimmy McLarnin. Millar would drink free on it. He assembled an album of clippings to prove his feat. McLarnin, as Foster said, had a few weaknesses. Sometimes he warmed up slowly -- a typical weakness of a decent man involved with a blood sport. Also, Jim could slip punches to the head, and had a granite chin. He was a little careless until he got tagged once. Three times he got caught this way, early in fights. The other times he had trouble, he got stunned with hard blows to the temple, but went 15 rounds.

At the opening bell, Millar sailed out and swung his famous left hook. McLarnin pulled back his head enough to avoid the blow's power, but the punch swept across his cheekbone with terrific velocity. A horrible gash opened under McLarnin's eye, down to the bone. Blood streamed down Jim's face. "I'd never been hit quite like that before. I never cut badly in any other fight. It felt weird. It felt like a knife blade had opened me up. I honestly, to this day, think that he had something in his glove," said Jim. "Oh, it was a good punch, but I wasn't stunned. I might have been better taking it. His hook was hard, and I don't believe in taking any punches. Anyway, it was as if a razor blade had been drawn across my cheekbone. They couldn't stop the bleeding." Jim was handicapped not only by blood obscuring his vision, but also by the necessity to change his style, to protect his eye. Jim couldn't make Millar miss all the time. Millar realised that his best chance was to keep hitting Jim on that cut until the referee had to stop the fight and award it to Millar. It's cruel, but it's the way to win a pro fight, and Millar isn't to be blamed. Every time Millar caught Jim there, the blood would fly into the air and cover both fighters. Millar's gloves were sopping wet with Jim's blood. After eight rounds of this, Pop could stand it no longer. He threw in the towel. Millar had done the impossible; he had stopped Jimmy McLarnin for the one and only time. Ray was a ten day's wonder. McLarnin was never knocked out in well over 100 fights, and this was the only time he was stopped. Perhaps this is why Jim's mind was so clear. The punch must have come in over Jim's right glove. "I don't know," said Jim, "It's one of the few punches in my career that I didn't see clearly."

"But you moved back," I persisted.

"Well, I could tell by his body movement that there must be a left hook coming, but I didn't see the punch itself."

Millar fought some good fighters, Canzoneri and Ross, and he won a lot more pro fights than he lost, and he caught a lot of other guys with his superb left hook, but he never cut one just like this, and it does make one think. I can only guess, but it might have been the peculiar angle of the twist of a left hook with the movement of Jim's head that caused the terrible cut, for Millar was a clean fighter, or he might have seen a great opportunity. Being stopped on cuts never happened to McLarnin again. Some fighters cut easily. The Englishman, Henry Cooper, might actually have beaten Ali at his peak had he not been a "bleeder."

"I had a small scar under one eye for years but I massaged it and it disappeared," said Jim, for he was proud of the fact that he hadn't a single cut or scar tissue or sign of his trade after over 100 pro fights, some early ones unrecorded. McLarnin was a great defensive fighter, one of the best. After the fight, Pop and Jim went to the hospital to get Jim sewed up and begin to plan to fight Millar again. "You learn something every fight, and I learned exactly how good Millar's hook was."

It was to be different when they met again. Most great fighters improve in rematches.

1929 was the year of revenge for Jim. He decisioned Glick on January 11 and came back to knock him out on March 1. That is the way a great fighter operates. The public was eager to see the fight. They were matched for October 9, 1929. "Dangerous left hook vs Dynamite right," said the New York papers. Big Apple fans wanted to see what McLarnin would do with the only man who had ever stopped him. Sportswriters picked McLarnin because he had just K.O.ed Joe Glick, who had a great left hook also, and I suspect that Pop got those fights with Glick to prime Jim for Millar. Nevertheless, they said Millar had the best left hook since Charlie White, who had caught the great Benny Leonard in his prime, put him through the ropes, and nearly beat him. Unfortunately, the fight was not the great contest that was anticipated because Pop and Jim had Millar figured out. It didn't take Millar long to realise that Jim had him. A minute into the fight, Millar began to grab Jim as he moved in. After a couple of rounds, Millar had had enough of Jim's fearful body punches as Jim moved in close with his gloves high by the sides of his head, blocking any hook and pounding both hands to the body. Millar's strategy for this was to grab Jim and wrestle him. Millar refused to box. However, several times Millar seemed to hit low deliberately, almost as if he wished to be disqualified. The crowd began to boo. When Millar threw his left hook, McLarnin moved forward and down and drove his right hard into Millar's body, making Millar pay so dearly for his hooks that Millar almost stopped throwing them. When he did throw them, McLarnin wasn't there and Millar missed. The scar under Jim' s eye from the previous fight was visible from ringside, but Millar wasn't able to lay a glove on it. Not usually a dirty fighter, Millar was warned several times for low blows. This can be the action of a fighter who knows he's beaten. Throughout the fight, McLarnin jabbed and crossed Millar. In the 7th round, Millar was pinned against the ropes and Jim hit him with a right that buckled his knees, but Millar held on. Jim grew arm weary, wrestling out of Millar's clinches. Now, Jim began to humiliate Ray by beating him at his own game, left hooking. Jim was hammering Ray as the final bell sounded. The New York Times sports page headline the next day was, "Vancouver boy lands decisive beating to Chicago boxer. Loser wisely refuses to mix."

Jim was avenged for one of his two losses in 1928. On October 9, Jim knocked out contender Sammy Baker in one round. Jim showed complete confidence in knocking out Baker, who was a tough trial horse.

Jim and Pop wanted to meet Mandell again and beat him. However, Mandell and his manager had learned a lesson from McLarnin's treatment of Millar the second time. McLarnin was poison in a 2nd match. Jim's memory was too good and his manager was too smart. In order to get his rematch with Mandell, he had to come in over the lightweight limit so that, win or lose, Mandell would retain his title. Jim did take off a little weight, and showed up for the weigh in at just over 139 pounds, four pounds over the lightweight limit. Jim fought Mandell three times and improved his performance each time. Before the second fight, he was asked by the scribes what change of tactics he and Pop had planned. Jim said that he had probably committed a tactical error in going after Mandell hard, so early, and this time he intended to conserve his energy, and pace himself, especially after he had lost so much weight to make the lightweight limit. Again, Pop and Jim had figured out their opponent. Jim slipped most of the "Sheik of Rockford's" left jabs, coming in with hard body punches as he had with Millar. It's difficult to catch a good boxer with punches to the head, but it's very difficult to move the body and slip. You must block, which immobilises that hand for counters.

On November 4, on Mandell's home turf at Chicago, McLarnin took Mandell, the lightweight champion of the world, to pieces. By the end of the fight Mandell was almost out. "I'd have had him too," said Jim, "if I hadn't had a glove that didn't quite fit me. My hand kept moving around in it." Despite that, it was a decisive win for Jim.

The rubber match was staged in Chicago on March 1, 1930. This time, McLarnin was overwhelming. Even the Chicago papers said that only Mandell's skill saved him from a K.O. Jim kept the pressure on all ten rounds, and to do this he had to be in top shape. Jim was always well trained, except for the year he had jaundice. Jim's weakness about training was that in his dedication, he sometimes over trained, as in the first Mandell and Ross fights. For this fight, he was just right. He staggered Sammy in the 2nd round with a left hook to the jaw, followed by a left and right to the head. Mandell appeared to be on the point of going down, but the bell rang as McLarnin moved in. Again, in round six, Jim caught Mandell and buckled his knees. By the final bell, Sammy was bleeding from the mouth and from a bad cut over one eye. The question of who was superior was now settled. Each fighter received $40,000. McLarnin was richer and more marketable. Mandell was still lightweight champ. Independent manager Pop Foster still didn't have a championship in his control. All was right with the pugilistic world. McLarnin was given a civic reception in his hometown. That should be enough for any independent fighter in his early twenties.

Hometown papers hung on every scrap of information now about Vancouver's own Jimmy. Vancouver papers picked up a photo of Jimmy.

By this time, Jimmy was an excellent dresser. Mandell can't have hit him much, because after the fight there is no evidence on his face of cuts or even swelling. Jim looked to be bursting with energy. He was no longer a boy and looked ready for anything. There is a short write up. The reporter is impressed that this outstanding fighter from his town is no scarred pug. McLarnin was said to have a book of poems by Tennyson and Byron. It was said that he liked dancing. Jim's brother Bob told me that Jim was a terrific Irish step dancer. I've seen Jim mimic the "Ali shuffle" and other steps. The report continues that Jim has gramophone records of the popular Irish tenor John McCormack. The family attends the Methodist church in East Hastings. Jim seems to have struck the reporter as an anomaly. He was sent to interview this pro fighter who turned out to be polite, well-dressed, knowledgeable, unscarred, and to have a decent, intelligent family. With so much going for him, the reporter was interested in Jim's social life. Jim was not seen regularly in all the social spots in Los Angeles. Yes, Jim admitted he did get letters from ladies eager to make his acquaintance, but he didn't go out much. He had his training to think of. All that would come later. The reporter said that Jim had a trunk full of letters from ladies, but really didn't have much time for them. Jim found it hard to get away from reporters after a fight, but slipped away to phone home, then off to a hotel for a night's rest. The reporter had seen Jim fight and been told about him and now he had met a very different young man.

In between the last Mandell fights, McLarnin had knocked out the handsome and brilliant Jewish boxer, Ruby Goldstein. In many ways, McLarnin and Goldstein resembled each other. Both were intelligent and decent men in a rough sport. Nobody ever looked better sparring in the gym. Goldstein had classic moves. He had the best training, from Benny Leonard, among others. He was clean living and trained hard. When his career was over, he became one of the greatest of referees. Unfortunately, he froze for one notorious moment when Emile Griffin had Benny Paret trapped in a corner, and briefly unconscious, sitting on the ring buckle, and Griffin beat him to death just before Goldstein stopped it. Griffin was incensed, for Paret had called him a "fairy" just before the fight. Ruby hesitated and considered too nicely on the event. Most actions in a ring must take place instantly.

But McLarnin and Goldstein seemed an ideal match, two beautiful fighters with fine records and boxing styles -- the ideal young Jewish boxer against the ideal young Irish boxer. Two sensational rounds were all the fans got. Unfortunately, just as Ruby was boxing beautifully, Jim nailed him with an overhand right on the jaw and followed it up with another, as Ruby stopped momentarily and "the Jewel of the Ghetto" was out, on December 13, 1929, in New York, in front of a full house of startled Irishmen and Jews. McLarnin was simply tougher. Some fighters are tough far beyond the average human being.

The old lightweight champ, Battling Nelson, was one of the toughest sentient beings ever. Once asked how he took such punishment, Bat replied in all seriousness, "I ain't human." McLarnin had met the fearsome Nelson, for he had dropped around to Jim's camp once. McLarnin was closer to Nelson than Goldstein was. McLarnin was tough beyond my comprehension.

Interviewed before the fight, Jim said that he was looking forward to meeting Goldstein, and that after that he would go home to his family for Christmas in Vancouver. In front of a packed house of 20,000, Goldstein made the house roar when he caught Jimmy twice on the chin with beautiful rights. Both times, McLarnin had been coming in with hands held, as the scribes said, "like the claws of a lobster."

This seems to have been Jim's stance at this stage of his career, his right held high beside, not in front of, his jaw, and his left held just above waist level, almost a yard from his right. This is the exact opposite of what I had been taught in college where we were instructed to hold the hands high and fairly close together, with elbows close to the sides. I asked Jim about this and he illustrated how his stance was excellent for slipping punches and for countering with looping rights over lefts and body punches with the left to the ribs under the right lead. He rapped me a few to the jaw to prove his point, as I punched from my college stance. Jim's stance also allowed him to block left hooks easily, and counter with the right, and in the movie of his fight with Benny Leonard he stands this way, almost straight up. His defence depends upon his ability to slip punches by moving his head sideways, and make his opponent pay with counters for body blows. Indeed, it forces a young boxer to learn the skills of defence, and not just hide behind his gloves. Gene Tunney makes just this point in an essay for the Encyclopaedia Britannica on the advances in the science of boxing. Later in his career, Jim's stance is more orthodox, and the movies of his fights with Ross show a more closed stance. It appears more effective for fast straight punches. Ross's left is higher than Jim's, and straight. In the third Ross/McLarnin fight, these two boys appear to be the greatest defensive fighters, except for Willie Pep, the incomparable "Wisp", or perhaps Billy Conn at his best.

In the first round, Goldstein took advantage of this open stance with straight punches to the head. Dale Walters, Canada's Olympic bronze medallist, did this same thing in his pro fight against Tony Pep at the Agrodome in Vancouver in 1986. Goldstein won the first round. But in round two, as Ruby slid in, Jim hit him with a looping right with all his weight against the side of Goldstein's face. Goldstein sank to the canvas, with his eyes looking off centre. He arose at the count of nine, just on time, with, as the scribes said, an aggrieved and hurt look on his face that somehow he had been dealt with unfairly. This was not supposed to happen. Had he not been boxing superbly? Goldstein fought back. Jim pursued him with an intense look, chin in, eyes staring intently. McLarnin stepped in and hit Ruby with a left hook, a looping right, a short left hook, a short right chop, and Goldstein pitched limply to the floor, then rolled back over the bottom rope of the ring. Fans never knew if Jim would treat them to a dazzling display of the subtleties of the sweet science or a devastating knock out. McLarnin was now the biggest draw in boxing. Between the times of Dempsey and Louis, the fans would rather pay to see Jim than any other fighter. This was a remarkable achievement for a man 5 foot 7 and 150 pounds. Certainly Jim's good looks, fine manners, and Irish ancestry didn't hurt his popularity.

Now, however, three weeks after his second victory over Mandell, Jim met a tough accomplished black, Young Jack Thompson, who was to win the welterweight championship from Jim's old California rival, Jackie Fields. Thompson's only loss on his road to the championship was to Jim. They met in New York on March 28, 1930, in Madison Square Garden.

The papers report that despite the fact that McLarnin's win was unanimous and decisive, McLarnin was extended by Thompson. To extend McLarnin in those days was considered a moral victory. "That smiling Celt, Jimmy McLarnin, had a hard battle on his hands in the 10 round donny-brook with the muscular Jack Thompson." Jim's right was so famed that many fighters got caught with his superb left hook while they watched his right. It's a standard move that John L. Sullivan used. Sullivan went to the head. McLarnin often went to the body with that hook, and, as Thompson watched that right, Jim stepped in, and sunk his hook into Thompson's body almost to his backbone, depositing Thompson on the canvas where he lay until the bell rang and his handlers raced out of his corner. There was no argument about the decision.

Newspapers said, "McLarnin is today the greatest drawing card in the fight game. Fields with his welterweight crown can no longer duck this Irish bruiser." Oh yes he could! The loser of that fight, Thompson, immediately signed for a championship fight with Fields. McLarnin got called the uncrowned champion – but no title shots. When Thompson won the crown, he wanted no part of McLarnin. Thompson couldn't forget that left to the stomach. No Irish need apply!

It would be years before Jimmy got his shot at the welterweight title, and they thought they had just the right kind of awkward fighter who could smother McLarnin's brilliance. Pop signed to meet new lightweight champ Al Singer. Singer had knocked Mandell cold in 1.46 of round one. Singer had lost only 8 of his 70 pro fights, but he was knocked out four times. On September 11, 1930, in New York, the odds had shortened. Singer looked sensational in training and McLarnin had not. There were rumours that Jim would quit after this fight. Singer was confident because it had taken McLarnin three fights to master Mandell. In round three, McLarnin shook Al with a solid left hook. Then Singer threw a hook to the body and ran into another left hook from Jim. If an opponent hooks consistently, you get used to it. With the second hook, Singer's head snapped around, and down went Al. Jim was sure that Al was out cold, so over McLarnin went into his victory somersault. Landing on his feet, he was presented with Al Singer standing right in front of him with his hands up ready to punch. "Holy Smoke," said Jim as he told me about it laughing, "I was never so surprised in my life. I had to knock him out then. Did I look stupid! Fortunately, Al was still a bit groggy. I went after him and finished him. If Al had lasted, they would be laughing at old Jim today."

Singer was dragged to his corner by his heels, for now he was really out. Then Dr. William Walker worked him over. Walker said that Singer was out longer than he should have been and had suffered a partial paralysis. Singer later met Jim. "You nearly paralysed me," said Al, "You're the hardest puncher I ever met."

On May 21, in New York, McLarnin met the toughest man he ever fought, the high plains assassin, Billy Petrolle, nicknamed "The Fargo Express" for the way he rolled over most fighters like an express train. They had three incredible fights. Petrolle was built like a short block of granite, covered with muscle and hair. He was a touch slower and less skilful, although he hit as hard, or harder, than Ross, Canzoneri, and McLarnin. At any other a time than boxing's golden age, he would have been a great world champion. Petrolle was managed by that master of ballyhoo, Deacon Jack Hurley, from Seattle. Back in 1930, the Deacon had Petrolle, who could hardly be hurt with a newly sharpened axe. "Billy was the toughest man I ever fought," said Jim. "You could hurt your hands hitting the end of his nose."

Nat Fleischer, the editor of The Ring, and then the ultimate authority on boxing, called the first McLarnin/Petrolle fight one of the half dozen most thrilling fights he had ever witnessed in his long career, and definitely the greatest exhibition of courage he had ever seen. Fleischer said, "No one who saw that mill in the Garden will ever forget it."

The sportswriter who did the best job writing about McLarnin was the Toronto writer, Trent Frayne. In the book *Great Canadian Sport Stories,* Frayne writes with his usual gusto, "Petrolle was a man who could hide behind his scar tissue. He was a veteran of 152 fights." There was nothing fancy about Petrolle's style. He wore an old black wool sweater instead of a shiny silk robe with his name on the back. Petrolle came to fight, not to show off. When he pulled off his sweater, he was covered with dark chest hair and muscle. Pop Foster, who had glanced away momentarily, thought he still had the sweater on. Pop shouted at the referee, Patsey Haley, "Good Lord, Haley, make him take that sweater off. What is this?" Jim calmed Pop down.

In round one, Petrolle came out of his customary flat-footed half crouch and caught McLarnin with a hard right, cutting him under the left eye. It was a portent of a long night for both. McLarnin took Round One. In the second round, disaster struck the classy Canadian. McLarnin saw Petrolle's jaw open and threw a hard right, one of the hardest he ever threw, says Jim. Petrolle ducked in time and Jim's right hand exploded on the top of Petrolle's head. Intense pain shot along Jim's arm. McLarnin had broken his right hand. Petrolle was on him like a tiger. Men had broken their hands on the old Fargo Express before, and Billy sensed what was wrong with Jim. Billy threw a barrage of punches at Jim's chin, catching him several times.

Jim retreated, jabbing hard, holding his right high as if there were nothing wrong. McLarnin rallied in the third, jarring Petrolle with hard lefts. Jim knew he had to put everything into his left because he no longer had a right. You can box with just a left, but not just a right. In the 4th round, Petrolle moved right and hit Jim with a twisting left hook. Down went Jim, for one of the very few times in his career. Jim reeled to his feet at the count of eight, and Petrolle met him with solid lefts and rights. Jim slowly crumpled to the canvas and then arose to absorb one of the worst beatings that any pro fighter has absorbed. "If I hadn't been in shape, I'd have taken permanent damage," said Jim. The veteran fight crowd in Madison Square Garden was appalled at what followed. Al Golden, part owner of King's Park Race course in Montreal, suffered a fatal heart attack from the excitement. In the 5th and 6th rounds, Petrolle worked Jim's ribs and then his chin.

By Round 7, Jim's face was a swollen mess. At the end of that round, New York's mayor, Jimmy Walker, got hurriedly to his feet from his ringside seat, and remarked, "Well, I don't see how McLarnin can take this, because I can't," and left the arena. He had come, as he always did, to see McLarnin's fistic artistry for, as he said, "It's a thing to behold." He hadn't bargained for this.

In the 8th Petrolle hammered Jim remorselessly. The crowd howled at referee Haley to stop it. Haley grabbed Jim, peered into his half closed eyes, and asked him, "Have you had enough, Jim?" McLarnin shook him away and called Petrolle in. No Surrender!

A friend of mine, Ron Manson, who boxed professionally out of Seattle, once cornered Petrolle's manager in the Olympic Hotel. In the course of the conversation, he asked the Deacon who was the toughest fighter he had ever seen. Hurley didn't hesitate. "Jimmy McLarnin, without doubt. He was a rock!" I believe the Deacon was thinking of the moment when, with his face streaming blood, his eyes half-closed, and his right hand broken, McLarnin shook off the referee, and called in murderous punching Billy Petrolle to do his worst. McLarnin was a fighter.

By the 9th round, the crowd began to go quite mad. Fights broke out all over the Garden. Both fighters were labouring, Jim almost unconscious and Billy tired from the punches he had thrown. McLarnin was fierce but clean and is still admired for it. "Gentleman Jim" is a fine name for a fighter.

Only Henry Armstrong and Marciano could punch non-stop for fifteen rounds, and sometimes hit low. They were not dirty. They simply kept punching. A. J. Liebling points out that in many sports the fierce competitor, who can get a little dirty if necessary, like Gordie Howe or Ty Cobb, is often admired. Boxing, however, like rugby and football, is so elemental that the dirty fighter is not to be admired. Concrete Charlie Bednarick, the last great two-way pro football player, put Frank Gifford out for a year, but with a perfectly clean tackle.

The great Petrolle/McLarnin massacre was a completely clean fight. After every beating, Jim kept plodding back into the barrage. Near the end of the fight, they would fall into a clinch, leaning on each others' shoulders, eyes almost closed, then separate and swing from the hips, all attempts at defence gone. The final bell was moments penetrating their clouded minds so they continued to punch after it sounded. After this terrible beating, Jim was on his feet and still punching. A true professional fights until he dies, for it is the job of the referee and his manager to see that this doesn't happen. What a fight! Petrolle won a unanimous decision.

In a hotel room afterwards, Jim, both eyes almost closed, his body aching, turned to his manager. "Well, Pop," he muttered, "I guess that's it!"

"We'll see, Jim," said Pop, "We'll see."

Six months later, McLarnin and Foster went to Jack Hurley, looking for a rematch with the fearsome Fargo Express..

Pop said to Jim when asked, "Yes, you can beat him, Jim, but only if you box him, not if you slug with him." So they got Petrolle twice more and beat him twice, each time bad and the last time worse.

"Speaking of that first fight," Jim said to me, "I got hit so hard I don't remember any of the last nine rounds."

All the great fighters but Marciano, perhaps the greatest, have taken some early losses and profited from them. They were big men demolishing much bigger men and they looked like gods doing it. Now and again they ran into a smaller man who was faster and could take a good punch and have a good defence. Louis suddenly looked incredibly slow against 169 pound Billy Conn.

Jim shook his head about Ali, who would take punches to prove his courage and endurance. "Never take a punch you don't have to," said Jim. "When I got hit, there was a mistake someplace," repeated Jim. Tyson's great old boxing coach, Cus D'Amato, pointed out that Ali jabbed and then always moved the same way. Cus said that Ali would do that once, maybe twice, with Louis and then he would get hit with a terrific combination.

Speaking of Mike Tyson, who was, like Petrolle, tough but not quite good enough, Tyson was at a party in London where the great philosopher A. J. "Freddie" Ayer was also. At one point, a young lady rushed into the room saying that her friend, the supermodel Naomi Campbell, was being assaulted in the bedroom by Mike Tyson. Philosopher Ayer went in and told Tyson to desist. Tyson replied, "Do you know who the fuck I am? I'm the heavyweight champion of the world."

Ayer replied, "Yes, well I'm the Wykham Professor of Logic at Oxford, and as we are both pre-eminent in our fields, we should discuss this." Fortunately, Naomi took advantage of this to slip away. Socrates, a good fighter and veteran of battles, could not have put it better.

Like Schmeling watching Louis, McLarnin and Foster had watched Petrolle. Before the next fight with Petrolle, Jim explained, "I made the mistake of trying to back away from Billy's long left hooks and got caught on the jaw. This time I'll keep my head down and force the fighting. When he cocks the left, I'll shoot over my right. He had me out on my feet in the first three rounds."

Foster talked about how Jim had trained. "Last time Petrolle floored Jim twice for the count of nine. We'll move in close and counter and that won't happen." Often, in contact sports, it is dangerous not to move in close, although all your instincts are telling you to get the hell out of there.

So on May 27, 1931, in New York, McLarnin again glided out to meet his terrible conqueror, the old Fargo Express, one of the toughest men ever to lace on a boxing glove. Boxing with care and artistry, Jim beat Petrolle to the punch again and again. Speed was what Jim had, incredible speed. I saw the echo of that speed when he was 77. Petrolle couldn't match it. Every time Petrolle set himself and shifted his weight to hook, Jim stepped in and slammed a right into Billy's face. He took no chances, and won a careful decision.

The public demanded a show down between them. This time, Pop and Jim had Petrolle completely figured, and McLarnin created a masterpiece that sent the aficionados into ecstasies. He was like the greatest matador, Joselito, with a fierce Muira bull, playing him within inches of destruction. In his 2nd and even more in his 3rd fight with Petrolle, McLarnin covered him with the web of his boxing skills and hit him only sparingly, to avoid chances of hurting his hands on that hard rock.

McLarnin began the 3rd fight smoothly. By the 4th round, repeated body punches began to draw Petrolle's guard down. Then Jim opened up as he hadn't in the 2nd fight, and beat Billy even more grievously than he had beaten Jim in the first fight. Some of those great fighters like Barney Ross beat Petrolle, but none the way McLarnin did that night. He would fake his right and hook a left, and every time Billy set himself to hook, Jim would step inside and smash him with a right. Jim Murray of the L. A. Times said, "McLarnin hooked Petrolle into a blood clot." He didn't have to hit hard. Boxing gloves were invented first for the protection of the hands, and secondly for humanitarian reasons. After a fight, the first thing you do is plunge your hands into an ice bucket.

Most of boxing's elite were at this third fight, and they were ecstatic. The great old master of boxing technique, James J. Corbett, was amazed at Jim's artistry. "I've seen hundreds of fights, but outside of my own victory for the championship over Sullivan, I was never so thrilled as when I watched Jimmy beat Petrolle. I never saw more beautiful timing or countering."

Grantland Rice, the dean of American sportswriters, who wrote such immortal lines as those about the Notre Dame backfield, "Outlined against a grey October sky, the four horsemen rode again", at this time, penned the lines: "Pound for pound, McLarnin is the greatest fighter in the ring today, maybe of all time."

Later, this phrase was stolen with no acknowledgement and applied to Sugar Ray Robinson. Robinson had won the middleweight championship from Jake La Motta. Ray was leading light-heavyweight champion Joe

Maxim when he ran out of gas. Ray looked so good winning, sportswriters thought if he were a bit bigger, he might win the heavyweight championship. The same was true of McLarnin in the thirties. So they snipped Grantland Rice's articles on Jim and, lo and behold, they had invented the idea, and Robinson was "pound for pound " the greatest fighter. Ray lost his title to Paul Pender, in his thirties, who beat him twice with a left jab. Robinson was not a good defensive fighter. Now, even in his hometown, East Vancouver, if you ask an Irish Canadian fight fan on Commercial Drive, a block from Jimmy's old home, who is "pound for pound" the greatest fighter, he'll tell you Ray Robinson. How soon they forget!

I asked Jim how he thought he would do against Robinson. "Possibly a bit big for me," said Jim modestly. But Jim knew Ray when he was a large middleweight and was probably thinking of him that way. At 147 pounds, the welterweight limit, McLarnin would have beaten Robinson with his superb left jab and moved inside Ray's long jabs.

The papers called for Jim to be given, finally, an honest chance to win a world championship. "The Vancouver boy should be in line for a shot at Black Jack Thompson's title." Several New York writers called McLarnin the greatest welterweight in the history of boxing. But Black Jack Thompson was no fool. He wanted no part of Irish Jimmy McLarnin. Thompson remembered Jim's terrible body blows that had laid him on the canvas. Gentleman Jim Corbett was interviewed as the most intelligent and articulate expert on boxing, and he gave a detailed analysis of Jim's style, saying that Jim was "the perfect ring man. McLarnin has no major weakness."

When Corbett came to McLarnin's camp to watch him train, he would chat with Jim about the subtleties of the sweet science, Hayden to Mozart. Fighters have to be not only good, but tough. Ruby Goldstein was good, but not tough enough, and Petrolle was tough, but not good enough. "Jim Corbett told me something I always tried to remember and live by," Jim told me, looking straight at me. "A fighter can always afford to be a gentleman." The legendary Corbett explained that all professional fighters, even those stylists like Goldstein, are tough, real tough, and they should remember that they don't have to prove it. The rest of us may have an excuse to make tough noises now and again.

Corbett was a close observer. He also used to go to Tommy Loughran's camp. Loughran was light-heavyweight champ and a beautiful boxer, so good that at 5 foot 10 and 173 pounds, he could outbox almost every heavyweight. He outboxed the murderous punching, superbly built, later heavyweight champ, Max Baer, 6 foot 3 and 220 pounds. Loughran became leading heavyweight contender for the crown, held by Italian Primo Carnero, 6 foot 6, 250 pounds, and strong as a horse. He had been a circus strong man but his crooked managers stole all his money, so he became a wrestler and recouped his money. Primo was a better fighter than he has been given credit for. He developed a strong long left which worked well as long as his opponent couldn't move too fast. His skills were similar to those of Larry Holmes. Primo developed a strong uppercut, easy for a big strong man. But after Carnero knocked out 6 foot 2, 210 pound Sharkey, there was a cry from sportswriters and fans to create a "super heavyweight" division. We all like to think of the heavyweight champ as a huge man and not under 5 foot 10 and under 190 pounds, as the greatest of them, Rocky Marciano, was. President John Kennedy was amazed when he met him, to find that Marciano was smaller than he was. The reason Ali was special was that fast heavyweights have been 6 foot 1 and 190 while Ali was fast at 6 foot 3 and 215.

The size in the boxing bubble burst when Loughran outboxed Carnero for the heavyweight title, but lost a questionable decision. After the fight, Tommy said that the only time Primo had hurt him was when he stepped on his toe. The mobsters who controlled Carnero had gotten to the judges, but sportswriters realised that a 175 pound man had beaten the giant and that was the end of the "super" division. Finally, Baer and Louis nearly killed Carnero.

McLarnin had so impressed New York fight fans and writers that there was no denying him a decent title shot, to keep up the appearance of fairness. What to do with this unbeatable youngster from Canada and his incorruptible manager? So they lined up three of the most awkward and difficult fighters in the history of boxing, who happened just then to be in Jim's divisions.

In 1932, Pop and Jim signed to meet the heaviest fighter that Jim fought publicly (of course, he had sparred with heavyweights), middleweight champ Lou Brouillard, 160 pounds to Jim's 145. Brouillard, a French Canadian, had been welterweight champ, beating Jack Thompson. He was a rough, tough fighter. He was at the peak of his career when he met Jim outdoors in New York. That was to be the key point, outdoors. Pop and Jim thought that he could have outboxed and outsped the heavier man. Jim is sure he could have slipped most of Lou's punches to the head, and moved constantly and blocked his body punches, jabbed and hooked, and won an easy decision. All great fighters have a good left. The only great heavyweight who didn't was Dempsey – his left hook wasn't great, it was incredible. Jack bobbed and weaved and crouched as he came in, but because of his left, he could be caught by a quick right, if the hook could be anticipated. Tunney did this.

McLarnin was set to add to his legendary career by beating the champion of every division from flyweight up to light-heavyweight -- mind boggling and unmatched!

However, in the early morning of August 24, 1932, it began to pour rain in New York and onto the outdoor ring. Then, as the dawn broke over the towers of Manhattan, the rain slackened and by fight time had become a light mist. The fight could proceed, but this was before the days of sports field coverings. When Jim and Pop stepped into that ring, it was a water slide. You could stand still and punch or shuffle, but if you shifted your feet suddenly, you fell on your face or your fanny. Before the rain, the odds had been two to one on Jim. Now, at ringside, there were desperate attempts to change bets. The papers had favoured Jim. "Jimmy is well rested after his great victory over Petrolle. Foster sees that Jim stays in quiet hotels. McLarnin will win because he is the best defensive boxer of modern times."

But nobody had thought of this rain overnight in August. Brouillard was a short-armed, stocky middleweight and a cruel body puncher. As the fight began, it was soon seen by everyone that neither fighter could move quickly on this skating rink. They simply stood in front of each other and punched. McLarnin ducked and slipped punches to his head, but you can't slip body punches like that and Brouillard soon bulled in close and punched the heart out of McLarnin. "I couldn't move. It was a tough fight. He cracked some of my ribs and kept punching them." McLarnin stood toe to toe and punched with the heavier man -- with a cracked rib -- for 12 rounds. I cannot imagine doing that! "Well, I just might have caught him one really good one. I still wished it hadn't rained. He thought he could make me quit and I wasn't going to!" Naturally, Brouillard won the decision and Jim had to settle for being the uncrowned champion of only the welterweights and lightweights.

McLarnin's eminence, strangely, did not sit well with a certain living legend and idol of fistiana. The immortal Benny Leonard was apparently irked by Jim's many conquests of fine Jewish boys, many of whom he had coached. Leonard had retired as the undefeated lightweight champ, perhaps the greatest ever. Everyone always said "the great" Benny Leonard. Leonard, however, had lost most of his money in the Great Stock Market Crash of 1929. He was still only 35, and in good shape, and decided to make a comeback, recoup his fortune, and perchance get a chance to teach that Irish kid, McLarnin, what a really great fighter was like. He had nineteen bouts before he signed to meet the most dangerous man between him and his old title. That number of fights can be a whole career for a contemporary fighter. Benny's comeback was well prepared.

Why should Leonard particularly want McLarnin? Perhaps because the 1920s and 30s were the decades in which that brilliant and indomitable race was rising from the ghettoes and slums of the inner cities of America and making its way to influential and powerful positions. The influence of its thinkers was already there. Consider only Freud, Marx, and Jesus, let alone Spinoza and Moses Maimonides. An athletic Jewish boy could take a short cut to fame and fortune for the despised and minority races -- pro boxing. It gave them pride before they could shout, "Help, My son the doctor is drowning." When Jimmy McLarnin climbed to the top, it was over the prone bodies of many skilled young Jewish boxers, many friends of Leonard. I know that Jimmy never gave a thought to the fact that so many were of one race. Indeed, Benny Leonard had been young McLarnin's idol because of his all around ring mastery.

A similar thing happened to Rocky Marciano. He went through a string of great black fighters on his road to the crown, and Joe Louis had been his idol. When you see him beat Joe terribly and leave him lying senseless on the ring apron, he rushes over, worried that Joe may have received a serious injury. Later, he went to Louis's dressing room and almost apologized for knocking out the old champion. Louis was impressed and often remarked about it when Rocky's name came up.

Leonard began to plot the downfall of that irritating Irishman, and Jimmy was blissfully unaware. Jimmy always thought the best of anybody when he first met them. The Irish are known for long memories. "Yes, well, you wouldn't say that if you had been here when Cromwell was here," an Irish gentleman said to me in Cobh, Ireland, some 300 years after the events.

Benny Leonard was one of those classic athletes who, once a knowledgeable sports fan sees them in action, he never forgets.

There is a wonderful article by Bud Schulberg, the author of the classic boxing novel based on the life of Carnero, *The Harder they Fall*, about when his father tried to take him to see the great Benny Leonard fight Ritchie Mitchell. They had tickets but couldn't get Buddie past the door because he was not yet 16 and so shouldn't see violence. His dad had to send Bud home in a taxi, but he came home right after the fight, without his usual beer with the boys, to tell his son of the brilliance of Leonard. "My father had caught lightning in a bottle and brought it home for me," says Schulburg. Mitchell had floored Leonard and Benny had arisen battered and dazed but talking, "Is that your best punch, Mitchell?" And as Ritchie drove in, remarked, "Try to keep them up, Ritchie." As Ali did, he talked his opponents out of their rhythm, recovered, and finally knocked tMitchell out.

Leonard had been born Benjamin Leiner in New York in 1896. He boxed from 1911 to 1924 with a comeback in 1931 and 32. He fought 209 fights. He had a sensational reign as lightweight king and was the toast of America for his intelligent athletic artistry. Leonard made a point of understanding his opponents to conquer them. Benny knew the great left hander, LewTendler, to be a completely clean fighter and very proud of it. At one point in their close fight, Tendler temporarily paralysed Leonard with a left to the stomach. "Keep them up, Tendler," he snapped, implying that it was a low blow. Tendler was so shocked that he stepped back, giving Leonard time to recover. Leonard retired in 1925, saying that his mother didn't want him to fight any more. He became an outstanding referee, but died, poetically, of a heart attack, in the St. Nicholas Arena in 1947, where many of his great victories had taken place. The question has always been, "Who was the greatest boxer ever, Joe Gans or Benny Leonard?" A fight at their respective peaks would have been the greatest boxing match ever. Now, however, Leonard had lost his money and an Irishman had beaten all the Jewish boys he had coached.

It was ironic, since on his way up, Pop had tried to get an exhibition match with Leonard but was turned down. Now, Leonard wanted McLarnin, and said so. Much of what he said may have been hype to insure a great gate, but Jimmy was still a bit hurt. Benny said he was going to beat

McLarnin "to regain the honour of the Jewish race". This romantic racism strikes Jim as repugnant nonsense and said so. Despite what Leonard had to say, nobody ever saw him, as a referee, give a decision on the basis of race. Leonard's comeback wins were mostly K.O.s and he looked very good until he met McLarnin. Suddenly he looked old. He was 35, but a number of men have won championships at a later age. Early in his comeback, he had visited Jim's training camp and watched him work out. Leonard's analytic mind did see something that he could use as he watched Jim work out and he filed it away for when he would sign with Jim. In McLarnin's technique, there was one small mistake. Sometimes, in order to avoid a right hand punch, Jim would duck under a right and move in closer himself. But, if Jim could be faked into that duck, and then the right hesitated, he could be hit with the right hand if it was repeated fast and just at the instant when Jim's eyes were down from the duck and not looking at the fist.

"I probably caught him when he was a bit past it, and needed money," says Jim.

At any rate, on October 7, 1932, in Madison Square Garden, the greatest Jewish American boxer would fight the greatest Irish Canadian boxer. In the city of New York, full of Irish and Jewish fight fans, the Garden was full, for McLarnin was at his peak and Leonard seemed to have returned to his.

Fortunately, a full length movie of the fight remains. In this film, both fighters look their age. Jim is in his mid twenties and Leonard is in his mid thirties. Leonard's hair is receding a bit, but there is no fat around his middle. After all, Benny had had more fights in the last year than Jim. Leonard looks confident. He is coming off 18 straight wins, mostly K.O.s, and, above all, he thinks that he has found a weakness in McLarnin's technique. Leonard expected to knock Jim out when Jim made the mistake he was looking for, because a fighter doesn't lose his Sunday punch. He may be a touch slower, his timing could be a bit off, and he may not be able to take a punch as well, but he will hit as hard as ever. George Foreman was 45 when he K.O.ed Michael Moorer, to regain his championship.

Benny planned to bide his time, although he knew that he may have to take some punishment. His timing looks good. As he comes out of his corner, he moves in that smooth old Leonard slide, with no jiggling of flesh at his waist. Surprisingly, his left often paws at Jim and is sometimes open-gloved like Ali. Also, like Ali, he often leaves his left out to push off his opponent. McLarnin looks quicker and more aggressive. Jim's stance is wide, with his left low for hooks, and he often throws a combination hook and jab. His right is cocked beside his jaw, wider than you would expect. He is relying on slipping punches to the head. His chin is tucked in tight and he stares with concentration as he moves in, his hands held like a fiddler crab. He is hunched forward. Leonard looks like a veteran, with something in mind, and indeed he will use his secret knowledge earlier than probably even he expected. As the fight begins, he tries the obvious move of jabbing between the wide gloves of McLarnin. He isn't fast enough to reach Jim. Jim seems to have no fear of Leonard's punches. However, early in the fight, Leonard sees his chance. They are in close, and Leonard throws his right. Jim does exactly what Benny hoped. He ducks under Leonard's right hand. The move will put one in close for good body punches, but there is a moment when one loses sight of the opponent's right hand and one's face is more toward the floor than on the opponent. Leonard reacts so quickly that it is a difficult to see in the film, for it is a complex move. I don't think I would have figured it out if Jim had not explained it to me so that I could follow the action. What you see is Leonard twist the right side of his body for what must be a low right hand blow. You see Jim duck lower than his usual stance. Then suddenly Jim's legs collapse, and he drops down, but then recovers, just before his knees hit the canvas. It is a peculiar sequence, even more odd than the shift of Fitzsimmons just before the famous solar plexus blow that knocked Jim Corbett into paralysis. What had happened, was that just as Jim ducked the right hand that he saw Leonard start to throw, Leonard had pulled it back and quickly thrown it again, but lower, in almost an uppercut style, bent his knee slightly, twisting his body, flexing his right trapezius side muscle, and driving with all the force he could off the ball of his right foot, turning his right hip, and turning his glove sideways. It was a beautiful punch -- maybe the best Jim ever got hit with. The punch caught him squarely on the side of his jaw. McLarnin testifies to the effect of it, "I saw stars."

But nobody ever knocked out Jimmy McLarnin, especially with a punch to the jaw, for Jim had a jaw like a rock.

Then Jimmy stands up quickly, and you can see a look come over the face of Benny Leonard. He had found the only chink in McLarnin's defensive armour, exploited it brilliantly, thrown everything he had into it, and stunned McLarnin, but Jimmy McLarnin was still standing there, looking squarely at him. The look on the champion's face shows that he knows that he is in for it now. From now on, McLarnin pursues Leonard relentlessly. He inevitably catches Benny and drops him. Benny shakes his head and kneels on the floor. He looks suddenly old, not 35 but 55. There is a special look the old fighter gets when he gets caught. He knows the punch should hurt, but not that way. It shouldn't stun him that much. Dempsey tells of sparring with a big soldier at a base in WWII and getting caught like this, having to knock out the boy because he couldn't take another like that anymore. Benny was still a relatively young man who had just finished beating up and knocking out 18 young men in their 20's, but now he was in with one that was tough and a superb boxer and he knew that he was no longer the greatest. Benny got up, and, being well-conditioned, ran, jabbed, circled, and held, and prepared to take his beating. With luck, he wouldn't be permanently damaged, but he could look forward to weeks of painful recovery, and an older man heals slowly. You can tell that he knows how serious this has become, and he intends to use his skills and knowledge to escape being permanently damaged. From the look on Benny's face, you know that he considers that a distinct possibility, being in with this young tiger, and he probably remembered that one world champion had died after a fight with "the killer with the baby face".

In round six, McLarnin caught him again, and Leonard was left standing, but without his senses, not knowing where he was. He looked wistfully, somehow desperately, toward the ceiling. The crowd, McLarnin, and the referee, knew that Benny was helpless. McLarnin asked the referee to stop it. Then, with a blank look, Leonard raises his hands instinctively to fight. As Joyce Carol Oates says, "They are trained to fight until they die." It is the business of the referee to see that it doesn't happen. He must decide instantly. He put his arms around the old champ and said, "That's enough, Benny." Benny had put up a fight.

The movie is interesting. Benny stops often to hitch his trunks, and Jimmy halts his attack to let him do that. Benny will often rub his nose and slick his hair. Does he do this to gain a rest? He still has the body of an athlete but the face of stockbroker. Jim looks young, but no longer boyish. Both men feint numerous punches and then watch to see the reaction. They are both "thinking men's fighters". Jim moves in while Benny circles.

Of all opponents, I would like to talk to Benny about Jim. Mostly I would like to talk to him about Jim's right hand speed, which doesn't seem that fast, yet Benny has trouble avoiding it, even when he sees it coming. After the fight, Jim goes to Benny's corner to see if he is all right.

Hand speed of boxers is interesting. Mickey Walker, middleweight champ, beat most of the leading heavyweights because he said he just waited until they threw a punch and then punched them before their punch got to him. However, when he fought champion Max Schmeling, who had just K.O.ed Louis, he realised that Max's right was coming in faster than his own and he knew he was in for a long evening. In most sports, if your timing is right and you are faster than the big man, you can beat him.

Present day boxing is being destroyed, not only by the lack of sportsmanship from not taking Jim Corbett's advice, but also by the multiple pseudo divisions and championships. The oldest and most nearly respectable title of this "junior" sort is the junior welterweight title. Quite a few good fighters fall between the lightweight and welterweight divisions. Jim, himself, was a small welterweight, just too big for the lightweight divisions. The junior welterweight king of that day was a fine fighter, and one of the few Jim had not yet beaten, Boston Sammy Fuller. On December 16, 1932, they fought in New York. Of course, Fuller's title was not at stake because Jim might have taken it, but a pleasant amount of money was involved. Fuller had a large contingent from Boston. 12,000 fans filled the Garden. Sammy Fuller, the champion, never had a chance. He was not in McLarnin's league. By the third round, Jim had had Fuller down twice with left hooks to the jaw. Suddenly, he nailed Sammy with a terrific right to the jaw, sending the Boston fighter half through the ropes and onto the ring apron. He was counted out and the ring doctor leaped into the ring to see if he was all right. Fuller eventually came around, and remained undisputed junior welterweight champion and Jim made money and added another champion to his list of victims.

There was now nobody left between McLarnin and the welterweight championship. There remained only the welterweight champ, Young Corbett III. If it had been anybody else, McLarnin would not have gotten a title shot, but in this man, the dark lords of boxing knew they had a fighter, finally, who could defend against the fearsome McLarnin, and probably take a close decision from Jim with a little correct refereeing and tallying from the judges. They thought they finally had Foster this time, and that would end the menace of this deadly Irishman from the Coast and his uncontrollable manager, because Young Corbett was a different kind of fighter.

PART IV
Winning The World
Championship

Chapter 20
The only Kind of a Fighter worth Being, a Champion of the World

There have been young Jack Dempseys and young Joe Louises, but none of them have achieved prominence like several men who have taken their nom de guerre from James J. Corbett. Young Corbett III was an Italian American from Fresno, California. He fought out of San Francisco. His real name was Ralph Giordano, he was born in Potenza, Campanza, Italy, and the Italians of Frisco had given him their hearts. Jackie Fields, Jim's old California rival, fought Corbett twice, and complained bitterly of the difficulty of beating Corbett in Frisco. The fans were always behind him and he got the benefit of the doubt, and it was there he won the welterweight title from the slick boxing Fields. But Corbett had more than that going for him, much more, for, as one examines his record, one realises he was one of the most difficult and awkwardly effective fighters who ever laced on a glove. McLarnin and Corbett are, really the end of an era. McLarnin was born in Ireland and Corbett was born in Italy, and they were the last of the champs from the old sacred soil. Old Irish and Italian boxing fans who had been born and been young in the old lands had a special feeling when they watched these boys fight. Both boys had been raised on the West Coast and that was where they were at home. The Corbetts are always associated with San Francisco, back to Gentleman James J. himself, and preferred to fight there. Young Corbett III was muscular at 5 foot 8, and sometimes fought as heavy as 170 pounds in the light-heavyweight division, taking on genuine contenders, some of whom were 185 pounds and contenders in the heavyweight division, such as Gus Lesnevich. Nevertheless, trained fine, and for a short period of time, Corbett could fight just under 150 pounds and defend his welterweight championship. His strength and awkward clutching defence made him capable of giving a good account of himself against any man in the world at any weight. Corbett fought middleweight champ Fred Apostoli and just missed winning a split decision. He had traded punches with Lesnevich, light-heavyweight champ, and beaten him with the title not at stake. Lesnevich had given Ezzard Charles a good fight after Charles had beaten Joe Louis. And the man who beat him was the man McLarnin had to fight. If Corbett could handle a big man like that, one would think he would not have much trouble with "wee Jimmy McLarnin". Could 146 pounds punch harder than the 5th ranking heavyweight?

Fields explains Corbett: "He would hit and hold. You couldn't get a good second shot at him." Seldom do you knock out fighters with one punch. He was an excellent defensive fighter. Pictures of Corbett show a tough looking, muscular fighter with a broken nose. Pictures of Jim at the same time show a choirboy face, straight nose, curly hair, and a charming smile. Put your money on Corbett! Some ring historians refer to Corbett as a "mediocre" champ, but that is all hindsight after McLarnin had beaten him. Nobody at the time thought so, and the wise money was on Corbett. The dark lords of boxing would never have let Pop Foster's independent fighter into that ring if they thought he had a ghost of a chance of winning a championship. The change in Corbett's reputation came about after he had let the promoters down, and allowed himself to be beaten by the Outsider and his independent manager. They never forgave him, nor did the media.

In her book *On Boxing,* Joyce Carol Oates points out that when a fighter moves up a division, he sometimes leaves his punch behind him. Also, a bigger man absorbs a punch better. The largest of champions, Willard and Carnera, made admirable punching bags. The wise money thought Jim would be stymied by Corbett's size and style. Jimmy could knock out lightweights, but Corbett? They also remembered Jim's loss to middleweight champ Brouillard, and Corbett's even fight with middleweight champ Apostoli. They seemed to have forgotten that rain had made the ring so slippery that Jim couldn't move quickly. Corbett was left-handed, and it was felt that Jimmy had trouble with lefties. Hadn't left-handed Ray Millar been the only man to stop Jim? They ignored how easily Jim had dealt with Millar, subsequently. Nevertheless, Pop filled Jim's camp with lefties for Jim to work with. People thought Jim was right-hand crazy. They remembered Jim hammering Benny Leonard around the ring with right hands. They didn't think that would work on tough, left-handed Young Corbett. They forgot the knockouts Jim had had with a left hook. Corbett fought out of a tight defensive shell of muscular arms and elbows, threw his punches and then moved in to hold on with his strength. It is a boring but effective way to fight. It nullifies flashy fighters like McLarnin. It was very reasonable to put money on Corbett. But Jim's manager was Charlie "Pop" Foster, and Jim could hit a ton! Bigger fighters who sparred with Jim came away remarking, "He hits like a heavyweight."

Corbett had beaten the incredible Mickey Walker, who had fought to a draw with heavyweight champ Jack Sharkey. Corbett had shut down brilliant boxing Billy Conn, before Conn went on to defeat middleweight champ Tony Zale, light heavyweight champ Gus Lesnevich, and then, for 12 rounds, heavyweight champ, Joe Louis. That was Conn's finest hour. Louis was at his prime, aged 28. Having listened to the fight on the radio with my dad and every other sports fan, in 1939, I had the impression that Conn had moved constantly, as one would expect of a lighter man, but in video, Conn remains in front of Louis, slipping, blocking, ducking, countering, and beating Louis to the punch. He did this for 12 rounds, and in the 12th he began to stagger Louis. This performance by such a light man against perhaps the greatest fighter of all time, is surely a remarkable athletic achievements. As Conn weighed in, promoter Mike Jacobs said, "We can't announce Conn's weight at 169. Put down 175 for Conn and 199 for Louis, instead of 215." He was afraid the huge weight difference – nearly 50lbs – would ruin the gate. Legendary trainer, Eddie Futch, says, "You want to know how to box? Watch Conn beat Louis for 12 rounds. Today, with 12 round championship fights, he would be champion."

McLarnin had been at these fights, for Mike Jacobs had sent him tickets for him and his friends. "Heck of a fight. Conn was wonderful."

"Were you pulling for Irish Conn?"

"Heck, no, Joe was a friend of mine!"

Corbett, who had beaten the incomparable Billy Conn, was the man our Jimmy had to beat for the welterweight title. Corbett himself thought he would have no trouble with wee Jimmy, for he was too small. How were Jim and Pop going to deal with this formidable champion? Corbett would poke a left, move in and tie Jimmy up, punch to the kidneys, rabbit punch, and only break when the referee made him. The answer, of course, was that there was nothing Jim could do in the ring to get Corbett to open up.

Pop suddenly realised they would have to do something outside of the ring. Pop started to work first on Jimmy. "He's a hard man to fight," said Pop one day early in Jim's training. "We've got to find a way to get him to open up and fight." Suddenly, Foster glared at Jim, "Corbett is a rotten fighter, Jimmy. He can't beat you and he knows it. He's afraid to fight you. He's afraid to mix with you."

Jimmy couldn't believe it. "Oh, no, Pop," said Jim. "He's a good fighter. Look at the men he's beat!"

Pop lowered his voice. "We know that, but that's not what we're going to say. We're going to say that Corbett is a cheese champ who is afraid to fight you, and that you can lick him easily. If any reporter asks you, and they will, just say Corbett is a coward who is afraid to fight you. Say he's scared of you and will run away from your famous right hand punch, and hide from the beginning. Get it Jim?"

"O.K., Pop," said Jim grinning wryly, "Do you think that might open him up?"

"It just might," replied Pop. "There's a chance they might fall for it. We'll get him mad enough to want to kill you, instead of fighting his fight." And that's what they did.

From the McLarnin camp came a line of scurrilous insults to a fine champion. It made good copy on the sports pages of America. It was a surprising change from the usual copy that the McLarnin camp put out, and the papers loved it, even in Fresno, California, Corbett's home town. Corbett stewed. Ali wasn't the first man to call his opponent a big ugly bear.

Bob McLarnin used to run with Jim. He told me that Jim always began his training at home in Vancouver for a couple of weeks. He showed me pictures of Jim in cap and heavy sweater, out running through the streets of East Vancouver. Then Jim would move closer to where the fight was to take place, to "acclimatize". Jim trained for his championship fight mostly in Oakland. Bob said L.A. would often get too hot to train in. Then, for the last couple of weeks, they moved to Los Angeles. During all this time, Jim was telling sports writers what a lousy fighter Corbett was, that the only way he ever won was by clutching and grabbing because he was afraid to take a real punch. Jim said Corbett wasn't going to give him any trouble. He would just take Corbett out with his famous right hand. No problem.

Corbett was a proud man, a champion and a fine one. He had beaten pros twice the size of Jim. His friends and supporters called upon Corbett to teach this young man a lesson. The Italians are a proud race with a great history, culture, and athletic tradition. They don't have to listen to little Irishmen putting them down. Corbett was advised to fix McLarnin and fix him early. Just winning wasn't going to be enough. They wanted him knocked out and shut up. The old magician, Pop Foster, had worked his magic and Jimmy was going to get his fight. The champion was going to come out punching!

The Vancouver papers were full of "hype" for Jimmy's second legitimate championship fight, even though he had fought so many champions -- more than any man in the history of this deadly sport. The papers analysed Corbett. They were concerned that Corbett was an awkward left-hander, and Jim had had some trouble with left-handers before. They had forgotten how easily Jim had beaten Millar in the rematches.

I have been struck, in my reading of McLarnin's career, how, time after time, his best performances are passed by, as if they never happened. His poorer performances are marched out as if they were his best, even by those most sympathetic. It is passing strange how even his well-wishers and most distinguished reporters refer to his off nights as his peak. Let us set the record straight. The McLarnin/Ross fights are what ring historians take to be McLarnin's peak. These fights took place when Jim was in a letdown after winning the crown after so many years, and a two year lay off, and when he was courting his wife to be, and getting involved with the social life of Hollywood, and really learning that he preferred hitting a golf ball. Even Ross said that, "Jimmy has had it all. He's not hungry. I'm glad I didn't meet him a few years earlier." Historians don't deal with his victory over the legendary Pancho Villa, flyweight champion before he was 20, his mastery of Mandell in his 2nd and 3rd fights, and his last fight and victory over Lou Ambers. But, above all, his peak really is his sensational K.O., in record time, of the tough Young Corbett III. It is one of the most sensational and unexpected of boxing's victories, ranking with Louis's K.O. of Schmeling in a round in their 2nd fight, and Willie Pep's great masterpiece in the 2nd fight with Sandy Sadler.

The fight fans were to see the cool, deadly punching McLarnin at his best, and the unbeatable, cagey Corbett walked into the old magician's trap.

So pour yourself a straight John Jamieson's Irish whiskey, breathe in its smell of Ireland, and savour the most brilliant of West coast Irish Canadian Jimmy's victories. As you now see, the wizard could see the future.

The local newspapers commented the day before the fight that McLarnin liked to come in punching, and Corbett was an excellent counter puncher. They were wrong, for it was Jim's left counter that won for him. The bout was to take place in the open air on Wrigley Field, Los Angeles, and was to be promoted by Jim's old friend, Jack Doyle. In Vancouver, you could get instant fight results by calling Seymour 5131. Of course, you could get all the details, comments of various experts, round by round, with post fight reactions of the fighters and their managers, and the experts in the newspapers all over North America for three cents a paper. Jim was quoted as saying he would knock out Corbett within three rounds. I doubt that Jim really thought that, but it was all part of the psychological warfare. "I really liked Corbett."

Jimmy's dad, Sam McLarnin, age 60, came down to Los Angeles for the fight, but later had to admit to his son that he hadn't seen the high point of his son's life, for he dropped his glasses just as the fight started, and was fishing for them under the seat when everything happened.

It had been five long years since Jim had fought Sammy Mandell at the Polo Grounds in New York, on the other side of the continent, for the light-weight title. Serious sports writers had said that McLarnin was so good now that he would never get another title shot. Every champion was afraid of him -- except Corbett. "I regard McLarnin as over rated," said Corbett. Jim and Pop's quest had begun with that trip to San Francisco on the Dorothy Alexander, the run that Canada had promised in perpetuity when B.C. joined confederation. Now they got their shot on March 9th, 1933.

Jimmy was in great shape for the fight. He was built up and muscled, well under the welterweight limit. He was not weakened by making weight as he had been for his other fight for a championship. Corbett had weighed in that afternoon at 147 pounds, bang on the limit. He had trained down just right. Jim sat silently in his corner, with Pop massaging the muscles of his neck and upper back to keep him loose and warm for instant punching, because Jim's key moves might be early and sudden and that can tear cold muscles. There was a rising hum of expectation in the slightly chill night air, filling the stadium with that tingling electric feeling that precedes a great and closely matched championship contest, especially a pro boxing match. This was it for Jimmy McLarnin and Pop Foster. They had made enough money to last them a lifetime, but this was for more than money. This was for the glory that they had dreamed of. This was for the promise that Foster had made to the McLarnin family when he took their teenage son. Once you are champion of the world they can never take that away from you. You are, forever, the champ.

Foster continued to talk in his tight-lipped way to his boy. Jimmy flicked a glance across the ring at Corbett. The champ was slouched on his stool, feet shuffling impatiently, shoulders twitching under his robe. "He's edgy, Jimmy boy. We've got him mad. He'll come out fighting, just like we wanted."

Jim nodded, "I think you're right, Pop."

Did their minds go back to the long road they had travelled? Pop's probably did. Jim would be visualizing just what he expected to do. He was going to put on a fine job of acting, as fine as John Barrymore or Paul Muni, the two actors Jim had met and admired most. Jimmy would be a little nervous, as he was always, until "somebody got hit". Then all tension would leave him. Jim sat there, eager to start, knowing exactly what he was going to do. Corbett also sat across the ring, knowing what he was going to do. There were only people in the ring who had business there. Pop had been over and checked Corbett's gloves.

Suddenly they heard somebody shouting, "Jim! Pop!" Down the aisle came Jim's young brother, Bob, easily seen because he was over six feet. He was trying to get past the guards to the ring, shouting to them that he was Jimmy McLarnin's brother. Bob had been in Corbett's dressing room as the designated man to watch the taping of Corbett's hands, to see that nothing was taped inside but hand. Bob told me, "They didn't know who I was. They were busy. Corbett was boiling mad at James, and said that he was going out there and take that little Mick out of there in short order." Pop's plan, although simple, had worked. Yes, the old magician had worked his charms and changed Corbett's style. Bob fought his way to Jimmy's corner and breathed out his message, "He's coming out punching! I heard him say it!"

Pop said quietly to his fighter, "All right, Jimmy. You know what to do. Show him that right. Then when he opens up, get him!"

Jimmy looked across at Corbett. "Yeah, right, Pop."

Pop continued, "Now wait until you get the right shot, then give it everything. If you don't take him then, he'll cover up and you might not get another good shot."

"Right," said Jim grimly, then the whistle blew to clear the ring, then the bell, and out went Jimmy McLarnin to Glory. Jim still chuckles over how pleased Pop was when the crusty old Yorkshireman saw that Corbett had swallowed the bait, hook, line, and sinker. The press was taken in, also.

Foster couldn't keep from grinning as he checked Jim's mouthpiece. Corbett was already up and anxious to get the kid who had called him a cheese champ. Pop whispered, "Look at him. He's fighting mad. We're going to get our fight just like Bob said. He'll come out punching."

As Jimmy slid out of his corner, across came Corbett, throwing punches, right on top of McLarnin, bouncing both hands off Jimmy's ribs and hooking hard to his head. "Oh, he could punch," said Jim to me. The crowd was on its feet, cheering the wild pace as Corbett bored in. This was no opening round of feeling each other out. It was Corbett making the fight as McLarnin back-pedaled, bobbing, rolling with the punches. "He was big and tough. He seemed like a middleweight. I could see that, but I could also see that he would make a mistake sooner or later because he was so busy punching. He was mad. He was looking to take me out right now." McLarnin looked as if he were afraid as he retreated before this furious onslaught. He held his right hand ready in an obvious position moving it just slightly. "We showed him the right hand and got ready with the left."

Then it happened. The great defensive fighter, in his anger and frustration and confidence, made a mistake. "I saw an opening," says Jim, "as Corbett let go a left, just after I had ducked a right." Ringsiders saw McLarnin duck and then step in. Even Pop was confused about what happened, but Pop's eyesight wasn't good. However, Jim remembered it. He looked in front of him as he told it. He was seeing it again. In he stepped, as Corbett gave him a few inches and Jim came up from ducking, his eyes always on the champ, staring at his face, but seeing peripherally, all of him. Corbett's missed right hand began to pull back just a bit low, his left hand going out to where Jim had been and suddenly finding him close, he glanced at Jim's right hand that he had been told to watch, leaving the right side of his head wide open. McLarnin's split second reaction was the product of hundreds of the same situations from the streets of Vancouver to the rings of Oakland, Chicago, Detroit, New York, and Los Angeles. Jim rose from that duck (you punch hardest coming up and pressing your feet down, and close). Jim threw a very tight left hook to the right side of the champ's jaw, landing full and flush on the side of Corbett's jaw. Suddenly, the champ's offence stopped before the crowd realised it, and the champ was on the floor. Yes, Young Corbett III, the unbeatable welterweight champ, was down. Corbett, who never had been knocked down by the fifth ranking heavyweight contender, was on the floor from a single blow from a 145 pound challenger. The startled crowd, which had just recovered from Corbett's opening rush, was on its feet. What a reversal. At the count of four, Corbett rolled over to one side, eyes glazed, struggled to one knee, his back supported by the ropes in the neutral corner. Just before the count of nine, he wobbled to his feet. McLarnin sprang across the ring as Corbett got up with the help of the ropes. "I knew I had him," said Jim. Jim never let his man off the hook. This time, he didn't have to fake a right. He rammed a solid right to Corbett's jaw and the champ was down again and again he hauled himself up -- trained to die rather than quit. In came the relentless McLarnin. Struggling desperately and gamely to get up, the doomed champ clutched the ropes. "Oh, I was sorry for him, but after," says Jim. Corbett was reeling around the ring, away from Jim. Chasing him, Jim hit the champ with a series of lefts. Then he cocked his right hand but stopped as he looked at the beaten champion, and turned to the referee, "I think you should stop it, Mr. Blake," said Jim quietly. Blake shook his head. This was a championship fight. Corbett continued to reel away from Jim, trying to raise his hands in defence as Jim followed him. He nailed the champ twice more on the chin with no reply from Corbett. Referee George Blake leaped between the two men and stopped the fight. He seized McLarnin's right hand and raised it over his head. "The winner and new welterweight champion, Jimmy McLarnin!" shouted Blake. The arena erupted with a roar! What a finish! What a surprise! What a great day for Vancouver, the

West Coast, and all the Irish. It had taken 2 minutes and 37 seconds, a new record. The old wizard had made the boy into a champion. Don't tell Jimmy and Pop not to dream the impossible dream.

Jim went over to Corbett's corner to see if Ralph was all right. Corbett looked up and nodded, and Jim walked back across the ring and the old man was there to throw his arms around his boy, "Oh, Jimmy, Jimmy."

"I knew I'd do it," said Jim. "Then the press was all over me. My old pal, Bill Forst, was there for the Vancouver Province, and I didn't see what was going on elsewhere in the ring." His handlers all crowded around shouting.

Jim's dad climbed into the ring grinning. "Darn it, Charlie, I didn't see the punch. I dropped my glasses."

"I didn't see it either," said Pop. "I think it was a right, wasn't it, Jim?" But he got no reply, for the reporters were all but smothering the new champ.

"Everything came true," said Jim again to me as we talked about his apotheosis. "I couldn't have done it without Pop. He made me what I was."

Pop was talking to Jim's dad while the press swarmed over the sensational new champ. "Well, he did it just as you said he would, Charlie," said Sam.

"He did as he was told, Sam," said Pop. "He's a good boy."

"Well, yes," said Sam, "but he keeps getting into these fights and his mother is worried how he will turn out."

"Yes," said Foster to his old friend, "I can understand Mary's concern." Then, after a pause, "But his fights don't last long." And they both burst out laughing, and shook hands and slapped each other on the back and once more spat on their hands and shook hands and grinned. Would to God I had been there, but I've talked to several people who knew Foster well and I think I have the measure of the man. You didn't really get it from Jim, who was still somewhat amazed by him.

Jim K.O.s Champion Corbett in Round One

The dark lords of boxing began to look again for the ideal opponent who could smother some of McLarnin's brilliance, for judges who could make the correct decision believable, and cooperative writers to report the fight in the correct manner. But this was Jim's greatest fight. He wanted this one. He never wanted one as much again. Now he had it all. Jim had had a complete career. "We didn't owe anybody anything."

Incidentally, Jim didn't blame fighters like Jake LaMotta, who had to throw a fight to the rising young black, Billy Fox, in order to get a championship fight with Marcel Cerdan, the fine Frenchman who beat the great Tony Zale. "Some fighters have to do that," Jim declared. "We were lucky that we could play it straight." Then, as he often did, Jim slipped in a snippet of boxing lore. "By the way, Cerdan was killed in a plane crash over the Atlantic. And did you know that Edith Piaff, the beautiful French songstress, was Cerdan's mistress?"

But honesty, hard work, and dedication had won Jim a championship. "It's a great story," says Jim. Yes, and a clean one, Jim! It's something a man can be proud of all his life, and his family afterwards. Vancouver, B.C. had its hero. It has never had a world boxing champ since, but it always dreams of another. Canada had a great hero, but oddly, I have talked to Eastern writers and publishers who always say that McLarnin was only sort of Canadian, not really Canadian, because he didn't come to Canada until he was two and then was raised in Vancouver.

Every Irishman, the world over, had a new hero. I remember my father was ecstatic. Now the line stretched from Brian Boru, the Irish king, who at the age of 80 beat the Vikings when nobody else in the world was doing it, down to Jim McLarnin who could beat anybody in the world under 150 pounds, and almost everybody over that.

Also, and this was to affect Jim's life more, Hollywood had a new hero who did great deeds in real life, who was as handsome as a movie idol, well-mannered and modest, and very welcome at Hollywood events.

Pop Foster said, "Jim was never quite the same fighter after he got mixed up with that Hollywood crowd." Not that Jim drank heavily or caroused late, but he relaxed and his mind was not always on fighting. Pop was a born Spartan and a Stoic. He confronted life with an antique courage and death with a Christian hope.

But what a great day it was! Vancouver rejoiced. There were crowds gathering in the bars along Hastings Street to drink the health of the new welterweight champion as soon as the news was heard. Cars honked to each other . People shouted on the streets. Streetcars clanged their bells. The street car that ran out Hastings to Commercial Drive, where Jimmy would go home, rang its bell the whole way out and then back into town to Granville. In several of the larger movie theatres, the movie was suddenly stopped and the announcement made to cheers that McLarnin had won in round one by a K.O. The soccer game at Callister Park was stopped for the announcement and then a celebration.

Jimmy was interviewed in the dressing room. "I knew I could do it," he told reporters." I feel sorry for Corbett. I'm the happiest man in the world. Yes, I did ask the referee to stop it. Yes, my left did it. I knew I had him then."

Then Jimmy was away to phone his mother and to telegraph her. "Dearest mother, Hope you are all fine. Always thinking of you. Hope family is well. I'm fine. Am happy Mrs.McLarnin's boy is champion. All my love, your loving son, Jimmy." Sounds like a college boy rather than a professional fighter. The press was around Jimmy's house in Vancouver on William Street, the one he bought for his family. His sister Margaret said they could soon talk with the new champ himself, as it was Jim's custom to come home after each fight.

For some weird reason, Corbett's manager felt that his boy had been fouled. Harry White said he intended to protest the result. He never did. However, the annihilation of Corbett was a little hard to believe. Nobody but Pop and Jim thought it could be done by a welterweight until Jim did it. So Foster took a walk over to see Corbett's manager in his dressing room. With a straight face, Foster said to White, "That's a fine boy you have there. You want to see that he doesn't get hurt like that again."

Now, a delightful new note enters the reports of Jim's life. "A certain person" is often asked how she feels about developments in Jimmy's career. The coyness of the media, in those wonderfully innocent days, contrasts with the present attitude. The media had almost too much respect for the privacy of a developing affair of a celebrity. Amazing! After Jim's championship fight, reporters asked this person how she felt about it and "the certain young lady" (she was never identified, as it was nobody's business but the young couple's) admitted she was tremendously pleased. When asked about the impending engagement that was rumoured, the certain young lady replied that she would rather the announcement came from James. Respect for a lady was part of the world that Jim was brought up in. That Victorian view lasted into the 1940's. The certain person in question was no bimbo or groupie Jim had met in his travels. Jim admitted to me after questioning that there were always girls interested in him as he became famous -- a few starlets around Hollywood, and a few stars, among them the redoubtable Mae West herself, the reigning sex queen, who seems to have had the "hots" for Jim after she saw him stripped to his gym trunks. Pop shewed her away and he must have been some man to throw Mae off the scent. But the certain young girl was a college girl and a schoolteacher who lived just around the corner on McLean Street from the McLarnin's on Williams. They went to the same church, the United Church just off Commercial Drive on Venables. Jim was immediately smitten, and never got over it.

Jim's brother, Bob, and his dad, Sam, were introduced to the press. Sam said that he didn't even have time to pray before Jim had won. Movie stars George Raft, Mae West, and others were interviewed and asked how they like the fight. Mae said she liked a man who could strike when the iron was hot, as only Mae could. They were all enthusiastic, for Jim had become, in the last few years, a Los Angeles and Hollywood star. The crowd outside Jim's dressing room shouted ,"Speech!" Jim came out, but just introduced his dad again. Jim kept a picture of his dad in his study, with all his other mementoes.

Mae West, constant spectator and admirer at Jim's fights

Other notables were at the fight, old heavyweight champ Jim Jeffries among them. Jim liked Jeffries. He was probably the fleetest heavyweight, for, at 6 foot 3, and 225 solid pounds, he could run 100 yards in around 10 seconds. Jim wouldn't celebrate yet. Pop had told Jim to get a good night's sleep after a fight and then celebrate.

There is a change in Jim's appearance. In pictures, you see a different look on his face – more mature and less intense. His hair is longer. He dresses smartly and is very stylish. He still dressed well when I met him -- shirt, tie, and jacket each day. One of Jim's pejorative phrases was, "you round haircut". As a young fighter, Jim had short hair that could be cut by putting a bowl on his head and then trimming a "round." Now he had a good barber. The world had changed for Jim. Jim became socially sophisticated, but Pop didn't give an inch. That old Spartan didn't tempt fate or waste a penny.

The Vancouver papers were ecstatic. The fight appeared on the front page of the Province, not the sports page. "Jimmy Brings Title to Vancouver by K.O. in First Round." Underneath was a picture of Pop and the champ.

There was on page four and a story by Bill Forst telling Jim's reactions to the fight. As a boyhood friend of Jim's, this fine newspaperman was perfect for The Province to send to cover Jim's fights. I asked Forst why he had never done a life of his famous friend. "I suppose I should have. In my day, everybody knew all about Jim's great career." The sub-headline was "All Vancouver to honour Jimmy." Forst's feature was "Jimmy very happy." Forst said Jim drew the champ out by feigning to be set up. Jim said, "He took me for a pigeon." Forst goes on, saying Jim hooked a terrific left on the jaw at the first opening. Corbett didn't know what hit him. The article ends, "City crowds jubilant as Jimmy wins. Mayor Louis B. Taylor plans civic reception."

People who were in Vancouver that night told me they would never forget it. Everyone was out walking around grinning.

The Mayor of Vancouver, BC, welcomes new Welterweight Champion, 1933

Chapter 21
Bringing Home the Welterweight Championship and What that Meant

Jimmy McLarnin arrived in triumph at his home on Williams Street at the front of a long police motorcade which had gone to escort Jim from the border at Blaine, Washington. He was accompanied by the police pipe band, and the cheers of a huge crowd. Jim hopped out of his car and held out his hand to his dad, saying, "Hello, Dad, it's great to be home." The neighbours flocked around and two pipers played "The Wearin' o' the Green". What a day! W. C. Mainwaring, president of the Rotary Club, of which Jim was a member, said that the Mayor of Vancouver, Louis B.Taylor, would be giving Jim the key to the city.

Vancouver had its undisputed world champion of boxing. It has never had another. The old heavyweight champ, Tommy Burns, from Quebec, later made his home in Vancouver and is buried there. He defended his championship all around the world. Burns was also a fine lacrosse player, and in his day, Vancouver and neighbouring New Westminster were lacrosse crazy. The biggest crowds, before the coming of the B. C. Lions pro football team and the Whitecaps pro soccer team, were for lacrosse. It used to draw 15,000 for games outdoors. Newsy Lalonde was paid $6,500 for playing lacrosse. Cyclone Taylor, the top NHL hockey star, was paid $1,800.

Burns achieved leading status in his division when it was not at its peak. McLarnin would have been champ at any time in history. Indeed, it would have been easier at any other time than the highly competitive one he had to go through to the title. Part of the reason why Jim could put more people into a boxing arena than any other boxer was that never at any other time in boxing history were there so many top, all time boxers in those lighter divisions. This was not true of the heavier divisions. There was a lapse between Dempsey and Louis, who would have beaten the champs in between them. Sharkey, Schmeling, and Braddock were competent boxers.

That night in May of 1933, in Los Angeles, Jim stood, with the "home crowd", from where he had been living and fighting, going wild around him. He had knocked out a great champ from San Francisco, the rival West Coast city to Los Angeles. McLarnin stood with his arm raised over his head by Referee George Blake, and Pop Foster climbing into the ring, his face wreathed in smiles, after one of the most dramatic knock-outs in boxing history. At 80, Jim still sparred with precision, for Jim was a fighter whose mind was engaged. He was welterweight champion of the world when that really counted. The welterweight division goes from 135 pounds to 147 pounds and the men in this division stand from about 5 foot 6 to 6 feet. If such men are in great shape, they can weigh just under 150 pounds.

When Jimmy was a boy, he dreamed of being the lightweight champ. When boxing began in Britain, in the 18th century, it seemed not sporting to expect a small man to fight seriously against the biggest, so the lightweight division came into existence. Even in bareknuckle days, the welterweight and middleweight divisions were recognised to allow the average sized man to show his skills. But what is a welter? The Random House Dictionary says that "welter" means "to writhe, roll, or tumble about, or be drenched in something," likely blood. "Well," said Jim, whose mind still moved fast, "that sounds like some of the boys I've had to deal with."

These three central divisions will have more boxers registered than any other, and the pressure of competition will make the champions of those divisions superior. It is probable that if you watch a welterweight fight, you will see a better fight than a heavyweight one. The best fighters are usually large middleweights like Billy Conn, or small welterweights like McLarnin or Oscar De la Hoya. Unless you are a fairly skilled observer, the speed may make you miss some of the key action. The present preference for heavyweights is that the contemporary fan is less knowledgeable than in Jim's day, and is more comfortable following the slower heavyweights. The average Japanese soldier in WW11 stood 5 foot 3 and weighed 120 pounds, and Jimmy's pal, Barney Ross, could tell you how tough they were in the South Pacific War.

Watching a closely matched welterweight championship fight is a bit like reading James Joyce, another Irishman with a great sense of humour to top his artistry. You must have some idea of what he is up to. Would the McLarnin/Ross match overflow an arena today? Then, most men had done some boxing in a ring, and watched more. They could appreciate the subtleties. But everybody would love McLarnin's knock-out of Corbett.

What kind of a division was this of which Jim was now the undisputed ruler? What was the history of the kingdom? The welterweight division is an old and honoured country, and perhaps the greatest fighters, pound for pound, have been fighters in this division, the division that Jim ruled now, as he stood with his hand raised, acknowledging the shouts of that tumultuous crowd.

Boxing was a great advance in civilisation in the 16th and 17th centuries, in Shakespeare's day, when the next poet to our Will, Kit Marlowe, was killed in a knife fight, and men fought with swords and knives and killed each other. There was boxing and wrestling in the classic Greek Olympics and Rome, but the line is broken, and modern boxing really goes back to Britain.

In the early days, it was standard for the top men in the middle and welterweight class to fight heavyweights. As late as Jack Johnson's day, he gave middleweight champ Stanley Ketchell a shot at his title, and, as Ketchell was an outstanding fighter, the public assumed that he had a chance. Only Johnson knew he didn't. In the fight, a fine movie of which still exists, Ketchell catches Johnson with a beauty and down goes Johnson. Ketchell was used to people he hit with his Sunday punch staying down. Johnson leaps up and Ketchell is unprepared, and the heavyweight champ takes the middleweight champ out. It is an interesting fight to watch, for it pits perhaps the greatest heavyweight against the greatest middleweight. The great middleweight goes a respectable twelve rounds and floors the heavyweight. However, when the great heavyweight floors the great middleweight, he stays down.

How would Jim have done with earlier welterweight champions? Joyce Carol Oates says all great fighters are contemporaneous. I once memorized one of Ray Robinson's favourite beautiful combinations. I threw it to see what McLarnin would say. It was just before dinner at Jim's son's place, and we were having some Bookwalter wine. Jim's daughter has married into the family that runs that excellent winery in Eastern Washington. Jim watched, pointed his wine glass at me, and grinned a wry grin. "I'd catch you between that hook and that uppercut. You're wide open then. Throw that and I'd kill you in there." When Robinson was a welterweight, I'm sure Mclarnin would have caught him. In Robinson's two losses to Irish Paul Pender, Pender beats Ray again and again with his left, which is not as good as McLarnin's. But most telling is Robinson's loss to welterweight champ Carmen Basilio after Ray was middleweight champ. Basilio was 145 pounds and 5 foot 7, just Jim's size. Manager Jack Hurley said nobody was tougher than McLarnin. Hurley's fighter, Billy Petrolle, said he never fought a fighter faster than McLarnin. I'm certain that McLarnin's defense would baffle Robinson. But, on May 29, 1933, in Los Angeles, Vancouver didn't just gain its only world boxing champ, but it got a greater one than it has ever realised. Robinson never fought a boxer as skillful, especially on defence, as McLarnin; I'm certain that McLarnin's defence would baffle Robinson. Robinson's own defence was only average. He was a great flashy fighter.

Sport is morally serious because one of mankind's noblest aims is the contemplation of worthy things such as beauty and courage. After witnessing a splendid athletic contest, one feels deeply that it has done one good. The average fan's reaction to an excellent move is to say, "Beautiful, beautiful." "We are restless until we find rest in God," says St. Augustine. A true sports fan finds at least momentary contentment in a great performance.

If an Irish boy today went from Ireland, then Vancouver, then Los Angeles, to the welterweight championship of boxing, we in this corner of the world would be very proud of him. Some time ago, I picked up a Ring magazine, flipped to the monthly ratings, and noticed with interest that 5 foot 7, 145 pound champion Buddy McGurt, was just Jim's size. Boxing is no longer front page news. But, in the first two thirds of this century, it was. The welterweight champion was recognised anywhere.

The modern era of that most competitive of divisions came into existence when rough, tough Mysterious Billy Smith knocked out Danny Needham in 14 rounds in San Francisco in 1892.

Just prior to World War one, two magnificent Irish boxers dominated the lightweight, welterweight, and middleweight divisions – Mike Gibbons and Packey McFarlane. These two boxers met in one of the most artistic fights ever, in 1915, just before entering the army, resulting in a no decision or draw.

McFarlane, from around the Chicago stockyards, was a big lightweight like McLarnin, who fought mostly in the welterweight division. He fought all the top men and had one hundred and forty fights and lost just one, early in his career. Despite all this, McFarlane never managed to get a single championship fight! Champions knew they would not only lose, but look foolish. "Why fight McFarlane?" an anonymous champ said, "You'll just lose." McLarnin told me that he was afraid that he might end up like McFarlane. But Jim got a break. When they signed Jim to fight Corbett, they were sure they had a man who could make Jim look bad enough that they could give him the decision. Nobody, thought the wise guys, knocks out Young Corbett, not even legitimate challengers for the heavyweight championship – except McLarnin! So began the search for another great spoiler who could make it close enough for cooperative officials to slide the title out from under the brilliant West Coast fighter and his awkward manager.

I chatted with Jim about who the greatest welterweight might have been. "Well," said Jim, grinning, "how about Mrs. McLarnin's little boy, Jimmy? Well, Mickey Walker or Jack Britton. Did you know that Britton fought 300 fights from around 1905 to 1930? Did I see him? Sure. Listen, he was so good, nobody could hurt him. Hardly make him work. Unfortunately, I always feel bad when I think of Jack Britton. You see, when I was a headliner, Jack brought his son, who was just starting out as a boxer. He wanted to start right, so he brought him to my camp to watch me work. Then he asked me if I would go a few rounds with his boy. Well, he turned out to be a good tough kid, so I stopped fooling around and I hit him. He wouldn't stay down, so I kept hitting him. After, Jack came over to me and said, 'Jimmy, you were pretty tough on my boy.' Oh, I felt bad. I could have carried him and boxed him, and showed him a thing or two, but you know the old ego. A man should be big enough to rise above it. But he wouldn't stay down," said Jimmy, lamely. "Darn it. I still feel bad about it."

Jim's next choice, Mickey Walker, thought nothing of fighting professionals who weighed 100 pounds more than he did. "The bigger they are, the harder they fall," as Bob Fitzsimmons, 178 pound middleweight, light-heavyweight, and heavyweight champ put it. Fitz, by the way, was still fighting in his 52nd year, and, like Gordie Howe, still winning.

Finally, Walker moved into the heavyweight class, still standing 5 foot 7, where he beat contender Bearcat Wright, a murderous black with muscles on his muscles, who outweighed Walker by 120 pounds. Yes, 120 pounds!

Then Mick fought a draw with heavyweight champ Jack Sharkey, who had just had Jack Dempsey beaten when he turned to complain of a low blow and got knocked out. Walker was leading Max Schmeling, who had just knocked out Joe Louis, when Max tagged him with a terrific fast right, and Mick got knocked out in the 8th round.

After Mick retired, he took up painting. He became a critically respected "primitive" artist and could demand a good price for his works from people who had never heard of the great "toy bulldog" of boxing. Well, Mick was always a touch primitive. I can't help being impressed with a welterweight who could fight top heavyweights. But I know that if your timing is correct, and your form good, and you are in good shape, you can bring down the biggest man. But if you lay off and lose a bit of timing you will get killed by a good, big man.

The next great ones were McLarnin and Ross, followed by Henry Armstrong. Armstrong was a featherweight, lightweight, and welterweight champ, all at the same time. Nobody else has done that. Others have held junior this and super or partial that of several titles at different times, but nobody has held three legitimate titles at the same time and been able to make weights to defend them. Armstrong was eventually beaten by Lou Ambers, whom McLarnin beat in his last fight. Foster thought McLarnin could counter with such pin point accuracy, and hit hard as Armstrong came in that he could have caught the rushing Armstrong on his way in close, and stopped him early, but they just missed each other.

The spectacular Cuban, Kid Gavilan, held the title in the early 50s. The crowds loved his useless but spectacular bolo punch with a big windup that telegraphed it to any decent boxer. Jim laughed about that punch, "It's ridiculous." He was actually badly beaten by the competent New York Irishman, Billy Graham, in the Garden, in 1951, in what is often referred to as the worst decision of all time, but there was more money for the dark lords of boxing in the flashy hot shot Cuban than in the intelligent, competent Irishman.

When one considers welterweight champions, Ryan, McCoy, Walcott, Langford, Britton, Walker, Lewis, Corbett, McLarnin, Ross, Robinson, Duran, Hearns, Leonard and add the fine champion 5 foot 5 Parnell Wittaker, who befuddled the fierce Julio Caesar Chavez, one can conclude that welterweight has been, "pound for pound," the finest of all divisions in boxing. Perhaps this is because the average fighter in the world would fall into this division. Any of the above mentioned fighters could be considered in the top ten of all fighters ever. The welterweights have been the most competitive of all the divisions of boxing.

Jimmy said he wouldn't like fighting Robinson because he was too big, but Jim was thinking of the Robbie whom he saw fight light-heavyweight champ Joey Maxim, at 6 feet, 167 pounds. There is no doubt in my mind that Jim would have had no trouble with Robinson when he fought at 147 pounds.

When Jim was 145 pounds, not yet married or titled, with Pop Foster in his corner and still "hungry", not yet relaxed and golfing, and having two or three good fights that same year, I believe that McLarnin could have beaten any welterweight of any era. I believe he was one of the ten top fighters of all time at any weight.

This brings us back to where we started talking to Jim, with the famous classic fights of McLarnin and Ross. But let us examine first the theme of our book. Aristotle said that happiness is not a condition that stands on its own, but a frame of mind that accompanies an activity. Happiness is the pursuit of excellence in a vocation. Jim and Pop must have been happy at this time. McLarnin's mind moved very quickly, like his hands. He was a benevolent and decent man, but not an extraordinary man, except in athletic ability. I know that is a little like saying that all Paganini could do was play the violin.

A workout on the heavy bag before fighting Ross

Chapter 22
Second Thoughts About the Famous Ross/McLarnin Fights

The dark lords of boxing found in Barney Ross a fighter who, although he probably could not beat McLarnin, was so fast and skilful that he would possibly not lose to Jim obviously, and so, with the proper judges and a cooperative referee, the desired result of prying him loose from his championship might be accomplished, and boxing could gain financially, if not morally.

Although Jim was the perfect age for boxing, in his late twenties, he was not at his peak. He knew more about boxing and was stronger than ever, but he had been fighting for a long time, as he had begun so early. Winning the championship so late had taken the edge off "the killer with the baby face". He was still a great boxer and a fine athlete, but he was no longer a killer. I talked about this with Jim and he couldn't bring himself to agree with me. He said, "I just hated to lose." I think Jim loved to win in his early fights and that he secretly had satisfaction in taking a man out cold. In his match with Benny Leonard, he looked like Wyatt Earp moving in on Buck Clanton at Tombstone, eyes intense and narrow, and he was going to kill him. But as McLarnin matured and achieved his goals, he became much less intense. He still enjoyed out-boxing and out-thinking an opponent but was no longer wild to beat him into insensibility. A leading West Coast bantam, Teddy Silva, once thanked Jim for letting him last after Jim had caught him with a "corkscrew" left hook, turning the fist and arm just before landing.

By the time he had won his championship, Jim had everything he had wanted. Usually, a young fighter makes his fame and fortune by defending his championship. Then he can demand high prices. But Jim had already been the ring's biggest money-maker of his era, between Dempsey and Louis. Pop and Jim had made a fortune with those over-the-weight bouts, with every champion from flyweight champ Villa to middleweight champ Broullaird. Jim could have made the weight and should have taken the championships, but they did get money.

Jim's life had changed indeed. He had fallen in love with his hometown girl, the beautiful Lillian Cupit. She looked like a Hollywood starlet, but she was a college girl and a young teacher in Vancouver, from Jim's area of town. He was proud to take her to parties in Hollywood. "She was such a lady," says Jim. Lillian was a fine influence on him. Jim's son, James Jr., told me that his mom took care of them all and, having met her, I believe it. Jim was an incredible athlete and a good man, but it never hurt to point him in the right direction. Foster had seen to it that Jim had enough money in the bank so that merely the interest would give a middle class life style for him and his family for the rest of his life. Oh, yes, and a membership in Lakeside, one of the best golf courses in Los Angeles. So when he won his championship, as the wizard had promised, Jim had it all. Jim lived a celebrity's life in Hollywood, and he had a great time. Coming from his neighbourhood and being naturally a bit deferential, he thoroughly enjoyed the fact that the famous stars of Hollywood now wanted to meet him.

Jim was still an active pro, so he didn't drink much. He still got up at six or seven, so he went home early. He still watched his diet. "I never ate much, so I didn't put on weight between fights." Nevertheless, as Foster knew it would, his comfort and lifestyle took the edge off the killer. His face became relaxed. McLarnin never really dissipated. Pop's training had never worn completely off. But his life had become "a bit easy," as Pop wryly put it. Pop did not believe in an easy life – semi-comfortable perhaps, but not easy. Jimmy had given up his youth, and he said to me, "I missed hanging out with the gang."

Before he defended his title, he took a year off. Then Pop said one of the few unwise things that the old wizard ever uttered. It was the most amazing mistake a wizard ever made since Merlin told that femme fatale, Vivian, his charms, and she locked him up inside a tree and there he is still. One day, some logger will be cutting and there will be the scowling wizard after 1,500 years of imprisonment.

Foster spoke to the media about Jimmy thinking of retiring soon. Nobody said much about this, retiring at the pinnacle of his career, but in the secret councils of the dark lords, those words were noted, commented on, and their possibility believed. "Yes, those two West Coast bastards will probably do just that, and there will be no more money to be made out of them. He's not going to be a fighting champion!" I believe that it was decided that the first time Jim had a close fight for his championship, the decision would go against him, and the sooner the better. With a different manager, Jim might have been champion for years, like Joe Louis -- and ended up broke, like Joe. That's why Dempsey was sent to tell Jim to get another manager. Dempsey thought he was helping Jim.

McLarnin also suffered from a problem common to most knock-out artists. They will sometimes string together so many good fights that they last only a very short distance or the opponents are so badly stunned that the winner actually gets very little practice in the hard fighting which keeps professionals sharp. Exactly this happened to two potentially great fighters, George Foreman and

Gerry Cooney. As a result, when Foreman had to box Ali, he was made to look foolish. Later, he learned, and re-won his championship. McLarnin knew his basics, but it had been almost three years since he had been extended, so he was rusty. Now he took a year off. Again the wizard made a miscalculation. Foster, like McLarnin, seems to have relaxed, once he accomplished his goal. He should have chosen an easy opponent for Jim's first title defence to warm Jim up.

Probably, like another genius, Robert E. Lee, at Gettysburg, he had come to believe that his boys could do anything. Jim, like the army of Northern Virginia, was incomparable, but circumstances could be created in which they could be had. Lee realised his mistake during Pickett's charge at Gettysburg, took off his hat, and rode out to the shattered returning troops shouting, "It's all my fault, boys!" They had just missed taking the key ridge, and the battle, and probably the war, for the road would have been open to Washington, but they had taken appalling casualties, which the South could not afford like the North. Would that other generals would admit such a thing! I suspect that Foster, too, feared a mistake, but could not deny his boy, Jimmy, some rest and fun after all the years of strict regimen and violent battles. It may have been against his better judgement, but it is always staggering to see all-knowing men like Lee and Foster make mistakes. Wizards, like prophets, are partly human, too.

Jim had had only a little over a minute fighting Corbett. His two fights before, against Fuller and Leonard, were not long. When Jimmy climbed into the ring to defend his title against the great Barney Ross on May 28, 1934 – the fight that my dad and I had listened to when I was a child – Jim had not had a tough fight since he had fought middleweight champ Broullaird in 1932. Even then, he could not practise his moves, because the ring was so wet and slippery. The last good fight he had had was against Petrolle, three years earlier, in August 1931. McLarnin might as well have been retired for three years, for all the fighting he had done.

Nevertheless, Jim was in good condition. He had trained extra hard, probably too hard. I suspect that Pop realised what hit me, also, as I looked at Jim's record, in an attempt to understand how a new champion comes into a ring rusty, with a lacklustre performance, in his first title defence. Jim was over- trained, rusty, rich, and famous. He was happy, satisfied, and in love. I suspect he couldn't wait to get this unpleasantness over with and get back to California for a golf game with Bing or a party with Bogey and Stanwyck. The awesome McLarnin was ready to be taken.

Nobody had written it that way, but I think Barney suspected it. "Jimmy's had it all," said Ross to a reporter. Ross anticipated his great-est victory.

At this point in their careers, ring experts did not consider Ross in McLarnin's league. When Jim lost, there was even talk of a fix. Certain inside connected gamblers had made money. Ross's reputation as a ring great is based mostly on his two wins over McLarnin. He had wins over Petrolle and Canzoneri, but the win over Canzoneri was suspect, as was the third McLarnin fight. Canzoneri was as adamant that he won the fight with Ross as McLarnin was that he had won his third fight with Ross. Ross seems to be the beneficiary of several somewhat smelly decisions. This is not to say that Ross was not one of the greatest fighters in ring history, but this combination of favourable decisions in close and important fights makes one think.

Perhaps Ross's best win was over middleweight champ-to-be Ceferino Garcia. Ross did a great job on the larger man, beating him to the punch, the way Jim did not get a chance to do with Broullaird because of rain. The expert rating of Ross always leans on his two wins out of three over McLarnin. But when they met, it was not this way. Ross was an outstanding lightweight champ and McLarnin a great welterweight champ. You could get good odds putting your money on Ross, the underdog, and some gentlemen made considerable money. One wonders about a lot of things to do with those fights. I think that Ross's shrewd managers, Pian and Winch, realised what few others did, that the awesome McLarnin was now assailable. I think that they realised that Jim had not had a good fight for three years or they wouldn't have let their boy into a ring with a heavier man. They were shrewd matchmakers. They got Barney good fights, and his final fight with Armstrong was their only real mistake. He was a bad style for the light-hitting Ross who could not keep Henry, who bored in close, away from him enough to use his great boxing skills. As Armstrong came in, he would have been a great target for someone like the hard-hitting McLarnin. I suggest that a messenger was sent to Ross's managers that Ross was the man they were looking for, and now was the time to catch McLarnin, and slide the welterweight championship out from under the control of that too independent and foxie Charlie Foster, who had been respected as man of his word, but not liked as one of the "reliable" managers. Pian and Winch may have been startled until they began to think about it. Then they talked to Barney.

There was little money to be made from a retiring McLarnin, but Ross, although not the drawing card that Jim was, would make them more money as a new champ who had beaten Jim.

Everyone who counted in boxing wanted Jim to lose. Ross was superb at smothering the hard blows of a power puncher, and at piling up points with numerous light punches that could be scored by sympathetic judges. "He could make you look foolish," Jimmy said to me seriously, nodding his head. An expert like GeneTunney might leave the ring holding his nose, but the general public could think that it was only the Irish or Italian fans who booed those decisions, and the sportswriters would be paid to write it that way. It takes quick reflexes and a mastery of defence. It wasn't often that Jim met a man with reflexes as fast as his. Sammy Mandell was close. However, Ross could not hit nearly as hard as McLarnin, but he did take a good punch, so he was a good bet if you could get odds. Ross had out-sped Miller, Petrolle, and Canzoneri on his way to the lightweight championship.

Canzoneri, however, swore to his dying day that he had beaten Ross in the rematch. His comments sound just like McLarnin's. I believe that Barney just had to make it look close. Sympathetic judges and writers could cover any slight discrepancy. But it would have to be close.

Boxing fans waited in suspense for those two greats to meet. Promoters waited for Barney to win so they could have a rematch, for they knew Foster and McLarnin would retire with the title if Jim won. If Ross could manage a win, who knows how many more fights they might get out of the crowd-pleasing McLarnin, as well as Ross. In the meantime, Jim was living a pleasant life around Hollywood, and flying to Vancouver to court Lillian.

When the match was made, Jim trained hard, perhaps too hard, to make up for his lay off, and, I suspect, his lack of intensity. He was no longer a "pit bull" dying for a kill. He had become, except for the six weeks before a fight, a gentleman of leisure.

Nevertheless, there is a certain poetry that accompanies those hungry fighters. The chase creates a beautiful animal. Only a God as great as He is incomprehensible could forage not only creative forces but destructive forces as well. Animals, like tigers, share this terrible destructive beauty with the great athletes of contact and blood sports. There is a fascination in watching a black panther stalk his prey, and, indeed, one great black boxer whom Dempsey's manager wanted no part of, Harry Wills, was called the "Black Panther".

McLarnin always trained hard and was always in top shape, "You do that, or you can get killed," Jim would tell anyone. "The mind's a delicate thing. Two or three bad beatings and you can end up a ward of the state."

Jim entered the most famous and best-remembered stage of his career in full command of his boxing powers, but no longer the killer. He was more mature but not nearly as single minded. Jim's and Barney's three contests were magnificent exhibitions of boxing skill. They have never been forgotten by boxing historians. But only in the third was Jim close to his best. It was a knowledgeable crowd that appreciated all the nuances. In each of those matches, the crowd was on its feet, giving a standing ovation to both fighters, not for the violence, but for the artistry.

Barney Ross put it as well as it could be put when a scribe asked him what he thought of the fight after the first one, "God, wasn't it great?" The invocation of the Deity is not blasphemous in this occasion. Ross knew it was the fight of his life. Only in the last round of the third fight do you see that Ross is completely gone and hanging on and faking his punches, after all those incredible 45 rounds. The answer of promoters to modern fighters' laziness was to cut championship fights to 12 "sissy rounds", as Joe Frazier called them.

The question remains, "Who won the classic trilogy of McLarnin and Ross?" You will have an answer, but, as Jim said, the fights were great and they made a great deal of money, and the fans got their money's worth. The Greeks considered their Olympic Games triumphs to be sacred occasions, and when witnessing a great athletic battle or artistic performance, thought, "Blessed is he who has seen these things before he goes into the hollow earth." Blessed is the fight fan who saw McLarnin fight Ross.

A great boxing match enlarges the spirit of man. It becomes, at the peak, almost a religious experience of cool skill in danger. Hemingway speaks of grace under pressure. How many things of such excellence do we see in this life that passes like a dream? We are different after witnessing a great contest. Nietzche said, "Are we not, with this tremendous objective of obliterating all the sharp edges of life, well on the way to turning mankind into sand? Sand!" Boxing is a sharp edge.

The majority of writers and experts seem to have reached a consensus that Barney won the first, and Jimmy the second. I have read no reputable boxing historian who did not think that McLarnin did not win the last fight. I used that double negative because a few writers would have settled for a draw.

Bill Corum says, "There was no choosing between those two great welterweights, but in the last fight McLarnin had just enough of an edge not to lose his title." A close boxing match is a hard thing to call unless you are a super expert like Gene Tunney. There is, however, no doubt in my mind that Jim did enough to keep his title in the last fight.

Foster was bitter at the decision at the time. Perhaps Jim should have been pleased, for it is the only very bad decision that went against him in his long career. But it was the decision that he wanted to quit on, and those are the ones that hurt. The "big boys" knew this, and they didn't like a "money maker" quitting at the apex of his earning power, especially with all his brains and all his money. This offended them deeply. Promoters, not fighters, are supposed to make the big money from the sweet science. Jimmy doesn't seem to have been as upset as Foster, although he obviously thought that he had won. He gave his victory somersault before the verdict came in, but then looked surprised. Nevertheless, he congratulated Barney, and both boys walked across the ring with their arms around each other, looking at the audience as if to say, "Well, we put on some show for you, didn't we?" I suspect that Jim thought that he would get Barney even better next time, and that it would be written up by all as really his win, but there was to be no next time.

In the video, Ross looks completely spent in the last round, and as he goes to his corner he looks as if he thinks he has lost. But Jim was young and rich and famous and in love. He simply told writers that he thought he had won, and left it at that. Foster, however, raged, "Jim can't get a fair decision. There's no point in his fighting any more. We're retiring! This was set up before the fight. I was told there would be a different referee. We were double-crossed. We wanted to pull out but Jim wouldn't disappoint the crowd." Jim just sat in his dressing room and let his manager talk. Why should it bother him? Jim had achieved his goals without getting hurt, and now he was to get married. Famous champ marries hometown sweetheart.

Yes, he really did, for Jim's whole story, since he met the wizard, has been right out of a storybook. It is too good to be true, but it happened. Now is the time to think about the fairy tale romance and that beautiful wedding. McLarnin wouldn't say much, for he was a private man about his family, but the newspapers in Vancouver were ecstatic about Jimmy's wedding to the beautiful hometown girl, when they were half-afraid he would marry some Hollywood starlet. Jim said, misty-eyed, to me, "I met her on the tennis court in East Vancouver and she was as pretty as anyone in Hollywood. I loved her until she died. Hell, I love her still. I never thought my sweet Lil would go first."

Let us return to Jim's summer. The Vancouver papers went into details about the wedding and the society editor had a wonderful time describing the bride's wedding dress. Jimmy was thinking about some of that and it took the sting out of his loss to the man he knew he could beat. Jim had a wonderful future. He need not work unless he wanted to. He had great pals in Hollywood and friends to play golf with, and he had a half a million dollars in the bank. He had his sweet Lillian. Later, I think he felt as Pop had, that night long ago and only yesterday. He said to me quietly and with conviction, "Des, they stole my title. I tell you, they stole it." I asked how he felt about the decision at the time. "Well, I was the most surprised guy in the arena. But I let Pop do the talking. He was boiling and red in the face. After he cooled down and the newspaper guys had gone, he said to me, "What the heck, Jim, we're rich." Jim was not bitter. Boxing had been good to him.

I talked to everybody I could, except Barney, because he had died by then. Dave Brown, the most authoritative man on boxing in B.C. said, "Yes, Jimmy won that third fight all right, but they knew what they were up against. The benefit of the doubt always went against Jim, as an outsider, and, as Jim says, a "Canadian Wetback". Jim had to beat Barney really well to win, and Jim couldn't get that involved. He had even played golf when he trained for Ross. Pop couldn't object because Jim got into good shape anyway. Even when I met him, he did pushups in his kitchen each morning.

Jim sent his usual family telegram. In Vancouver, evidence of the changes in Jim's life surfaced. Miss Lillian Cupit, Jim's fiancée, said that Jim would fly back to California, and then proceed home by car. She expected Jim in about two weeks. "Well, I didn't like to go home with my face swollen," said Jim to me. "By the time I got home, I looked fine."

Perhaps the most surprising thing about the fight, I found as I researched it, was the reporting in the New York press, even the respected New York Times. These papers taunted Foster repeatedly. I quote James Dawson of the Times, "Foster is a blind, crippled, bitter old man who knows his boy can never beat Barney Ross. Ross is infinitely better than this bitter, old, blind cripple's fighter from the West Coast." They hated Foster for his independence and now they could finally crow and sneer at his limp and squint. There was no courtesy for the handicapped, even those, like Foster, with honourable war wounds, when attempting to blacken the character of an uncooperative manager. It is embarrassing to read today the things written about Foster by the establishment writers. We were urged to laugh as this "blind old fool limps back to the West without a championship."

Independent writers, especially Hype Igoe, who, Jim said, "couldn't be bought," agreed with the intellectual champ, Tunney, who said McLarnin had won 12 out of 15 rounds of that last fight. Yes, Jim won big and they stole his title. "Well, it's ancient history," said Jim. Yes, but it's history and that is the stuff that should be researched and put right. That is what history is all about.

Foster, I believe, wanted fame for Jim as much as money, and in the long run, as the ancient Greeks would tell you, that is more important. Homer said that fame in battle gives immortality, and that's why Achilles went to Troy, knowing that he would not come back. Beau Jack and Sam Langford, both of whom ended up broke and homeless, said that the memory of being great was more important than the money they lost. "If I hadn't fought," said Jack, "I'd have been a shoe shine boy who was never a champion." He had gone back to shining shoes. Langford said every fight was a pleasure. We mediocrities who have played sports know that we wouldn't trade those brief moments when we played really well and felt like champions. What must it be like to know, for a few years, that you can beat any man in the world? It is the spirit of man striving for perfection, for infinity –if you are religious you would say God. You transcend time and space. The imperfect human momentarily vanishes.

Jim and Pop felt down after the third Ross fight, but Jim didn't stay down long. He began to think, as Pop did, that he should have had that third decision corrected in the record book, and when he saw Barney ranked one above him in the all time record ratings, as often happens, he said to himself, "I could beat Ross nine times out of ten." Jim told a reporter, "Barney Ross was a good boxer and a remarkable man, but he didn't beat me in that third fight, and if there is a Valhalla for old fighters after they die, after all, they have done their time in the hell of pro boxing rings and days of recuperation, there's one more fight I'd like to have and Barney Ross would be in the other corner, and if I don't win, I'll cheerfully take the next elevator down."

Jim didn't retire. When he fought, he fought the greatest fighter of his time, other than himself, the great little Italian American fighter, Tony Canzoneri. The Italians loved him as the Irish loved Jimmy. Canzoneri and McLarnin, "They were the glory of their days."

But first, Jim got married! Jim had courted Lillian for several years, and then, when she was twenty-one, the proper age, they got married. Jim was twenty-seven.

Chapter 23
Inside the Classic Ross/
McLarnin Fights

"Jim," I opened, "you are remembered for those three barn burners in the New York rings, with Barney Ross, for 45 rounds of the most incredible boxing that masters of the sweet science ever put on. Never mind, Jim, that they came at the tag end of your career, and that you went into them rusty, and that your sensational knock outs were behind you. Those fights remain in the memory of boxing historians. One of the main purposes of our book is to redress that balance."

Despite all his other victories, perhaps over better fighters than Ross, Jim remains in those New York rings of 1934 and 35. At the height of the Great Depression, 125,000 excited fans gathered to watch Irish Canadian McLarnin fight Jewish American Ross, and, as Barney said, "Wasn't it great?" All three of those fights were masterpieces. Jim winces a bit at that, for he remembers what it was like to spend time denying all pleasure and company to train, then to be hit for 45 rounds. Jim was not pretentious at all, but some fighters will not deny that aspect of their craft. Alexis Arguello, the classy lightweight champ, said, "I'm not a fighter. I'm an artist."

The setting for these fights was equally artistic. It was the golden age of boxing. It was the era of the Great White Way of Central New York, its most creative time in music, art, and sports of Dempsey and Ruth. Because of numbers and competition, sparring partners were so good that many could have been headliners today. New York fight fans, especially the Jewish and the Irish, packed Madison Square for those three fights, the first in May, 1934, the second in September, 1934, and the final in May, 1935. William Butler Yeats, the Nobel winning Irish poet speaks of the creation of a poetic masterpiece, "Gather me, into the artifice of eternity." Great artistic physical performances, be they dance, sport, or poetry, partake of that eternity.

Ross's comment on his fights with McLarnin remind me of Ali's comment after he fought Joe Fraser for the third time in the "Thrilla in Manilla". "Lord, he's great, Joe Fraser, Joe Fraser!"

In Jim and Barney's fights, all three decisions were violently disagreed on, but nobody disagreed with the decision that each fight was a classic of fistic artistry. Naturally, the partiality of the Irish and Jewish fans made complete agreement in any close fight out of the question. Jim and I covered those fights in detail, referencing movies and newspaper accounts. I've said that Barney won the first, Jim won the second by a bit more, and Jim won the third decisively but not overwhelmingly. Remember, neither of these fighters had ever been knocked out in his career. In short, each was a master of his trade and could take care of himself in any situation. The third decision against McLarnin is not really so surprising when one realises the politics involved. Jim was a rich, independent champion about to quit the game, with an independent, unpopular manager. Ross was a rising star with smooth managers who had good inside connections. Foster was enraged at the decision, but Jim seemed just surprised and disappointed after the fight. He sat in his lucky green satin robe and said, "Yes, I'm upset." But he had a great life to look forward to.

For sports fans of the time, boxing and baseball were the premier sports, and the controversy over the Ross/McLarnin fights could arise as a topic of conversation at any time. "Westbrooke Pegler and Hype Igoe said I won" declared Jim, "and they could not be bought," implying that others could be bought. Before the first fight, Damon Runyon had written, "McLarnin should lick Ross..." Since Pop's suggestion that Jim would retire soon, Jim had suddenly become a bad business bet, so the Lords of Boxing wanted him to lose and Jim had fought only a little over one minute in over two years. Jim and Pop had pursued their dream of a championship and a fortune with single minded and shrewd determination, but they didn't seem to have considered the retention of the title. Foster was mostly considering the retention of their fortune. Jim should have taken on a couple of standard welterweight challengers before turning to a difficult fighter like Ross. After they had achieved their goal, Jim lost his mental edge.

Friends after 15 fierce rounds

Chapter 24
Barney Ross, World Champion and World War II Medal Winner for Outstanding Bravery

Barney Ross – what magic that name brings to men who lived through the 30s and 40s. His life was such a fantastic story that they made a movie out of it, *Monkey on my Back*. Unfortunately, it wasn't a very good movie, and both McLarnin and Ross's lives were so heroic and dramatic that they deserve a good movie - like *Body and Soul* with John Garfield. Indeed, that movie began as a biography of the life of Barney Ross, with the murder of Ross's father in the corner store, but it changed as it was shot, and became fiction. Like McLarnin, Ross was stunningly good looking as a young man, a fine dresser, well mannered, and charming.

The promoter and writer, Murray Goodman, tells of his meeting with Ross twenty-five years after Barney had retired. Goodman tells of having gotten to know Ross, realising that he needed money but hated to ask for handouts, so he hired Ross to talk knowledgeably about a fight to visiting newsmen, for he knew that Barney would have something intelligent to say. Goodman promised him a nice cut of the take, and Barney asked him for a little "walking around" money. This is not unusual. Goodman gave Ross a couple of hundred, but in an hour's time, Ross came back and asked for another hundred. Goodman asked what happened to the rest. Barney explained that he was a heavy tipper. Goodman said that he couldn't help but laugh. He said that you just couldn't get angry with Ross; he was so pleasant. Men who have been through that many battles have a certain quiet at the centre. "Anyway," Goodman said, "whatever he got, he earned it somewhere along the line. You looked at him and his bashed-in nose, his wisp of a smile, his grey hair, his sad eyes, and you thought of all the battles that man had been through in the ring and the war, and you said, "What the hell.""

Jim had always spoken well of Barney as a fighter and a man, but once, he muttered something. Barney had hit Jim up for money several times. I saw cards of thanks from Ross to Jim. Barney apparently never paid Jim back and McLarnin couldn't help thinking, "That guy steals my title and then spends my money and doesn't pay it back."

Goodman took Ross home one night and his wife was charmed by Barney. The two rivals, Ross and McLarnin, had many similarities. Unlike Jim, though, Ross didn't talk about his life with his lovely wife, the former Cathy Howlett, whom he married twice. The first ended in divorce, and they remarried after he kicked the drug habit. Ross said that his wife, Cathy, and his daughter, Noreen, were the reason why he was able to kick drugs. Goodman was amazed that when he thought Ross had been drinking water all day, he had been drinking pure Vodka with hardly any noticeable effect. I saw McLarnin drink several vodka and orange and show no effects of it. These men were not just strong, they were born hard to wear down. Besides being boxers, Ross was a martial arts expert and McLarnin was an expert street fighter. He told me, without threatening, that he could kill me on the street, although I outweighed him by twenty-five pounds. I didn't doubt it.

Barnet David Rosofsky was a small, skinny, asthmatic kid brought up with stern discipline in an orthodox Jewish home in the Chicago slums. His was one of the many good, hardworking, honest, poor religious families who rose out of those slums in a generation or so. His father and his mother disciplined him physically when they discovered that Barney had been fighting. The kids called him "runt". Little Barney learned never to cry. At 7:30 A.M., two young punks held up Isadore Rosofsky's grocery store, and when he pointed out to them that he had worked hard for the money in his till, they shot him. He died the next day. Barney lost his faith for a few years. Goodman suggests that this all contributed not only to Barney's determination but also to some of his compulsions. Ross threw away thousands as a compulsive gambler and gave almost as much to friends in need. In 1929, Ross won the Chicago amateur featherweight title. To support the family and to get his brothers and a sister out of an orphanage, and encouraged by his friend, Jackie Fields, who had won the world welterweight championship, Barney turned pro. Barney depended on his toughness and speed.

He talked Gig Rooney into managing him, and then Sam Pian and Art Winch took him over as he became successful and the old manager was dumped, the way the dark lords wanted Jimmy to dump Pop. They didn't make a killer out of Ross, but, by shortening his punches, they made a respectable hitter out of him, capable of knocking out all but the toughest opponents, but never developing what is called a knock-out punch. By 1932, he had a fantastic year. He beat Ray Miller, Bat Battalino, Billy Petrolle, and Featherweight, Lightweight, and Junior Welterweight champ Tony Canzoneri twice. He began to put on weight and decided to move into the welterweight division, especially as its unbeatable champ McLarnin was known to be considering retiring. However, McLarnin's manager, Foster, was always open to a good money-making offer as long as there was no great physical risk involved for his boy, Jimmy. Shrewd Pian and Winch were keen for the match and promoters were ecstatic about matching the leading Irish fighter against the leading Jewish fighter in New York, in front of a packed house of Irish and Jewish fans and any other fans who could squeeze in. Promoters were rubbing their hands with glee. Ross was taller than McLarnin but not as husky as the awesome Jimmy, as writers put it in comparisons of the day. Experts thought the hard punching McLarnin would break Ross with body punches and then knock him out. Ross defended his lightweight title and then his junior welterwweight, but the money, as Ross's managers knew, was in fighting McLarnin. McLarnin's sudden thunderous K.O.s made him gold at the box office, and after all, Pian and Winch reasoned, Jimmy won't hurt either of the managers, and it will be the biggest pay day yet. Besides, even Barney was keen, for he had large gambling debts. Really, Pian and Winch didn't think Ross was ready for McLarnin, nor did the experts, but one wonders if Pian and Winch thought that Jimmy might be rusty and a bit complacent after over two years without fighting, and so their boy would have a chance. Barney trained at Grossinger's, where he met and married his first wife, Pearl Seigal. He also met the rich advertising executive Milton Blackstone, who helped his career. After his epic battles with McLarnin, he twice defeated middleweight champ to be, Ceferino Garcia, a considerable feat, and defended his title against challenger Izzy Jannazo. Ross was a busy fighter. He kept busy until 1938, when he met his nemesis, Henry Armstrong, the featherweight king and a remarkable fighter. Later, Lou Ambers and Fritzie Zivic both showed how Armstrong could be beaten, but Henry was the most difficult type of fighter for Ross. Armstrong came straight at his man, constantly punching, even burying his head on his opponent's chest and punching with both hands, his elbows, and his head, for fifteen rounds. Ross's punches were not hard enough to keep Armstrong off him and Barney's smooth boxing skills were nullified. This type of fighting takes terrific conditioning, but Armstrong had fought 27 times in 1937 and was absolutely tireless, like Marciano. The slim Ross was simply worn down by the late rounds.

Barney Ross was an extraordinary man and a great fighter to the end, until he fought cancer, which finally beat him. Although McLarnin was considered the better of these two great champions, Ross has always been considered one of the top ten lightweights and welterweights of all time. Moreover, he could always give even the greatest, physically superior champions, like Canzoneri and McLarnin, a rough night.

As Jimmy said, "He was a terrific boxer; he took a good punch. He was usually moving away from your punch or rolling with it to take the force out of it. And he was smart." To catch the judge's eye, Ross used the same trick that Ray Robinson used. Just before the round ended, just before the judges marked their ballots for the round score, he would throw a flurry of punches, whether they hit anything or not. Especially if the round was close, the judge would think, "Well, Ross finished strong," and he would get the round.

Robinson used to drive Jake LaMotta crazy in their series of close fights. Mind you, Jake was great, but never popular. As he said himself, he was often, "Lamotta non grata." He showed the brawling, tough side of boxing, while Ray showed the slick, classy side, despite the fact that there was really little to choose between them, all things being even, which they never are in pro boxing. They were even until Jake outgrew the middleweight class and had to weaken himself to make the weight. Many put Ray at the top of the middleweights, while Jake is never in the top ten. Ray got a great press. Both Ray and Barney were popular with the media. Barney fought often. As he didn't hit hard, he had no trouble with having to rest his hands. Thus he was always in good shape and his timing was always on. He was skilful and quick, so he was seldom hurt.

Paul Pender beat Robinson twice because he had an excellent left jab, could take a punch, and knew boxing, even though Pender was well into his thirties. It happens to the best of them. Robinson was not as adaptable a fighter as McLarnin. Ray had trouble with several good but not great fighters who had certain skills. Tommy Bell, an average but tall welterweight with a good left, gave Ray a close fight for the 147 pound title. Ralph "Tiger" Jones really beat Robinson in two fights with a hard straight left. Robinson was superb with fighters like LaMotta and Basilio, who came straight at him hooking, then Ray could jab and move and throw those beautiful combinations. He could be the matador to the bull, but Ray was not a great defensive fighter. I suggested to Jim, that for these reasons, Jim could have beaten Ray at the 147 pound limit. Jim was the same height as Basilio, hit harder, had a better left than Pender or Bell, and took a punch as well as Basilio. Jim was thoughtful, "Robinson was bigger than I was. He was a big welterweight who grew into a middlweight. I was a small welterweight."

"Yes, but look what Basilio, who was your size, did to Ray." Jim got to know Robinson after he retired and had put on weight and looked like a natural light-heavyweight of about 175 pounds. I could see that he was thinking of Ray that way. Really, Ray's best fighting weight was only about 157 pounds, only ten more than Jim's, and less than Lou Brouillard's, the middleweight champ that Jim would have beaten under good conditions. Robinson took a lot of punishment because he was not a very good defensive fighter and this adds up over the years. I met Ray at Jim's club and he wasn't looking well. I could see the effects of punches on his mind.

I'll match McLarnin against Robinson any day and put the family savings on Jim. Just as Jones, Bell, Pender, and Basilio upset Robinson, so Ross was a good bet to give the awesome McLarnin a tough fight, especially at this stage of his career. Every expert thought that they were overmatching Barney.

Ross, himself, said, "Jim's had it all -- a championship after all those years of being frozen out, all the big money purses, enough glory for any fighter. He's not hungry any more. Sure he could fight five more years, but he's not intense like he was a couple of years ago. I probably couldn't have stayed with him then." That sounds to me like his managers speaking to Barney. It often is, when a fighter makes a public statement. Barney made the statement after the 3rd fight, but I think Ross's managers said it to him before the first fight, and Ross was honest enough to repeat it.

Nevertheless, as Jimmy would say, "Barney was no flyweight." He had 81 recorded fights, 22 K.O.s, 51 wins by decisions, and only 4 losses. Like Jim, he was never knocked out. Only McLarnin knocked him down; even when he took that terrible beating from Armstrong, he never went down. This is a tribute to Ross's mastery of his trade, his durability, and his great heart. You will notice that Ross had 22 K.O.s, yet is called a light puncher.

That is all relative. Any professional fighter can punch your lights out, even flyweights, even if you outweigh them by 50 pounds.

I once boxed a pro sparring partner at the Western Sports Centre on Hastings, Vancouver. Having flicked his right over my head with my elbow and caught him, I grinned and tried it again, only to receive a blow high in the ribs close to the armpit. I also watched the tough but not heavy-punching George Chuvalo work out on the heavy bag, and as he punched, he buckled the bag! Chuvalo was in Vancouver to fight Ali. I went to see Ali work out. He was in the ring when I came in. There were some very attractive women hanging around ringside saying loudly to themselves and Ali, "Oh, he's beautiful! Isn't he beautiful!" Ali looked down while he continued to spar and said, "Tell me somethin' I don't know." He was indeed beautiful in more ways than one.

But, to return to Barney Ross. Ross had wins over greats like Miller, Petrolle, Garcia, and Canzoneri, but it is his fights with McLarnin that place him so high on the all time great list. On the other hand, it is the sweep of McLarnin's victories from flyweight to middleweight champions that secures McLarnin's place in the Valhalla of boxing. The fans wanted to see if Ross could stay with the Killer with the Baby Face. They were treated to a classic exhibition of the noble art of self-defence, one of the best of all time, and the debate concerning those three classic fights still continues among boxing historians.

Ross had fought his way out of the slums of Chicago after his father's murder had left the family penniless. Barney's younger brothers had to go to an orphanage to survive, until Ross began to make good money in boxing. Ross's widowed mother came to his fights and wept when he won, and wished his father could be there to see it. Barney was polite, unassuming, and a clean fighter, even if his management was, as they say, well connected. He had fought when he was a kid in the streets and he fought heroically on Guadalcanal in the South Pacific when his squad of ten marines was almost overwhelmed by the Japanese. Barney was hit and hit again, but he had been hit before by the best. In that engagement, Ross fought until twenty of those brave Japanese soldiers lay dead in front of his position, and he saved his buddies. When he returned with the Medal of Honour, he was put on drugs for his wounds, became addicted, and had to fight again. He conquered again.

When Ross was down and out, he asked Jimmy for money. Jimmy gave help, "Well, what can you do? We made a lot of money together." Ross and McLarnin never deliberately fouled each other or spoke ill of each other. I saw a Christmas card from Barney to Jim, sent shortly before Ross's death at 57. They had risen above their professional rivalry.

As Jim and I sat in Jim's big front room, I noticed two different tones in his voice, one for things he had spoken about hundreds of times, especially the first two Ross fights, and he would sit back with an ironic grin, and the other tone when I asked about fights that he hadn't talked about much, like his win over the great champion Villa when he was in his teens. He would sit forward and relate the events as if reliving them. Of his first fight with Ross, he said he overtrained, and felt a little weak. Indeed, Jim's left hook, which put Barney down, might have led to a K.O. if Jim had been a little heavier.

"Well, it's a tough business," repeated Jim. "I'm glad I did it, but I wouldn't do it again nor would I have my kids do it, just enough to defend themselves. I enjoyed it when I was a kid, but I'd sooner play golf."

"Your son James told me that you hated to lose at golf, even to your wife." Jim faked a left at my jaw.

Pop and Jim went back to Ireland after he won the title from Corbett. He saw his relatives in Belfast. They were royally entertained even in Dublin, then they went to Liverpool.

While in England, they went to see Jim's old friend, retired New York mayor, Jimmy Walker. "He was at all my fights in New York. He invited me to his office after I K.O.ed Sid Terris, who was supposed to be the next champ."

"One time we were flying East to train for a fight and we missed the plane and had to get the next flight. The flight we were supposed to be on crashed. Our names were on the passenger list and there were headlines in the paper "McLarnin killed in air crash." It's funny to read about your demise, and you shouldn't go cursing your luck. I sat in a hotel in Chicago and read about my own death."

Pop hugs Jim after the plane disaster report in 1935

For a possible fourth fight with Jim, Ross's managers, Pian and Winch, demanded too large a share of the purse. I suspect Pian and Winch did not really want to fight McLarnin again.

At age 33 Ross joined the marines and returned from the South Pacific as a badly wounded war hero. If you can believe in heroes in this ironic age, believe in Barney Ross, for he was a real hero. After he had been to the White House to receive a medal from the president, he publicly admitted that he had become addicted to the generous shots of morphine that he had been given in the military hospital for malaria and wounds. He signed himself into a hospital and came out cured. He remarried his wife from whom he had separated when he was on drugs, and so he was reunited with his wife and daughter. He died in his middle fifties, fighting cancer as bravely as he had fought Jimmy McLarnin, the Japanese, or the tough kids on the streets of Chicago. Red Smith wrote in his obituary that Ross, "a peaceful man, had fought ever since those two punks had murdered his father in his little grocery store on Chicago's Jefferson street, and finished his life like the champion he was."

Chapter 25
The Great Upset: Ross
Wins his Third Title

The great fight was to take place in that Mecca of fistiana, New York. There were two arenas for premier fights, Madison Square Gardens and the Garden Bowl. The bowl had been built as an outdoor facility to handle a larger crowd. Irish McLarnin, wearing a shamrock on his shorts, and Jewish Ross, wearing the Star of David, would mean an overflow crowd. There was always excitement in the air when Jimmy fought in those golden days of his fistic summer, and so it was this summer night. Promoters were singularly quiet about the fact that Jimmy was an Ulster Protestant, for New York was full of Irish Catholic fans, and he was Irish. Jewish fans came to support Ross.

McLarnin had risen to challenge Young Corbett by knocking out Jewish fighters Sid Terris, the "Ghost of the Ghetto", Ruby Goldstein, "the Jewel of the Ghetto", and Benny Leonard, the greatest of them all. Jimmy said Leonard's first fake just about faked his eyeballs out. Jewish fans would have satisfaction to see the terrible Celt get his clock cleaned. Jewish fighters predominated in all the lighter weights. They were noted for their intelligent approach to boxing. They mastered its difficult skills, for it provided a fast escape from the Ghettos. This was not only true of the States, for the welterweight boxer from England was the Jewish Ted "Kid" Lewis, who fought the great American champion Jack Britton an incredible twenty times. Indeed, the first skilful heavyweight champion was in bare-knuckle days, English Spanish Jewish Daniel Mendoza.

In short, New York fight fans were ecstatic when McLarnin and Ross were matched. There was a promotional battle between Mike Jacobs and management of Madison Square Garden. The Garden had the money, but Jacobs, a graduate of selling peanuts on the Coney Island excursion boats, and a powerful ticket broker, had the brains. He set himself up to rival the Garden with his 20th century Boxing Club. He made money promoting the new sensational K.O. artist from the West Coast, Jimmy McLarnin, and he didn't forget Jim. Jim wrote to "Uncle Mike" to see if he could get some tickets for the SRO Louis/Conn fight. Jacobs phoned Jim to tell him to come and there would be free tickets for the McLarnin party. "Just say how many there will be." This is something Al Weil wouldn't do for Marciano, even at his own fights, and even for Rocky's father.

The Garden was packed on May 29, 1934, to see the greatest boxers of their time meet. 60,000 fans came, at the height of the Depression, not to be disappointed. Barney's mother was there and Jim's dad had come from Vancouver. How proud they both were as Jim and Barney came down the aisles with their entourages, to the cheers of their fans. It was a gala event in New York, with all the rich and famous in their finest clothes. Barney and Jim were symbols of manhood and courage. They enriched the lives of their races in America.

Introductions took place. The whistle sounded. The seconds were out of the ring, and a hush fell as the long awaited contest began. "I was rusty so I had trained hard, probably too hard, which puts you on edge," said Jim. "I was lighter than I had been for years – more endurance but less strength than I should have had." A couple of rounds were spent "feeling out the opponents". Videos of the first round show them faking with their heads, fists, shoulders, and feet. Ross was particularly careful because of Jim's reputation as an early K.O. puncher.

Jim was slow because he was rusty. Sparring in training is not the same as one good fight. Barney would take no chances with a puncher like McLarnin. Through rounds 3 to 8, Barney realised what his cagey managers had hoped. Jimmy had boxed only a little over a minute in almost two years. His timing was rusty. His boxing and even his footwork were just a touch off. Jimmy probably took the first two rounds on aggression, but Ross, boxing beautifully, was making Jim miss as he hadn't since he was twenty. There was a low buzz of comment to that effect around the arena. In round nine, however, Jim began to loosen up after his long lay-off. Barney was still leery of Jim's famed right which had knocked out so many great boxers, greater ones than even Barney Ross. Suddenly, Ross was caught looking at Jim's right a second too long. A left hook goes just beyond your peripheral vision. You mustn't focus on the movement of the right hand. With a short slide forward and around, and a shift of weight to the ball of the left foot, a crook in the left elbow, and then a sudden contraction of the deltoid and trapezoid and triceps, a tremendous explosion of force beginning with a pressure on the ball of the left foot, and up through the calf and thigh bicep, hunching of the left shoulder, all taking place instantaneously and without conscious thought, at the lower level of the brain, Jimmy's hand flew through Ross's defences for the first real time, and Jim's wrist turned slightly down just before the point of impact on the side of Barney's jaw. Barney's head snapped back and forth grotesquely. Barney lost a second of consciousness and sailed through the air, dropping on the seat of his shorts. The entire crowd of 60,000 was on its feet, screaming and straining to see -- Barney's fans, in an agony of fear that he would not get up in time, and Jimmy's fans, in expectation of another stunning victory with a single punch. They expected that if Ross did get up, Jim would, with icy precision, finish Ross with a quick succession of accurate punches. After the knock down, Ross was momentarily stunned. Once on his feet, he charged Jim, threw a series of punches, and backed Jim into a corner. There, to avoid a left, Jim tripped and fell, without being hit. This picture, of McLarnin on the floor, was the one published in all the papers and was the lead over the story of the close decision to Ross. Nevertheless, it was a good symbol, for Jim, whose footwork was usually impeccable, had fallen without being hit. He was slightly awkward, as he hadn't been for years. His timing was just a touch off, enough to make his best punches surviv-able, not for your average fighter, but for a top fighter like Ross. Jimmy was visibly annoyed at himself. The "greatest fighter pound for pound" was a little off his game, not enough for Ross to dominate, but enough to let him manage nicely. Ross would throw a flurry of light punches with one or two landing, and then Jim would reply with a combination including a hard one. Then Ross would slide just out of range. Jim could not put together a combination to take Ross out. This "stick and move" is the best defence against a dangerous puncher. Billy Conn did this superbly. The old trainer, Eddie Futch, had a video of Conn's first fight with Louis. He showed it to young boxers saying, "That is how to box." Cus D'Amato argues that when Ali committed mistakes like pulling his head back instead of sideways to slip a head punch, allowing one to counter, a smaller quick heavyweight like Marciano would be able to pursue and tag him when he brought his head back. Ali was fast enough to get away with this with the big slow heavyweights of his day. Ali had trouble with smaller heavyweights such as Doug Jones, Michael Spinks and Henry Cooper. Jones, in reality, beat Ali, but Ali got the decision because there was little money to be made in a competent, unexciting fighter like Jones. The Associated Press called Jones the winner – 6 rounds for Jones, 3 rounds for Ali, and one even, and Ali outweighed Jones by almost 20 pounds. Ali was saved in the Cooper fight, after Henry had knocked him through the ropes, by the bell, and a quick thinking second who slashed his glove with a razor, allowing for extra time to get a new glove, and for Ali to recuperate.

Ross never established a pattern where Jim could expect him at a certain time. Such a fighter demands instant reactions. McLarnin hit the harder punches but Ross hit more light ones and made McLarnin miss. He would finish each round with a flurry. It impressed the judges.

Crucially, Jimmy lost the 9th round on unintentional low blows. Ross said after the fight that Jim's low blows were accidental. "Jim's not that kind of a fighter." Jim struck low several times because his long body blows were inches off when Ross moved back. Ross's ability to slip punches to the head was excellent, so Jim began to go to the body. No low blows hurt Ross, but

Referee Forbes warned Jim four times. The most obvious violation was in the 13th round. Jim followed the time-honoured apology – touching gloves, and nodding. Jim grazed Ross's jaw several times, but Barney's gloves were always up. In the 3rd, Ross drew blood from Jim's nose. Ross won the 5th, 6th, 7th, and 8th rounds on the number, not the power of his blows. But in the 10th, Jim jarred Barney with a blow to the jaw. In all the last rounds, Jim pressed the attack against a tiring Ross and seemed on the verge of victory. He lost the 13th on another harmless low blow, and at no time could he really nail the cagey Ross. Jim had hit harder, inflicting more damage, and had pressed the fight, but Ross had thrown more blows, and Jim had lost several rounds on low blows. The 15th was crucial. Barney again threw flurries of blows at the end.

Scoring a fight such as this is difficult. In an amateur or Olympic fight, Ross would have won for the number of blows. In most professional fights, McLarnin would have won, inflicting the most damage. At the end of the fight, Ross was in worse shape than Jim.In pro boxing, things being fairly even, the question is which fighter will make us the most money if given the win. An overwhelming victory is usually a victory, with a few glaring exceptions. However, in a close contest there is room for economic consideration before the verdict. If McLarnin had been overwhelming in the 15th round, he could not have been denied the title. But it was a close round, and the cagey Ross had made Jim miss, finishing with a flurry, a clever fight. The decision was split. The crowd waited in silence. But the scoring was comic. Judge O'Rourke gave McLarnin 9 rounds to 1, with 5 even. Judge Barnes called 12 rounds for Ross, and 2 for McLarnin, with one even. Referee Forbes gave Ross 13, McLarnin 1, and 1 even. Completely incredible! What fight were they all watching? Everyone in the arena, including Jim and Barney, but not the officials, knew the fight was very close. Foster thought Jim had won about 9 to 6. The newspaper scribes thought Ross had won 8 to 7, considering the rounds Jim had lost on low blows, and that may be about right. However, a champion's title is seldom taken away for unintentional fouls. Undeniably for Ross, the underdog, it was a moral victory.

The desired financial result had been obtained. Jim would have to "unretire" if he wanted to retire as champ, and another fight was inevitable. The controversy would make a rematch even more appealing – a great champ had been defeated by an outstanding challenger in a questionable decision. Sports fans around the world were arguing about who really won. The only way this could be settled was in a rematch at considerable reward to all, especially the promoters. How fortunate for all that Referee Forbes had taken those rounds from McLarnin. The fans had been on their feet often during the fight and would be watering at the mouth to see these two superb ring-men have at each other again. "Coves what loves a mill" around the world would follow with intense interest. Mike Jacobs must have been rubbing his hands and smiling at a job well done. He was a great promoter. Jim accepted the defeat graciously. He had been far from the "baby faced killer" with disarming smile and disabling punch that New York had grown to idolize. Pop Foster mildly disagreed with the decision and intimated, as he had before the fight, that Jim might still retire. Jim had been fighting professionally for over fifteen years and had made close to a million dollars in those days of low taxes and solid dollars. They had had the championship that Pop had promised "wee Jimmy" on that Vancouver street corner. Jim still had his health, his good looks, all his brains, and the world before him.

As Ross said to the reporters after the fight, when asked how he had beaten the most feared fighter of his generation, "Jim's not hungry any more. He's had it all. Probably two years ago, things would have been very different." What a decent man Barney Ross was. The enthusiasm for a rematch overrode all caveats. The six to five odds on McLarnin had made a few inside people a bit of money. It was a most satisfactory situation.

The real reason that Ross was able to eek out a close win, and I think Ross won, can be seen in the recent records of the two men. From December 16, 1932, when Jim knocked out Junior Welterweight Champ Sammy Fuller, until May 28, 1934, when he fought Ross, Jim had boxed not quite two serious minutes in the ring. During the same time, Ross had had thirteen fights, and had gone 135 rounds. He had fought all these and two all time greats, Billy Petrolle and triple champion Tony Canzoneri. Ross was primed for the fight of his life, and that is what he gave his fans. Jim would have had to have been vastly superior to Ross to have won this fight.

The older Jim got, the more he appreciated the art of boxing, but when he was in it, Pop kept reminding him that they were in it for the money. "Yes," said Jim over coffee, cookies, and profundities, "It was mostly the money and the promise of a good life for my family, but I hated to lose." Looking into his eyes and at his clenched fists, I was glad I was not in a ring, even then, with this old warrior.

Dr. Sam Johnson, the grand Cham of Literature, who brought out the first decent English dictionary, and who was handy with his fists, said that a man who wrote for anything but money was a fool. The same applies to pro boxing, yet there is a great deal more to boxing than money or ego or animal aggression. For a superb discussion on the values of boxing, the ultimate of sports, I recommend a few splendid books. Joyce Carol Oates, the novelist and most unlikely boxing fan, published, in 1987, for Doubleday, an amazing study of boxing's implications for mankind called *On Boxing.* Every intelligent human should read it for its comments on human nature and art. Pierce Eagen's *Boxiana* gives a wonderful survey, written in those times, of bare knuckle fighting and its times. A. J. Liebling's *The Sweet Science* and Gardner's *Fat City* give one the taste of boxing, and Red Smith's collected columns *To Absent Friends* introduces one to key figures. Of course, Nat Fleischer's *Illustrated History of Boxing* provides an essential survey.

Many fine writers have been fascinated by boxing. Jack London called for a white fighter to emerge and wipe the "golden smile" off the face of the superbly confident Jack Johnson. Norman Mailer has written perceptively about a sport that fascinates him. Ernest Hemingway loved to spar and admired the "grace under pressure" that boxers must have. He often sparred with his friend Gene Tunney. Once, he thought he had caught Tunney and set himself for a serious haymaker when he suddenly found Tunney's fist one inch from his nose and Gene staring into his eyes saying, "Don't you ever do that again, Ernest." Exactly that happened to me when I tried to catch McLarnin with a left hook. Nevertheless, still the best of all is in Homer's *Iliad*. Watch the Trojan champion Hector leave his wife and little son at the gate of the city and go out to meet the invincible Achilles. You will know why the invincible Mohammed Ali, after he demolished the gallant, good, white heavyweight Gerry Quarry, remarked to Quarry's little son as he sat at ringside with his mother, "Son, never forget your father is a brave man, never forget."

Why should so many people care deeply, and for so long a time, about a fight between two average-sized men for their day, Jim and Barney? These two young men inherited skills that had been passed down from the beginning of boxing in 18th Century Britain, peaked in the quarter century when McLarnin was fighting, and has declined slowly since.

David Halberstam, author of the best book about Viet Nahm, *The Best and the Brightest*, comments in his fine baseball book, *The Summer of 49*, "There was an ongoing seminar about the smallest details of the game. One of the ways in which the modern athlete usually differs from the old time athlete is in the area of single minded devotion to the sport. The modern athlete may often be larger and may work out with weights but his attention is divided. He spends less time thinking about his game. He usually spent less time in his youth playing his game." In the 20s, 30s, and 40s, boxers spent a long apprenticeship in small boxing clubs, with trainers who devoted all their time and knowledge to their craft.

Pop and Jim went back to Vancouver and then to Los Angeles to consider their next move. It was no time until an attractive offer for a rematch was forthcoming. I asked Jim why he decided around this time to settle in California when all his family lived in Vancouver. His wife, Lillian, kept her Canadian citizenship all her life. But Jim eventually became an American citizen. "Well, I love Canada, but I got $60 for my last fight in Canada and $60,000 for my last fight in the States." So Jim went back to Los Angeles and played golf with another Northwest athletic boy living in Hollywood, Bing Crosby, and then began training six weeks before the next fight with Ross.

Chapter 26
The Second Ross/Mclarnin fight: Jimmy Wins his Second Championship Decisively

The second of this great trilogy of fights took place in the same arena, in front of an even more excited crowd, on the night of September 17, 1934, just a few months after their first fight. Just a few months – that is the key to the second fight. I remember listening on the radio, for I had just turned five and my father 45. McLarnin now had fifteen tough rounds under his belt. Probably about 45 competitive rounds a year are about right, unless you take a bad beating. Jimmy always thrived on competition. He didn't get hit hard often, and it sharpened his timing. However, the great McLarnin, I found out, had one weakness. He hit too hard. He didn't cut or break easily but he was a welterweight whose straight right and left hook hit like a light heavyweight's. As a result, he broke his hands five times from the force of his own blows, even through the bandages and gloves. Jim had very broad shoulders and long arms for his height, but had the hands of a man weighing 150 pounds. His perfect timing and leverage placed terrific pressure on small hands. At one time, Pop was worried that this might end Jim's career, so they took a few months off, rented a fishing boat in Vancouver, and went up the west coast of British Columbia to the long fjords into which the giant salmon swim, to River's Inlet, still a great fishing spot. Pop knew what he was doing. Like my father, he knew how to do anything. How are some men like that? Jim pulled in line and nets and salmon with his hands in the salt water until his hands were strong and healed. He never had real trouble with them again, but still Pop didn't like to take a chance by having him fight too often. Nevertheless, Jim's record would have been even better, although not so sensational, if he had not hit quite as hard. I think he would have beaten Ross decisively three times if he had fought in between bouts, as Ross had. Early in Jim's career, in 1924, for instance, he had seventeen fights. There were times in his career when he was known more for his brilliant boxing than for his punching. Fame for his punching came later, when he went east to Chicago, then Detroit, and finally New York, and knocked out all the most brilliant boxers of his day.

In wrestling, you counter a move to the legs by going to the head and a move to the head by going to the legs. Basic sports rules are simple. In rugby, when in doubt, kick it out. If you can't give good ball, don't give ball. On defence, corner flag. In baseball, how do you pitch to Ted Williams? High, hard, and inside, or low and away.

In 1934, however, Jim had one bout and it lasted barely two minutes. Then he had his fights with his greatest rival, Ross. His timing could hardly have been worse. Quick K.O.s do not advance a fighter much.

McLarnin, on his rise to the top, had about six fights a year. Ross never fought fewer than five fights a year. In 1931, he fought 14. So now Jim was in reasonable condition for a good fight, after the 15 round first Ross fight. Having been defeated, he was motivated, as he hadn't been since his championship. It had taken Jim and Pop so many years of Jim's being the best fighter around until they got a good shot, that there was a natural letdown after they won, and Jim did fight some fights with better ring generalship and overall mastery after he was champion, but never with the same intensity. Nevertheless, Jim was famous, as have been most great fighters, Robinson, Ali, Louis, in that they fought every outstanding fighter of their day, often each several times, and always did better the second or third time they fought a man. Jim's masterful jobs on Lightweight Champion Sammy Mandell, to whom he lost his first crack at a title, and his masterful victory over that fearsome High Plains Assassin, Billy Petrolle, are examples of his ability to solve an opponent. Jim learned from his fights. It doesn't take long to realise that although he hadn't had much formal education, he had a quick mind, and above average intelligence. Indeed, it comes as a surprise to learn that he hadn't had much education, for his grammar, for one example, is almost always correct, more so than many university-trained people I know. It was true in the 1930s that many bright young men, who otherwise might have ended up in college, had to take any job coming, even the rough business of professional boxing, if they had any ability that way. I suspect that the general level of intelligence among professional boxers was much higher in those days than at the present time, unless they had had their brains knocked out, for most fighters fought many more fights in those days. Also, most intelligent fighters have a visual memory of previous fights. They can replay some of those pictures to analyse and discuss tactics with their manager, getting sparring partners to make some of the same moves. Louis said, when asked about a second Conn fight, "Well, he can run but he can't hide." Joe could simplify problems.

The excitement of the crowd for the second fight lay in the memory of how McLarnin always administered a thorough beating to anyone who had caught him when he was not at his best. Could Jimmy repeat the pattern now that he was no longer a hungry fighter? Could the younger Ross defy the pattern? Jim had had all the success he had dreamed of. "I wanted to be lightweight champion. I never thought I'd beat all those guys, make that much money, meet all those celebrities, and be welterweight champ. Barney was very, very good but I thought I could beat him. I was anxious to fight him again. I thought I had beaten better men. Besides, I made around $150,000 fighting him. He could embarrass you with his skills, but he didn't hit hard, so you didn't get hurt. Sure I had had all I wanted, but I hated to lose. I wanted to retire with my title. Money was virtually untaxed in those days. Barney and I couldn't miss. Jewish and Irish in New York was a sure fire attraction. That was why I fought so many Jewish boys, and they were top fighters, and most of them great guys. I never met a boxer I didn't like. Take Benny Leonard, for instance, one of the greatest fighters of all time. I met him when he was an 'old man'."

Benny was 35 when he met Jim in the ring. Benny had had 18 fights on the comeback trail and thought he was ready to take McLarnin. He wouldn't have fought otherwise. Leonard was smart, but he wanted to beat that Irishman. Benny said he was fighting for "the honour of the Hebrew race."

"What nonsense," said Jim." What has a prize fight to do with that?" Jim is the only Northern Irishman I've met who seems unable to understand what racism is all about. He was aware of what Leonard was up to. Leonard had coached a whole succession of Jewish fighters whom Jim had beaten. It stuck in Benny's craw. Jim reminded me that he had caught Benny reading Lillian's letters in order to understand Jim better. Jim was hurt. He had idolized Benny when he was a young fighter. He was the outstanding fighter of the generation before Jim. Jim would never have taken advantage of a friendship. Leonard, however, had always realised that there is a psychological side to fighting. Jim met Benny when Jim was first coming up and Benny was at his peak. Leonard was fighting exhibitions at the Pantages Theatre in San Francisco. "Pop asked if I could go a few rounds with the great man, but Leonard's manager told him, 'Sorry, we have our schedule, Mr. Foster.' I was boxing in Oakland then and it would have been very good for me. Benny was a likeable guy and a really great boxer. But he lost his money in the crash of '29. That's why he made that comeback. Benny became a top referee after he lost to us. He dropped dead of a heart attack while refereeing at St. Nicholas arena. He died in the ring. Maybe he liked that. Never fancied it myself. Well, maybe on the golf course."

Pop wanted Jim to retire as champion so that he could be called the greatest welterweight of all. Pop wanted to give his boy immortality as well as security. Pop loved Jim as if he were his own son. If Jim had been given the decision in the 3rd Ross fight, that's how Jim would be rated. As it is, he and Ross are both rated in the top ten. So, we in Vancouver remember our champion, but not how great he was.

Jim, in his 2nd fight with Barney, was great, again. This was the most dramatic of the three fights. He had Hollywood friends, golf, and a growing interest in a "certain young lady". Pop later said that Jim was never quite the same after he got involved with "that Hollywood crowd". Nevertheless,

Jim still did not drink, and never did overeat, and was never more that a few pounds over the welterweight limit. However, he was much more relaxed and sociable than the simple minded young assassin he had been. All his years of training and fighting had been fulfilled in two glorious minutes in the ring with now former champion Young Corbett.

At weigh in, Barney was asked what he would do about McLarnin's low blows. Ross said again that Jim had not meant to foul him, for he knew that Jim was a clean fighter, but that he intended to win decisively this time. "Thanks, Barney," said Jim, "but we'll see about who wins." Ross weighed 142 pounds and McLarnin 146, a good weight for Jim, leaving him stronger and still comfortably under the limit. Ross was a 2 to 1 favourite.

Weigh-in for one of the McLarnin/Ross fights, 1934

The wise boys expected this would be the end of McLarnin's long ring career. The fight attracted 25,000 spectators, despite the fact that it was held eleven days later than scheduled and was postponed four times because of torrential rains. It was felt that this would be to the heavier boy's disadvantage because he would have to keep his weight down all that time. The gate produced $115,000, a considerable amount of which went to the New York Americans' Christmas fund.

When the fight finally took place, Ross came in, confident that he alone could handle the "Awesome McLarnin". Part of the fury of these fights came from the complete confidence of both Ross and Jim that they could handle anybody in the world, short of heavyweight champs like Louis. Featherweight Champ Abe Atell once punched heavyweight wrestling champ Ed "Strangler" Lewis silly for five minutes, when wrestling was still straight. Such men have a quiet confidence that they can handle any physical situation, and that the rest of the world would be wise to behave itself. Boxing experts could not wait to see the display.

Fans wanted to see if the killer could catch the spoiler. Referee Arthur Donovan called the boys to the centre of the ring for instructions. Donovan was one of the best referees of all time. Joe Louis always asked for Donovan. He was a man of complete integrity, above suspicion of prejudice, and a superb judge of boxing. Sam Pian, remembering the first fight, whispered to Ross not to be lured into watching Jim's right and forgetting the left hook, especially after a right hand fake. Pop told Jim to ignore those light flurries, move right through them and nail him with a hard left jab and a right cross. Save the left hook for just the right time and then step in and throw it hard. Ross came out quickly. Jim came out with a look of determination. Ross's stance was more erect than in the last fight, more aggressive than the half crouch he had used so effectively before. Ross must have hoped to do what nobody else had done – stop McLarnin. He must have believed that McLarnin's rusty performance in the first fight was the result of ring aging from Jim's long career, rather than from the two year lay off, and so assumed that he would simply meet an even older McLarnin. It was to be one of the greatest fights of all time.

Despite Ross's confidence, McLarnin took the fight to him, spearing the Chicagoan with swift snappy left jabs, mixed with powerful left hooks. It was apparent that Jim's timing had returned. Near the end of the first round, Jim staggered Ross with a sudden hard right, followed by a left hook. Ross's knees buckled momentarily. Jim's fans were on their feet, shouting, but Barney, being in superb shape, recovered, and by the round's end was fighting back furiously. Jim came out in round two, determined to continue his mastery, catching Ross with left hooks. He wasn't saving them. Ross sprang back, driving both hands to the head. Pop and Jim decided between rounds 2 and 3 to use a different attack to stymie those point-scoring light flurries. Jim jabbed with his left, moved in with his left hook, and then chopped a short right. The hardest punches are not long punches, even when they are wound up and look hard, but short balanced punches with the body behind them. For the perfect form, look at Marciano's K.O. blow to Walcott in the first fight. To throw these in combination so that the opponent is hit in rapid succession before he can recover is the most effective offence. Ross and McLarnin, however, were two of the greatest defensive fighters. Both could slip, deflect, duck, fake, and block with the greatest masters like Jim Corbett, Gene Tunney, and the greatest of all, Willie Pep. Jim continued his mastery through the 4th and 5th rounds, but a long left that landed low cost him round 5. The 6th, 7th, and 8th were all McLarnin on everybody's scorecard. Again and again, Jim caught Ross with solid right crosses, but that indomitable little warrior refused to go down. The fight, however, seemed all McLarnin, for by halfway he had won every round. Back in Ross' corner, they knew that their title was slipping away. Barney cast caution to the winds and came out punching in the 9th and drove Jim before him with lefts and rights to the head. Now occurred something that nearly changed the course of the fight and called forth all the courage in Jim's Irish heart. The two fighters had bumped heads back in round one, causing a slight swelling, close to the nose, on McLarnin's eyebrow. This swelling was split by the desperate barrage of Ross, and Jim's eye began to bleed and swell closed. This situation separates the pros from the amateurs. The trainer may cut that swelling open with a razor so that you can see enough of your opponent to semi-defend yourself, for you can't see half of the punches coming at you with a closed eye. As Jim says, "It's a tough business."

The arena had been a bedlam of cheering all night from the rival camps. The Irish settled in the 8th round, satisfied that Jim was so far ahead that he could not be caught unless he were knocked out, and rock-jawed McLarnin had never been knocked out. The 9th round, however, brought Ross's fans to their feet because now all Ross had to do was spear that bad eye until Referee Donovan stopped the fight, fulfilling Ross's promise that he would stop the unstoppable Celt. It seemed that the 2 to 1 odds on Ross were about to be justified. This possibility was discussed in both corners, and it brought out one of the greatest displays of boxing ever witnessed. In the 10th round, Jim came out, blind in one eye, needing desperately to protect it from further punishment, and completely dominated the master boxer Ross, making him miss repeatedly and even awkwardly, using classic left jabs mixed with hooks. Ross came back in the 11th and 12th, nevertheless, throwing flurries with his boundless energy, and spearing Jim's swollen eye so that by the middle of the 12th it was completely shut. Ross's jabs landed exactly, or within an inch. As one looks at the films of these fights, one notices with surprise, that Ross and McLarnin punch with such precision. Most modern fighters will punch simply to the head. Ross will punch to the low section of the left side of the jaw and hit it consistently and without hesitation in the middle of a combination. The rock-jawed McLarnin had been stunned in the past by only one type of punch, a hard blow to the temple. In the middle of a fierce exchange in the 12th, Ross saw a brief opening, and threw everything into a hard right to the middle of Jim's temple. McLarnin's knees buckled momentarily. It was probably the best punch Ross had thrown, in all three fights. This fight, however, was won in the 13th and 14th rounds when Jim came back after that hard punch to completely outbox the Chicago master. When Ross got ready to throw a flurry, Jim would step in and spear Ross with a hard left to slow him, followed by a right to stop him, and then drive him back with a left hook to destroy his rhythm. Paul Pender did this to Robinson when he got set to throw those beautiful combinations, enabling him to beat Ray twice. I think Jim could have done that to Ray. With Ross coming in desperately, and Jim with limited vision, McLarnin established his superiority. Jim let down a touch in round 15, because both he and Pop knew he had it won. Short of a T.K.O. there was no way Ross could win. Barney threw everything at Jim's eye and Jim protected it, so Barney took the last round. Ross should have been able to stop Jim, given five rounds, but Jim's accomplishment of protecting such an injury was almost unique. At the same time he inflicted considerable injury on Ross. Both fighters were heavily damaged. Jim's eye was shut tight and he would have a glorious shiner for some time. Ross's eyes were also swollen, he was bleeding from his mouth, and his ribs were badly bruised. In short, it had been a war.

It had been Jim's habit, when he won by K.O. or a wide margin, to turn a handspring, from exultation and excess energy. His fans had come to expect it. So over Jim went at the final bell. He would be going home to Vancouver as champion of the world again. All of Vancouver rejoiced. You should have seen my father's face. You should have heard the relish with which he discussed the fight and sparred around to illustrate each point. "Yes, Ern," said younger brother, Art, who deferred to my dad's fighting experience. Art was a gentle soul, but, ironically, he had seen considerable violence as grey waves of helmeted German soldiers had swept around his trench and sometimes into it with the bayonet on the Somme in France in WWI, "that's how it must have been." They all looked into their whiskey and drank to Jimmy's skill, courage, and eternal glory, and wished they had been there at that great and famous victory.

Ross had fought superbly, as he always did. He never had a bad fight, except for his last one against Henry Armstrong. Nevertheless, this was Jim's night all the way. Jim's mastery began in round one when he staggered Ross with a left hook to the jaw and followed it with a chopping right. However, it was his uncanny ability to outbox Ross in the critical 13th and 14th rounds, with one eye shut, after carrying all the early rounds, that proved his superiority.

The distinguished short story writer and novelist, Paul Gallico wrote, "McLarnin simply outboxed and outhit Ross all night." Gallico knew his boxing, despite his ability to write touching stories. (His novella, *The Snow Goose,* never failed to bring tears to the eyes of my classes if I read it aloud.) He was a big athletic man who once got into the ring to spar with heavyweight champ Jack Dempsey, just to see what it was like to be in with the champ. In spite of Gallico's size and courage, he found it an unnerving experience. Once in the ring, Dempsey, a very pleasant, convivial man outside the ring, was never anything but mean. Galico said that as Jack came at him, he emitted a low growl, which Paul found most disconcerting. A quick left hook put Galico on the canvas and gave him a headache for several days. But he wrote a great article about it for his paper and it made his name.

At the end of this fight, McLarnin knew that he had won. He went back to his corner all smiles and said to Foster, "I knew I'd do it, Pop." Oddly enough, one judge, Charles Lynch, scored it 8 rounds Ross and 6 rounds McLarnin, and 2 even. One suspects that, like McLarnin, he had one eye closed during the fight. It was difficult to hear the announcer, the famous leather-lunged Joe Humphries, for immediately the fight was over, Jim's fans were so sure of his win that they began cheering for Jim and celebrating, creating bedlam, before the decision was announced. Judge Tommy Shortell voted 6 rounds for Jim, 5 rounds for Barney, and 4 even. However, it was the unimpeachable referee Arthur Donovan who voted about the way the experts called it after the fight, 10 rounds for McLarnin, and 5 rounds for Ross. Donovan later told reporters, "McLarnin outboxed Ross at every turn. Ross fought only in flurries and you can't win fights that way." Reporter James Dawson of the New York Times scored it 9 rounds to 6 for McLarnin. He said, "It was as glorious a battle as the intrepid warrior from the West Coast has ever waged." Then Dawson went on to marvel at McLarnin's ability to come back and beat anyone who had beaten him. Jimmy had established his mastery over every leading fighter from flyweight up to middleweight, from 110 pounds to 160 pounds, at a time when competition was at its very best. It is a record that has never been equalled.

Vancouver papers were ecstatic. "McLarnin smashes way back. Boxes six rounds with eye closed." Pop and Jim were rich. Jimmy had his title back. They had been longing to retire, and now was the time. However, certain important persons didn't think it would be a good idea for business if McLarnin were to retire with the title. As Jim said, "It's a hard way to make an easy dollar."

Bob McLarnin said, as we talked about those famous fights, "Ross never would have beaten Jim at his best. Jim couldn't get that interested after he won the title when he had waited all those years." Experts agree.

If he had won that championship early in his career, he would have had a long reign, but by the time he won it, he was really ready to retire from boxing. Jim boxed because there was an eager market for his skills, but he was no longer "engage" as the French say. Now he wanted more of the things that a dedicated boxer misses. He had fought not only for the money, but because Pop told him that he could be the best. By the time he was in his middle twenties, he must have known and felt in his heart that he was the best boxer under the middleweight limit of his day and maybe any day. Sports Illustrated rated him as the 2nd greatest welterweight of all time. A great fighter gets that kind of confidence. He didn't say it, but you knew he felt that he could beat anybody his size and more, no matter how good they were, and anybody any size unless they were damned good. "Fame is the spur, that last infirmity of noble minds." All he could gain from fighting Barney Ross again was money, and now he had more of that than he could probably use in a lifetime. Pop confirmed that, after his win over Ross.

Chapter 27
The Rewards of Excellence
and Hard Work

After the great victory, Pop mentioned to the press that since the Irish were so enthusiastic about Jim, they might like to see "the Belfast Spider" or "the Dublin Dynamiter," as he was referred to in the Irish press, in person. It would give Jim a chance to look up all his relatives and Pop a chance to skip across the Irish Sea and see some of his old friends in Liverpool. Pop and Jim had climbed to the top of their world and were beholden to no one, and so they sailed to the land of Jim's birth. "Come back, Paddy Riley" and so, like every Irishman's dream when he left the land of his fathers, Pop and Jim came back rich and famous, and they got a heroes' welcome. Jim couldn't believe the wonderful way they were treated wherever they went. There was no difference between North and South, Catholic or Protestant. "I was as welcome in Dublin as in Belfast. You'd have thought I was Brian Boru himself come back after defeating the Vikings." They also went across the Irish Sea, where Jim's little brother Sammy had died so long ago, to Liverpool to see especially Spike Robson. Pop's old fighter had lost all his money and Pop arrived to give him some more, enough so he would never starve. "God bless you, Pop," said Spike, almost in tears, when Jim and Pop were leaving. Jim said Pop often gave money away in large sums to people he thought in need and deserved it. Yes, may God bless Charles Foster, wherever you are!

By this time, young Jim had some ideas of his own, centered on that beautiful young lady from his own neighbourhood. He had been immediately smitten and never got over it. Jim was still smitten when I met them in their seventies. When I met Lillian Cupit a year before her death from cancer, she was still trim, attractive, sharp, and capable. Jim's son, James, told me his mother was the centre of the family and took care of most things. Jim accepts people at face value, but when I met Lillian, she was a touch suspicious about a combination high school English teacher, wrestling coach, and boxing nut, and asked me some sharp questions. I admitted to her that my combination of interests might be unusual. My mother had given me my love of poetry and my father my love of sports. Mother used to quote Walter Scott's *The Lady of the Lake* -- "The stag at eve had drunk his fill where danced the moon on Monan's rill, and deep his lair had made in lone Glenartney's hazel shade." Lillian took it up, for it was taught in all public schools at one time. "But when the sun his beacon red had kindled on Ben Vorlich's head, the deep mouthed blood hounds heavy bay resounded up the rocky way." She accepted me. I asked her how she got tangled up with Jimmy. She just looked at me and said he was Jimmy McLarnin – that is famous, rich, handsome, modest, and polite.

Lillian and Jim

Right after his great win, Jim phoned his mother to tell her that he was all right. He spoke to his mother and dad, and to some of his brothers and sisters. There were no celebrations until he had talked to his family. This time, Jim went home not only to see his family, but also because he was in love. Most old time fight managers claimed that being in love took the edge off a fighter, and that perhaps may account for the lack of intensity in Jim's ring work. Lillian was always referred to in Vancouver papers very coyly as "a certain young person who had news of Jim." Her personal privacy was respected, for she was a lady. By this time, they were engaged and the papers had announced that. They could report that Miss Lillian Cupit, Jim's affianced, said that Mr. McLarnin would be returning by way of California, that he would fly from New York to Los Angeles, and then he and his manager, Mr. Charles Foster, would motor north to Vancouver, and James was expected to arrive in two weeks. Theirs is a life long love story. This is not to say that it was all perfectly smooth sailing. Jim loved a good party, and while Jim retained his dignity, Lillian was more reserved. Lillian had her bridge club, and Jim had his business, and they both played golf, and had their family, and Jim considered Lillian's wishes. Jim's failings were good-hearted human failings, and he was full of affection and good humour. Jim liked celebrity parties in Hollywood and Los Angeles, where he was always welcome as a socially presentable, famous professional athlete who was good looking, well mannered, well dressed, and well spoken. Jim loved to take Lillian to parties with his Hollywood friends. The prize fighter and the lady, the title of a movie, stars the reigning heavyweight champ, Max Baer. Max knew you can get killed in a ring almost as easily as in a hockey or football game. Baer had been responsible for the deaths of two fine professional fighters himself.

Jim loved Louis for he was such a decent human being. Sportswriters used to say, with unconscious racism, Louis was a credit to his race. Jim often played golf with Joe, and Jim was proud of his golf game and would boast about it a bit, something he would not do about boxing, where he gives you unvarnished realism. He thought he could have beaten this or that fighter, but he wouldn't say so publicly. "Joe was a better golfer than I was. He could have been a pro golfer. He could hit it a mile."

Jim's fame as a boxer opened doors of the rich and famous. Jim said, "I'd have much rather have been on the golf course than the ring about that time."

Later, Lillian looked after her Jim. When I arrived with what I took to be a friendly bottle of Canadian Club, I could see her looking askance at it. Jim might have been a health nut, but after he finished his boxing career he liked a convivial drink with company and some good talk, especially about old times and boxing. "Oh, Jim," Lillian would say, "they don't want to hear all that old stuff."

"Yes, it's ancient history." Jim would laugh and stop.

Jim was devastated by Lillian's death. We were sitting at breakfast one morning and Jim was looking thoughtful. "I never thought my sweet Lillian would go before me," he said. I feel that they will meet again in wonder as they did on the tennis court in Vancouver long ago and if you can see through the 4th dimension and down the black holes of this universe, catch Leviathan with a hook, and tell me who clothed the horse's neck with thunder, then you can tell me they won't. But I think they will!

From the point of view of the ring historian, Jim should have retired after his smashing win over Ross in their 2nd fight. In nearly one hundred fights, Jim had never lost to anyone whom he had not come back and soundly trounced. Only Maricano who was never beaten but had half as many fights, and did not fight until he was mature, would have one better and I believe him to be the greatest heavyweight. Perhaps Jim Jeffries or Jack Dempsey, two incredible hard rocks and bigger than Rocky could have outlasted him, but I think Rocky could have outboxed them. Jim thinks Dempsey at his best could have beaten them all. He didn't want to say Jack could beat Joe Louis because Joe was such a great guy, but Joe could be hurt, while Dempsey could be knocked down or outpointed but not hurt, nor could Marciano or Jeffries. Perhaps Corbett or Tunney, those two most intellectual of champs, might devise a way to fight Rocky. Marciano was the best trained of champs. One afternoon, Rocky was resting with his eyes closed, after rounds of sparring, and a sportswriter noticed that his closed eyes seemed to be flicking back and forth. Thinking something was wrong, he asked trainer Whitey Bimstein, who told him that Rocky was doing eye exercises. The Rock was fanatical. Foster and Jim were also fanatical about training. Pop had Jim hold a weight by a rope with his teeth and swing it back and forth to strengthen his jaw and neck. One needs natural ability, dedication, and a master teacher trainer like Foster or Bimstein to reach this level. Now, Jim took one of his long lay offs, between his 2nd and 3rd fights with Ross. Ross was busy, having several challenging, but not exhausting, fights. As for Jim, a sportswriter commented that his eye injury would not be good for Jim's golf game.

Let us consider how a pro fighter feels after a fight, after fifteen rounds of being punched by an expert. Professional fighting is qualitatively different, even from games like lacrosse or rugby. A trained fighter doesn't feel as much in the heat of battle as you might think, as you sit at ringside and see the sweat fly from him as he gets hit. Rocky Graziano, tough even for the fight game, once remarked after seeing the movie of his 3rd fight with Tony Zale, the Man of Steel, "If I'd a known dat was goin on, I'd a left." Oh, there are blows that a fighter feels. Ringsiders could hear the brave Max Schmeling scream as Louis got him in the kidney in their second fight. Yet, it is after the fight that you feel it most. Jack Sharkey commented after his fight with Dempsey, not an especially punishing fight, and Dempsey was past his prime, "I came home and went to the hospital. I passed blood for a week." Jim said after his winning fight with flyweight champ Pancho Villa, "He had a great hook. Both my ears, not my eyes, were black and blue." Don't let the movies fool you. Get hit one good one in the middle of your face and you're not pretty anymore – don't consider 15 rounds. As Jim said, the fight itself is not so bad. It's the boredom of training away from family and friends and the weeks after. Sam Langford, the great Canadian Black, whom the great Jack Johnson wanted no further part of, despite the fact that Langford was little larger than a middleweight, said, "I fought maybe four hundred fights, and every one was a pleasure." Yet death is always waiting invisible in the ring, but that is true of every hard contact sport, for more young men have been killed in hockey and football than in boxing, and it has been said that turning left on a highway is more dangerous than getting into a ring.

The worst slaughter that I have seen is the Dempsey/Willard fight where the 189 pound Dempsey nearly killed the 6 foot 6 Willard, 75 pounds heavier. Jim told me that Willard came around to his house years later to insist that Dempsey had something in his gloves besides fists. Willard just couldn't believe that a little guy like Jack could do that to him. Jim asked Jack later if he had anything in his gloves and Jack said that he swore on the heads of his children that he had no metal in his gloves. "Well, maybe Dempsey had something else," said Jim. "Dempsey was just too fast and explosive for big Jess." Willard was no patsy. He knocked out Jack Johnson with a hell of a right. You can see it now in the video. Johnson didn't throw that fight in Havana. He got licked and good by Willard. Jim said, "That clears that up. They took that picture just after Johnson's hands went back over his head as he hit the canvas, making it look strange."

After Jim had gotten over the effects of this fight, they returned to the West Coast, to Los Angeles, and to Vancouver in triumph, and the West Coast and the Irish, and British Columbia rejoiced, for Jim was champion of the world again as he should be, for he was the finest fighter of his day.

The next fight, the 3rd Ross fight, is the key fight in how you rate McLarnin on the all time list. Don't say that a great fight, well and bravely fought, does not matter. The greatest of all dramatists after Shakespeare, the Athenian, Aeschylus, had fought in the epic battles of Marathon, and Salamis against the invading Persians, on foot, spear to spear, when he was in his forties. He produced his greatest drama, the *Oresteia* trilogy when he was sixty-seven. When he died, he didn't care if he was remembered as we remember him, the greatest dramatist of classic Greece. He asked that they simply put on his tomb "A Man of Marathon", the greatest fight he had ever been in. If Shakespeare had been in the English fleet that defeated the Spanish Armada during his lifetime, he would have wanted that on his grave, not the curse that is on his grave now. Men are peculiar. Cervantes, the author of the immortal Don Quixote, gloried most in the wounds he received at the sea battle of Lepanto, the defeat of the Ottomans.

If you agree with the official judges of the third fight, who voted for Ross, then McLarnin is an all time great who, at the end of his career, met an equally good man coming up. You may say that Jim could be beaten by a superbly great defensive fighter. Louis had trouble with the crouching Arturo Godoy, and so would have had trouble with the crouching Marciano. Jim said that doesn't mean Joe wasn't perhaps the greatest fighter. Ray Robinson had trouble with several fighters who had good left jabs, notably Ralph "Tiger" Jones. Ali had trouble with small competent boxers like 178 pound Doug Jones. McLarnin was faster than most opponents until Ross. Lord, he was still fast of fist when I met him in his late seventies.

However, if you agree with everyone who saw the fight, except the hired officials or the paid newspaper writers, who were out to make a little extra money from the right people, Jim won easily, establishing himself as a master of even the great Ross over three fights, proving himself the master of every fighter he had met, all the best in the golden age of boxing between the flyweight and middleweight limits. Looking at McLarnin this way, you then begin to argue whether he was better pound for pound than Robinson or Pep or Joe Gans or Benny Leonard or Jimmy Wilde or Mickey Walker or Sam Langford or Jack Johnson. Most papers of the day report in their lead article almost universal disagreement with the decision that night, and then carry a column of analysis where an established journalist reports that Jim was robbed. The lesser known columnists take Foster to task for his rage, and attack him personally, ad hominem.

Let us now consider that night. McLarnin was at the height of his physical powers and his knowledge of the subtleties of that most complex art, the sweet science, boxing. There was no move Pop had not seen, from Jem Mace, who taught the world scientific boxing, to the golden age of Dempsey, Louis, McLarnin and Ross. Along with Jack Blackburn, who taught Louis, and Whitey Bimstein, who taught Marciano, and Angelo Dundee, who taught Ali, Foster had become one of the greatest teachers of boxing.

Fans in those days were very knowledgeable. Every neighbourhood had its boxing club and most able-bodied young men had spent a few hours in a ring. It you were short of money, you might hang around the club on the weekly fight night and substitute in the boxing card if one of the opponents did not show up or if they needed another bout because someone had suffered a quick knock out. You will often see just this happening in old movies such as *City Lights* where Charlie Chaplin, desperate for money, takes on the local "champ". Young men would work if a boxer were short of sparring partners some days. Anthony Quinn, the great movie actor, once sparred a few rounds with McLarnin. Jim was training to fight middleweight champ Lou Broulliard, and wanted some larger sparring partners. Quinn had done some fighting and working in training camps to pick up a bit of money while he was only getting bit parts in Hollywood. Quinn was asked how he "did" with McLarnin. "Listen," he replied sourly, "one doesn't 'do' with a guy like McLarnin. He was so fast," Quinn said, looking amazed. My father spoke of sparring with a pro who snorted frighteningly through his nose for air just as he was about to sail into you. This broad first hand experience created a knowledgeable public. A few minutes in a ring make one appreciate good boxing. A contemporary crowd booed Gordie Racette of Nanaimo, who had few fights, but ranked in the top ten, when he lost to Jimmy Young just after Young had actually beaten heavyweight champs Mohammed Ali and George Foreman. If ever a fight prospect was rushed, it was Racette.

I saw Racette in a lacrosse game where he confronted a tough guy who just gave up and walked away after a few seconds with Gord. That's the difference between a sports tough guy and a pro fighter. Jimmy's ability to take out an opponent at his first mistake was just the icing on the cake. The fans were dying to put their money down at the height of the Depression for the privilege of seeing the artistry of Jimmy and Barney for the third time and probably more. The promoters kept offering Pop and Jimmy more money to defend against Ross again. Pop wanted Jimmy to retire, and Jim had half a mind not to come in off the golf course himself. Pop had the financial security for himself and Jimmy, and the title he had promised, and Pop had created a fistic masterpiece. He wanted Jim to retire with an unblemished record.

Both Pop and Jim had given up years of their lives for this ideal. Jim's sister Olive said that Jim had a great career but he was often lonely. Jim was naturally gregarious, although Pop taught him to be a little reserved, and he still was, even with his old boxer friends at his club. It did give him a certain dignity and his pals respected that. Foster himself had grown up inured to the Spartan life, fighting for his life in the boxing booths of English circuses run by his father and his uncle. Foster would stand on a platform at the circus and challenge all comers, any weight, to try to last with him. For each round they lasted, they made a pound, English money. Charlie must knock them out even if they were the toughest street fighters and Charlie did, although he was only a large middleweight.

"Mind you," Jim said, "punching most so-called tough street fighters is like hitting your sister. "

When the Boer War came along in South Africa, Foster enlisted and saw much action, as they used to say euphemistically, instead of saying that he saw many of his comrades blown to pieces before his eyes, and that he had killed many of his fellow men in cold terror. But that did not frighten Charlie Foster. He enlisted again in the army in 1914 for the First World War in France. He was decorated for bravery and some of his buddies who were there told Jim that Foster really should have been awarded the Victoria Cross, the Empire's highest award for extreme bravery. Pop was severely wounded, and still bothered by his wounds when Jim met him in the 1920's. However, he worked as a longshoreman, a physically demanding job, and went to the military hospital some days. Foster had been forged as hard as steel in the fires of battle, hand to hand combat, and killing. Despite, or perhaps because of that, he was a most humane man. His heart was large and his generosity was legendary. His mind was keen and analytical. He saw to it that his boys had as little chance of injury as possible. He wasn't the kind of manager who says, "Get back in there kid. He can't hurt us." The most delightful reversal of this was achieved by Oscar Wilde who, on tour in the old West, when told that they would tar and feather his manager if they showed up in town, replied, "Nothing you can do to my manager will intimidate me in the least."

In the first Petrolle fight, when Jim was hurt and slowed by a fearsome blow to the temple, Pop wanted to stop the fight. It was Jim who insisted on continuing. "If you stop it, I'll never fight for you again," Jim said. As they had no written contract, it was no idle threat.

"All right, son," said Pop, "but anytime." Fear was beneath Charlie Foster. He lived and died a man of infinite courage and ultimate humanity. He lived simply in a single rented room even after he had a quarter of a million dollars in the bank in the 1930s. He ate simply and healthfully and he drank water. He walked rather than rode whenever he could, although he bought a second hand car for fun, but Jim persuaded him against driving it because of his bad eyesight. He was one in a million -- no, make that ten million. With his Spartan life, he could have lain down beside Leonidas and his Spartans at Thermopylae. When the great Persian king told them that his army of hundreds of thousands would darken the sky with arrows over those 300 Spartans who blocked his way, Leonidas replied, "Then we will fight in the shade." I can hear Foster saying that. "Go, stranger, and tell the Spartans that we lie here obedient to their commands." Foster would like a simple epitaph like that.

But even Pop could use a break. McLarnin was not exactly a bon vivant, for Pop had trained him from age 16 to eat sparingly of mostly wholesome food.

Most of Pop's training took. Jim always woke early, even in his seventies, ready for roadwork. Even for the Ross fights, Jim didn't drink, but he loved a party, and was popular around Hollywood. He remained friends with many older stars of Hollywood's golden age.

There has always been a relationship between boxers and Hollywood. Male stars want to be boxers and most boxers want to be actors. Stars of that unreal world want to confront reality. If you have ever been in a ring, you realise you are in a "real" situation. I recommend it to Descartes when he wonders if he exists. You know that you are not alone in the world. There is somebody there who is going to smash your face. The boxer wishes for the cheers without the damn reality.

Jim enjoyed showing pictures from those days. "There's me and Lil at Clark Gable's. There's Clark, and there I am with Bogie. He loved boxing. He'd get me talking about some fight or some move and want me to go over it so he could learn it. There's Jean Harlow in my new car. That's Jim Farley, you know, Roosevelt's postmaster. He was a dedicated fight fan. That's my dad with Jack Johnson, down to see me fight."

Clark Gable and Jim

Jim with fan, Humphrey Bogart

It was a grand time for Jim. He went home every Christmas. His sister Olive told me he would buy hampers of food for poor families in East Vancouver to see that they had a good Christmas. I asked Jim about that and he said, "Yeah," but he didn't want to talk about it. Olive, however, felt he had done many good works around Vancouver. "They've forgotten all he did for them," she said somewhat bitterly. Jim told me about getting his good friend Bing Crosby to Vancouver for a benefit concert to build the Sunset Community Centre at 404 East 51st Ave. Dal Richards led the orchestra.

"Monica and I have danced to his band," I said.

"So have Lil and I," said Jim, and got off the subject of his good works.

But you couldn't party even as moderately as Jim did and keep your title in those days with many desperate and determined young men, the dogs of poverty snapping at their heels and just McLarnin standing between them and riches. Ross was still hungry.

After McLarnin, Ross defended against Henry Woods in Seattle, kept razor sharp, and always fought at his best. Meanwhile, Jim played golf, had an active social life in Hollywood, and thought about Lillian Cupit from his home town.

"You stayed in California, Jim?" I asked.

"I'm a Canadian wetback, but you can play golf 12 months of the year here. I have so many good friends in this town. Lillian saw that Glendale had good schools for the kids."

Jim wooed Lillian, played in the Crosby Invitational Golf Tournament each year, and mellowed. He had earned it. Pop didn't think much of the Hollywood crowd, but he approved of Lillian, "a good old fashioned girl with heart so true". Pop's trouble was that he only saw to the heart of things and had trouble enjoying the froth. Glamour and reputation meant little to him. Hard work and an honest heart impressed Foster, and little else.

Chapter 28
The Defining Contest

"One of the Major Fights of all Time"
New York Times on the last fight between
Barney Ross and Jimmy McLarnin.

"I don't like the smell of things."
Pop Foster to a *Vancouver Sun* reporter a few days before the fight.

"Jockey of Norfolk be not so bold
For Dickon thy master is bought and sold."
Richard III Shakespeare

After investigation, one comes to the conclusion that Foster did make one major mistake in his management of the career of McLarnin, and that gave the dark lords of boxing power good reasons to buy the great Jack Dempsey, the idol of fistiana, and sell the brilliant welterweight champion, Jimmy McLarnin, at considerable profit to themselves. Indeed, upon reflection, one realises that it was the only wise business move to make, and it's remarkable that it didn't occur to Foster.

When Jim and Pop returned from Ireland, they had accomplished everything they had set out to do and far more than they had ever dreamed of. They had their championship and they were rich and famous. They had been everywhere they wanted to be, and met everyone they wanted to meet. They had, between them, almost a million dollars in the bank, in the middle of the Great Depression. Celts dream dreams, but who could have imagined this, when they left Jimmy's newspaper corner on Main Street in Vancouver. They were both feeling extremely mellow, an unusual condition for Foster. For a moment, he had let his guard down in the tough business; that can be as fatal outside the ring as it can be suicidal inside it. They were both ready to retire in comfort and triumph to the West Coast. Pop admitted that they had that in mind, and gave reasons for it to the press. This was an aberration for Pop, who was usually very close mouthed, especially about Jimmy's financial intentions.

It is much better for the finances for promoters in particular to have an exciting new champion than to be left with a bunch of second best after an unbeaten champ retires. That this did not occur to Pop is surprising. He was approached with an offer of more than $60,000 for another fight against Ross. It looked like a good thing.

All fight fans and newspapers were calling for another of these wonderful contests. Why not a third "rubber" match? So, just one more easy fight to top up the bankroll, and then let the good times roll, they both thought. But, for a change, there were people thinking faster than Pop Foster.

So it was that Jim and Barney headed toward their third fight, the fight that defines their relative places in ring history. McLarnin's incredible list of victories over thirteen champions in all divisions from flyweight to middleweight obviously places him in the top five of welterweights ever. Ross's record places him in the top ten of all timers. In his all time ratings, Nat Fleischer of *The Ring* places McLarnin 5th with Ross 3rd, obviously on the basis that Ross took two of three fights from the awesome McLarnin, although his record is not as impressive as Jim's. Without that final loss to Ross, McLarnin would rank 3rd or 2nd, and who could deny that Jim might be the best 150 pounder of all time. Sports Illustrated ranked Jim 2nd of all time. Although Pop and Jim didn't realise it, Jim would have to completely overwhelm or knock out Ross in order to keep his title. Nobody had ever knocked out Barney Ross. In Ross, the boxing lords finally had a man who could stay close to McLarnin, and that was all they needed. Jimmy was the greatest money draw of his time, between Dempsey and Louis, but he was no use to promoters if he didn't fight. Even as champ, he fought seldom and now they were sure he intended, if he won, to fight no more. Give the promoters a good Black that they could starve if he didn't fight. That's what they did to the greatest of them all, Joe Gans, the old master, who died of T.B. from having to make the weight too often. A true hero and a wizard can come through it and win the Grail. If McLarnin lost, he would want to fight again. As fight time approached, Foster began to smell something of this. Pop had asked for Arthur Donovan to referee, but promoters put forward the name of Jack Dempsey, the heavyweight champ who had recently retired and was already running short of money. Jim liked Dempsey. He thought Dempsey was the greatest heavyweight, with Louis a close second. Dempsey was a faster, tougher, and harder hitting Joe Frazier, who came straight at you in a crouch, and so would have taken Ali, Jim thought. Besides, when Jim was known only on the West Coast, it was Dempsey who told the Eastern promoters that they had to get this Irish kid, fighting out of Los Angeles. Pop, however, never trusted Dempsey. Dempsey came out of a rough background and his manager, Jack Kearns, had lived on the edge of the law and had been mixed up with prostitution and the livelier aspects of the old West. Kearns and Dempsey were out of the West in the mould of the Earps and Jameses, and it can be argued who was on the right side of the law. Movie footage shows gunfighter Bat Masterson acting as an official in a championship fight. Wyatt Earp did the same. Dempsey could be a pleasant fellow to meet and he was a fine fellow when he could afford to be, but he came out of the jungle. He wasn't pleasant if he couldn't afford to be. He was probably the toughest of heavyweight champs. His first wife had been a prostitute, but eventually he married the beautiful actress Estelle Taylor. Before Pop signed, he was told verbally, "You won't have to worry about Dempsey." Pop assumed they would get Donovan.

Thus Pop and Jimmy went into the lair of Eastern power like lambs to the slaughter, in front of a packed house of glittering celebrities and sophisticated aficionados, and rabid Irish, Jewish, and mixed fans, and they were shorn of their championship. Another fistic masterpiece was expected, and there was always a chance that dynamic punching McLarnin might catch the wily Ross and take him out, as he almost had with a left hook in the first fight. They were not to be disappointed. It was a masterpiece of boxing, one of the greatest, and in the final round, Ross was probably the closest he had ever been to being knocked out, excepting his final fight with Armstrong. Ross did, however, keep within hailing distance of McLarnin, and that was all that was necessary.

Now let us remember that famous night at the fights on May 29, 1935, when they took Jimmy's championship and gave it to Barney Ross. "They stole my championship," said Jim bitterly, after all those years. He wouldn't say much more than that and he never blamed Barney, but it bothered him. At the time, it had enraged Pop and Jim had taken it philosophically. But not now. Old men think of eternity. Young men can console themselves with the joys of tomorrow.

My friend, Gerry Hale, told me of an interview he attended with Barney Ross, in Vancouver. Ross was accompanying singer Eddie Fisher. Ross was a perfect gentleman with white hair and a bashed-in nose. Asked about those McLarnin fights, he said that he thought that McLarnin probably should have had the decision in all three, but, "I wasn't going to look a gift horse in the mouth."

It was a nice thing to say in Jimmy's hometown, but he probably thought he was fortunate to win some of those fights. Barney had enough fame by that time. He had given Jim almost as good as he got, and it didn't hurt to be generous.

Jimmy has a remarkable story of a curious incident that happened just before this fight. It seems that one evening Sam Pian, one of Ross's shrewd and well-connected managers, came to visit them. He said that he had heard Jimmy and Pop were thinking of retiring, and he suggested that as McLarnin was an odds-on-favourite to win, there could be considerable money available for everyone concerned if Jimmy would just lay back a bit and let Barney win the fight. They were going to quit anyway; they would simply retire with a much larger bankroll. Pop exploded and told Pian that Jim was going to win this fight, and go home to the West with his championship. Pian looked serious now, and suggested that a man such as Foster might come to an unfortunate ending if he reported it to certain persons. Pop seized Pian by the shoulders, turned him around, and booted him out the door. Foster was shrewd but he lacked diplomacy. A perfect manager would have thanked Pian for his consideration, and gone to see the people to whom Pian had referred and explained his problem to them, as he had to Owney Madden, the underworld boss. Foster, however, was not only crippled by his war wounds, but also by an unshakeable morality. He was that oxymoron and contradiction, an honest fight manager. Most leading members of the fistic community have learned that flexibility makes things more pleasant. But Pop had created a fistic masterpiece, as well as keeping his promise to Jim and his dad. Jim had beaten every man who had beaten him, in return fights, and he was famous for his second fights. At this point, Jim had a perfect record. Now, however, ring historians could say that McLarnin might be beaten by a great defensive boxer and spoiler like Ross. This fight seemed like the one blight on Jim's incomparable record. But those ring historians should have been at the fight that night.

It had been a year since Barney and Jim had met last. There was a sell out crowd outdoors at the Polo Grounds, the old home of the Giants. A considerable amount of the take went to the Free Milk for Babies fund, of which Mrs. Randolph Hearst was president. Despite another long layoff, Jim remained the favourite. A few days before the fight, Sam Pian, one of Ross's "well-connected" managers, turned up unexpectedly at Jim's camp and wanted to speak to Pop and Jim privately. Pian said that he had heard that Jim was thinking of retiring, and, since the odds were heavily favouring McLarnin, he would see that considerable money was secretly laid for them on Ross if Jim would just "lay back" a bit during the fight. Ross could get the title and McLarnin could retire with a huge bonus, as he was leaving anyway. However, Foster was not only afflicted with war wounds, but also an unshakeable honesty, a serious handicap in the business. He seized Pian by the shoulders and propelled him from the room with a kick.

Then at ringside came the big surprise! There was Jack Dempsey to referee the fight!

They had switched referees on Foster and double-crossed him. This is a mysterious affair, and Jim didn't say much about it. He just looked glum. Jim admired Dempsey as a fighter and liked him as a man. Dempsey, like all human beings was many-sided. Outside the ring, he was convivial, except he had a strange penchant for giving people "the hotfoot," even giving a man named Lyons a hotfoot while he was shaking hands with President Roosevelt. Inside a ring, he constantly beat bigger men almost to death. Both 6 foot 6 Willard and 6 foot 4 Firpo were lucky to escape from Jack with their lives. In his early days, Dempsey said that if he didn't win in the ring, he didn't eat. There are few white fighters like that today. I mentioned to Jim that Jack must have been financially comfortable with that restaurant of his in New York. Jim said that Jack really had very little money, that he fronted for the restaurant, and that he had little of the millions he had made in the ring, and had to keep working, refereeing, and making "appearances", in order to maintain a good life style. Dempsey says as much in his autobiography. Manager Kearns had most of the money that Dempsey had made. Dempsey knew that Jim would be all right, even if he lost. It was hard for Jack to be sorry for McLarnin, and I realised that Dempsey would be better off financially if Jim "happened" to lose to Ross.

When McLarnin and his handlers arrived at ringside and saw Dempsey, as well as Ross, waiting for them in that ring, Foster grabbed Jim. "The fight's off!" shouted Pop and began to drag McLarnin from the ring. The first row of spectators sat with their mouths open, listening to Pop.

"We can't do this, Pop," shouted Jim. "Look at all these people! We can't back out now!" What a spectacle! Later, Jim realised what Pop did then, that Jim would have to knock out Ross if he hoped to win, and nobody had ever knocked out Barney Ross. So, against Pop's protests, McLarnin climbed into the ring to fight Barney and a stacked deck. As the crowd sat in bewilderment, Pop went shouting across at New York boxing commissioner, General Phelan, who was sitting at ringside to see that things went as they were supposed to.

"So the fix is in, is it, Phelan? " His angry complaints were heard by the front rows and partly reported in some newspapers, but in most there was deliberately nothing mentioned about all this embarrassment. Dempsey was not the only one who had come to realise that nobody would be much hurt and many would benefit if McLarnin lost the fight. A number of newspaper columnists had also suddenly been converted to this opinion. It had been seen that Dempsey had spent time at Ross's camp, and Pop then shouted to another official, Phil Brown, "You promised not to have Dempsey."

Phelan knew enough to say nothing, but he got very red in the face. He was famous for getting flustered and giving the wrong answer. When accused by a manager of dishonesty, Phelan had shouted, "There's no man in this state that can stand up and accuse me of honesty." He had once said to Joe Louis's trainer, Jack Blackburn, who had been talking while Phelan was explaining something. "A little less quiet, please, Mr. Blackbird." Phelan had just hit a new high before this fight. Ross's managers had accused McLarnin of using the rabbit punch, although Barney had protested that Jim was a very clean fighter. Phelan had illustrated a rabbit punch and dropped himself, nearly knocking himself out.

So Jim went to his corner in an unsettled mood, and Pop shrugged his shoulders in impotent rage under his old grey torn sweater that he wore to all fights. At least some fans at ringside had heard some very peculiar exchanges. The rest sat in expectation. "Those two fighters were closer than Gable and Lombard," wrote one columnist.

This fight told the story of the boxing politics that was hidden below the glittering surface of boxing's golden age. Foster was bitter, but he knew that he and Jim had been handsomely paid. Their lives would not be affected much by this treachery. They had been given good innings. But Pop knew that when you look back on your life, it is not the money you made, but the accomplishments that count.

So the big fight began. I think Jim later wished that he had let Pop drag him from that ring, but Jim generally liked to please people, and so didn't want to disappoint all his fans. Charlie Foster didn't give a damn what people thought, as long as his conscience was clear. The problem was between him and his God, and nobody else.

As expected, McLarnin was slow getting started after his long lay off. Jim said he felt tight and nervous. If you aren't of a naturally aggressive nature, you have a curious reluctance to strike another human being until he hits you. "I was tight until somebody got hit, especially after a lay off, even though I grew up fighting on the streets as a boy." Then fear falls from you, and you become liberated from self-concern. Violence is as liberating as a drug or a spiritual vision. Ross came out quickly, jabbing effectively, covering his chin with his right hand. He knew the force of Jim's blows and he took all precautions. In the first three rounds, Ross out-jabbed Jim at a distance and out punched him in close. Barney "herded" and rushed and threw punches, none of which hurt Jim, but counted with judges who were looking for points for Ross. When Jim did connect, it was much harder, and in the 3rd, he bloodied Ross's nose. By the 4th, Jim had warmed up and shed the rust. He caught Barney with a fine left hook that jarred Ross and put him on the defensive. In the 5th, Ross came out with a flurry, but Jim caught him with a hard left jab on the jaw, stopping his forward motion and his attempt to herd and win points for aggressiveness. This hard left broke the rhythm of Ross's flurries, and when Barney threw a right, Jim threw one harder, and surprisingly faster. This fight was the only time in Ross's career that he was often beaten to a punch. A few years later, Ross conquered middleweight champ Ceferino Garcia, beating him to almost every punch. In the sixth, seventh and eighth rounds, Ross continued his flurries, but his forward motion had been stopped and he had lost the initiative. In round nine, Ross began to look leery of the right that Jim had been hitting him with, and so Jim faked it and hit him with a left hook. Feinting is almost a lost art. In the tenth, all commentators agreed that Jim had outfought Ross at every turn. Indeed, it was after this round that it was seen that there was a flurry of men close to the ring moving around. These were the pro gamblers, who had odds on Ross, who were now trying to hedge their bets and change their odds to favour McLarnin, if possible. In these two rounds, McLarnin showed a mastery that neither had shown in all the 45 rounds that they fought. They were the only part of this series where one boxer seemed to have mastered the other. By the eleventh, Barney must have known that he was losing. He was badly bruised and cut by this time. After the fight, Ross said that this was the toughest of all his fights and that Jim was "hell out there". So Barney came out punching, but Jim slipped most of them, for Barney was slowing.

I have the opening round of this fight on a tape called "Greatest Champions", hosted by a group of boxing writers. It shows Ross and McLarnin feinting and slipping punches as they test each other. It is a lesson in the art of boxing. The Benitez/Leonard is the only thing I have seen close to it since. I doubt that Joe Gans could have done better. Indeed, Jim was hardly hit hard once in this fight, for his defensive skills were at their peak. In the eleventh, Jim followed three left hooks with an uppercut as Ross attempted to duck the expected fourth hook. The uppercut snapped Ross's head back. Then Jim cut Ross's left eye with a hook followed by a right cross. Barney continued to throw punches whether they landed or not, which sympathetic judges can score for aggressiveness, and which look good to the back rows. Those in the front rows knew what was going on. Ross did catch Jim in the twelfth with a hard left to the body. Jim continued, nevertheless, to slip most of Ross's punches and counter solidly, better than in any of the previous fights. These punches, which Jim threw just as Ross was about to throw his, and which hit harder than Ross's, were the perfect answer to the speed and durability of Ross. In the twelfth, Jim caught Barney with a hard left hook that made Barney blink. Jim then chased Ross to the ropes, punching with both hands. Ross fought back but got the worst of it. Ross, in desperation to hit Jim solidly, hooked several punches which landed very low, but referee Dempsey refused to take points from Ross as they had been taken from Jim in similar circumstances in the first fight. Mind you, Dempsey had thrown a few low ones in his time. Jim bobbed inside and drove both hands to the body. The fight was building to a terrific finish, worthy of the long rivalry of these two great champions. In the twelfth and thirteenth, they stood toe to toe and punched, ignoring defence for the first time. The crowd of 40,000 fans came to its feet cheering, with most standing, clapping and shouting, to give a standing ovation for this magnificent exhibition of skill, power, and courage. Those close to the ring could see the power of Jim's blows compared to those of Ross. These two rounds were equal in the number of blows, as Jim and Barney punched and feinted and slugged, but by the end of these rounds, the power in Jim's body blows began to drain all the strength from Ross. McLarnin came out for the fifteenth round and you can seen in the video that Ross throws his arms to simulate punching, but there is no power or even direction left in his punches. At times, Ross simply leans on McLarnin and swings his arms. Jim is dead tired, but still punching. When Jim connects, Ross falls forward and hangs on to Jim, in order to avoid going down. Jim is too tired to get out of the way. Ross will not allow himself to drop because he knows that if he does, he will not be able to get up. It is a remarkable round to see. The courage and determination of these two boys is amazing. Early in the round, McLarnin catches Ross with a hard right to the head, followed by a left hook that snaps Barney's head back. Ross is not even replying to most of Jim's punches, but he is rolling with the punches to take some of the force out of them. This becomes second nature with better pro fighters, so they will do it by instinct when they are nearly unconscious. Indeed, that is when they need it most. Barney's heart was all that was holding him up. He would not go down. McLarnin poured it on as Jim's supporters were on their feet shouting. "Take him out, Jim!" The whole crowd was again on its feet as McLarnin punched and Ross hung on. Suddenly, the bell rang, and the two fighters threw their arms around each other, and congratulated each other on one of the greatest fights of all time. Then Ross turned and shuffled to his corner. McLarnin leaped into the air, grinning from ear to ear and did his famous victory somersault Jim had some energy left. He had been superbly conditioned and had not taken the heavy body punches that Ross had. After watching the movie, there is no doubt in the viewer's mind that in the next two rounds, Ross could have been counted out. But Ross had done what had been asked of him. He had finished on his feet. The dark lords of boxing remembered that with gratitude and Barney has always received his due. It had been a gallant stand. The crowd stood cheering, minutes after the bell had rung – a standing ovation. At his ringside seat, intelligent, analytic, ex-heavyweight champ Gene Tunney turned to his companion and said, "Well, McLarnin 12 rounds to 3. No doubt this time!" But Gene was in for a surprise.

I mentioned this to McLarnin and Jim said, "Well, he wasn't as surprised as I was!"

Harry Ballough, the famous announcer, who was substituting for the even more famous Joe Humphries, collected the ballots. There was an unusual number of substitutions that night. "Judge Abe Goldstein scores it 8 rounds for Ross, 6 rounds for McLarnin, and one even. Judge George Lecron scores it 9 rounds for Ross, 5 rounds for McLarnin, one even. Referee Jack Dempsey scores it 6 rounds for Ross, 4 rounds for McLarnin, and 5 even. The winner by unanimous decision and new champion, Barney Ross.

There was a moment of dead silence over the whole arena. Then there was a roar of disapproval. All papers reported that, but most claimed that it was not the whole crowd, just the Irish, but there were no cheers reported. As the booing continued, Tunney was heard to say, "Five even? Unprecedented. What is Jack thinking about?"

The papers the next day were overwhelmingly in support of McLarnin. Columnist Hal Straight, implied that the fight had been fixed for Ross to win. He didn't say much more, we assume because he felt it might not be good for his health. Bill Corum wrote, "McLarnin is about to be married. He may get better decisions around home than he got last night. From where I sat, he retained his championship with a bit to spare." It was unfortunate that as brave and great a battler as Ross had to get back his title to a chorus of boos. Jimmy accepted the decision with a wry face and good grace. He went over and congratulated Barney.

Not so Pop Foster! He complained loudly that Jim had been robbed. "Jim won this by a larger margin than he did the last," claimed the white haired old Pop.

The reporter of the New York Times, James Dawson, couldn't bring himself to feel sorry for Jim. "Jimmy is wealthy. He is unscarred after thirteen years of warfare through five divisions."

Pop suggested that they would retire. McLarnin, himself, thinks he won the last two fights and deserved no less than a draw in the first, for you never take a champion's title on harmless fouls. He still says Ross was a hell of a fighter who knew his trade. Ross was asked if he thought McLarnin should retire. Ross, by the way, loved to fight, unlike McLarnin. "Jim? Retire? Why should he? He should just fight more often, not retire, that's all. He's only 28. He was hell out there tonight! Look at my face. Does it look as if I had an easy fight? He's got years left. Where were you guys?"

Ross knew what was going on. But conflicting reports appeared in the papers the next day. The older and more established writers reported that McLarnin had won decisively, and questioned Dempsey's scoring of five rounds even. Make up your mind, Jack.

Most papers began by reporting the booing and unpopularity of the decision. But James Dawson, at the New York Times, stated that McLarnin was "masterful", then went on to say that Ross had won easily, although he was exhausted at the end and badly battered. Extraordinary! Dawson stated that there was no point in McLarnin fighting Ross again, as he would simply be beaten more decisively the next time. I think the dark lords had decided that Jim had come far too close to knocking Ross out to allow him to try again, until he really got older and battered from other fights. Money, but no chance at the title. Dawson then refers to Foster as a "bitter, crippled, half-blind old man," a figure of fun whom nobody should listen to. Although he was declared the winner, Ross won, at most, three rounds. He led early. He hit Jim with a smashing right cross on the chin, his Sunday punch. In the sixth, Jim shook his head and won the seventh, eighth, and ninth, Ross retreating, and McLarnin in control. Gallico states Dempsey ignored Ross's very low blow in the twelfth. He quoted Tunney saying McLarnin won 12 rounds. Jim was positive he won nine rounds, at least. All ring historians call the fights controversial. Ross gave McLarnin more trouble than anyone since Taylor, when Jim was a teen ager in California, but I believe a close reading of the reports shows McLarnin pulling away from Ross as the series progressed, and by the end of the third fight, Jim had established superiority. I think Ross recognised that.

I have checked into the record of Mr. James P. Dawson, the scribe who was so strong for Ross, after the third fight. Time and again, Dawson will write for the fighter who is the darling of the boxing establishment. It could be a coincidence, but I doubt it. The most notorious example of this was the time Irish Billy Graham of New York overwhelmingly defeated Cuban Kid Gavilan for the welterweight title. Graham was intelligent and independent, and Gavilan was illiterate, but flashy. He had a bolo punch that the crowd loved, but every decent boxer could see coming a week before it landed. Give the promoters an illiterate from a minority group every time. Dawson was the only writer in America to say that Gavilan had won. Ring historians consider this the worst decision in modern times.

Jim wanted to fight Ross again. Pop thought Jim, with more work, might K.O. Ross, since he had come so close. However, when the time came and after Jim's win over Canzoneri and Ambers, and everyone calling for the fight, Pop still couldn't get reasonable financial split out of Pian and Winch.

"We don't have to fight for peanuts," Foster said to Jim. "We're rich. Let's go home." Foster persuaded Jim to retire – some manager.

Some evenings, if Jimmy had had a good shot of vodka and orange, he would tell you, "They stole my championship. Oh, I've got no complaints. I've had it all. Jesus loves me. But they really did steal it." And looked a bit wistful.

Jimmy and Des

Des, Beverley Scott, Bob Scott, Jimmy McLarnin, Billy Varga

Chapter 29
McLarnin and his Thoughts
after the Ross Fights

Top fighters and money winners like McLarnin are still robbed of obvious wins when it suits the dark lords. "Golden Boy" Oscar De La Hoya, top fighter and money winner, later easily beat Shane Mosely for the Junior Middleweight title. After the fight, commentator ex-heavyweight champ, George Foreman, stated Oscar had been masterful and overwhelmed Mosely, but Foreman had forgotten that De La Hoya was a rich, independent and popular white and Mosely was a "controllable" black. The decision and title went to Mosely, and, off camera, an official spoke to Foreman, who then stated that the decision was the correct one. George liked his job.

McLarnin did not retire after his loss to Ross. He beat two more world champions, triple champion and Hall of Famer Tony Canzoneri, and cagy, difficult Lou Ambers, who had just beaten the unbeatable Henry Armstrong, who was about to nearly kill Barney Ross and take his title. Suffice it to say that Jimmy McLarnin went out a winner, not a loser as most old champs do. He went out in the top of his form. In his last fight, he never looked better. Of course, the promoters and the public wanted him to fight Ross again after that wonderful and controversial third match. McLarnin was still a bigger draw than Ross. Foster talked to Ross's managers and the promoters when they contacted him about another match. "But they wanted all the money," said Jim disgustedly, so Ross fought Izzy Janazzio in the Garden and didn't draw flies. The public wanted to see Jim and Ross again as they wanted Zale and Graziano, and Ali and Frazier. "What the heck, Jim," said Pop, "we're rich. You don't have to fight for peanuts. We can't get a square deal anymore. There's lots to do in California."

With hundreds of thousands of dollars to be made, Foster persuaded his fighter to retire. What a manager! Pop put half a million in the bank for Jim and took the remaining money, paid off their trainers and sparring partners liberally, covered all their expenses, and had a quarter million for himself, with few taxes to be paid. They went home to California and Vancouver, and they never really had to work again. Jim had no scars, no cauliflower ears, all his teeth, a straight nose, all his brains, a beautiful new wife, and soon a family of three girls and a boy, living in a big Spanish style home in Glendale, outside L.A. He had a membership in the Lakeside Golf and Country Club and a great group of friends among the newspaper, athletic and movie stars of L.A. They lived happily ever after. Can you believe it? I told you it could have come from an old storybook. "Jesus loves me. I've had it all." That is not your usual pro boxer's ending. He had realised all his dreams.

80 fights and no broken nose

But I think it burned Pop that his boy did not have the title that he deserved, although he knew it was the best way to go. I doubt that it bothered Jim that much, at the time. "Never got to hang out with my pals. I hardly had a boyhood." Now, he could spend some time with his friends. But he wished he had had another crack at Ross. "I nearly knocked him out at the end of that last fight, you know. Taking nothing away from Barney. He's no ham and egger. He's in the Boxing Hall of Fame. Pop shouldn't have told them we were going to quit. Maybe he thought it would make them offer us more money to fight if they thought we would quit, but it didn't work out that way. They wanted to get rid of us.

Another thing, it's nice not to have to get up in the morning at five and go out and run five miles, work on the bag, spar, and be bored around camp for six weeks every three months or so; that's what staying on top of it is. I had enough of that when I was 28. I'd been at it since I was sixteen."

"Jim, how do you become a champion in a sport as tough and competitive as pro boxing?"

"You've got to train, and live clean. You've got to think of nothing but the championship. Tunney used to chant quietly to himself as he did road work, 'Dempsey, Dempsey, Dempsey'. You've got to have a good manager."

"Yes, Jim, and it must help to be lucky and not get hurt."

"Well, you make most of your own luck," said Jim, and if you learn defence well, you aren't likely to get badly hurt, even in pro boxing."

I suspect much of this was drummed into young Jim by Pop, when he was raising Jim through his teens to manhood. If you box professionally, you will sometimes be badly hurt, but if you are well- trained, really conditioned, and not over-matched early, you shouldn't get permanently damaged. "Sure," said Jim, "you meet the most peculiar people in the ring. You can tell they are put off that they haven't killed you. But I will say this. They come out of pretty tough situations socially and I've never met a boxer that I didn't like, after the fight."

It's the business of a referee and your manager to protect you. Mind you, funny things can happen in there.

"People have told me that Pop always matched you well."

"Yes, he did, but I had to carry through. Everybody thought I had been overmatched with Pancho Villa, the great little fighter who had just beaten the Jimmy Wilde, the greatest flyweight of all time. I was just a kid and he was world champ."

"Pop saw you had a couple of pounds on him."

"I needed them. He was tough inside. I was taller and I had the reach on him. I'd jab and move immediately. Then there was my fight with featherweight champ, Louis 'Kid' Kaplan. Even Pop thought I was overmatched but we needed the fight. We had to eat. We had driven by car from Los Angeles to Chicago – a job in those days, with no major highways, because I was frozen out in Los Angeles. Pop wouldn't pay off anybody. On top of that, I was growing and had jaundice a while. I lost fights to guys who couldn't carry my duffel bag. That year, it looked as if I was running out of gas, and some scribes in L.A. wrote it up that way. 'Is McLarnin finished?' Well, I was finished in L. A. for a while. So we piled our stuff into a car Pop bought, drove to Chicago, and signed to meet the featherweight champ, Kaplan. He'd just won the championship and he was tough. He thought he had an easy non-title bout against a guy who had shot his bolt. Well, it may have been the best fight I ever fought. I was down, and then he was down and finally I knocked him out, and every promoter in the East wanted me, but I didn't get his championship because we had agreed that I would come in just over the featherweight limit to get that fight. You know, I wish I could have fought Bud Taylor later. He beat me, and then I beat him. Then I beat him on a foul. He was a tough guy for a kid to fight. He's a Hall of Famer now. Even when you beat Taylor, you felt physically as if you had been clubbed all over. He worked you over and he'd do anything to win. I wish I could have fought him when I was twenty-five. He was tough, nasty, and good and he was then 25 and I was 18. A boxer needs some tough fights, but not too many and not in a row. Some fighters were never the same after a tough fight with Rocky Marciano, another punisher like Taylor. Archie Moore was never quite the same after that great fight he put up against Rocky. That's why Patterson took Archie out when they fought after Rocky's retirement. I see Archie around Los Angeles every now and again – a great guy. Maybe the greatest light-heavyweight. Marciano and Taylor didn't just beat you; they beat you up. Dempsey and Louis might take you out quicker, or Tunney or Ali might make you look worse, but nobody lumped you like Rocky. He hit you with his fist, followed by his forearm and elbow, followed by his head, at times unconsciously, in his relentless attack, and then hit you on the way down. Dempsey was like that, too. They weren't dirty, just wound up with destruction. Now Fritzie Zivic and Tony Galento could be dirty – thumb in the eye stuff. Zivic was a cold killer, but Dempsey and Marciano were in a rapture of destruction.

With Brouillard, in the rain, 'Adversity went against me,' as Yogi Berra used to say. He was a puncher and you box a puncher and punch a boxer."

"So, Pop really never overmatched you."

"Right, that's another reason why you need a good, smart, honest manager. Nobody should box unless they are well managed. Pop took 50 %, but he was worth it. Usually a manager takes 33 %. Anyway, he left it all to me and my family when he died, and it felt great to be a champ."

"Jim, once you have been champ, it's like being President, you're always the champ."

Jim grinned and said, "Right, champ. But how do you get to be champ?"

Jim often said this, in an odd way, and it seems to mystify him, as he feels there is nothing exceptional about him.

"Well, Jim, you were born around Belfast, a tough industrial town, and raised in tough East Vancouver."

"Yes," said Jim, "that's where boxers are raised, or in Hell's Kitchen or the Bronx."

"Champion of the world! It's a great feeling just to say you're better than anyone your size in the world at something difficult and daring."

"Yes," said Jim, "I could once go fifteen with the best in the world from flyweight to middleweight."

"McLarnin, you may be the only man who could ever say just that. Lord, I couldn't go fifteen rounds. How did you do it, Jim?"

"Well, you learn to pace yourself." said Jim, modestly.

PART V
Jimmy's Last Fight, Marriage, Family, And Business

Chapter 30
The Indian Summer of
McLarnin's Boxing: Epilogue

A: Jimmy gets Married.

Everything, except close decisions, went Jimmy's way now. He beamed when he talked about those golden days of the summer of his career. "I was called by M.G.M. to come in and talk about making a movie. Well, I lived just down the road from Hollywood and kept bumping into actors and execs from the studio and a lot came to my fights. I had lots of friends there. It was to be a Louis B. Mayer picture. I was asked to drop in on Mervin LeRoy. I went to his office and had a nice talk with him, but after I talked about it and thought about it, I told him that I thought that I had better stick to the profession I knew best, where I knew what I was doing. 'Well, if that's what you want, Jim,' Mervin said, 'and we'll talk about doing a movie on you and your career anytime.' Mervin was a nice fellow. I did take a small part in a movie, *The Big City*. I had a speaking part. I said, I think, 'They went that way', or words to that effect. I got paid more than others except the stars. I saw it in the theatre and heard some guy say at my scene, say, 'Isn't that Jimmy McLarnin?' They used to know me around this town. Well, it was much smaller in those days." I've seen Jim in that film. He did well.

Now to the real life romance. On July 11, 1935, there appeared on the front page of The Province, a picture, with the headline, "Jimmy McLarnin Weds". There is Jimmy, dressed in a tuxedo, beside his manager, Charles Foster. In front of them is his lovely bride, Lillian Cupit, in her wedding dress, and beside her, her bridesmaid, Miss Davies. Pop is husky, and several inches taller than Jim. Neither man looks like a fighter, although Pop looks solid and Jim fills his tuxedo with muscle. Lillian looks radiant. Pop, the best man, has the broadest smile. It is a lovely picture. The Province had a very smart article about it. "James J. McLarnin, twice world welterweight champion, has answered many bells in his twelve years of professional boxing, but he answered the most important bell of his life on Thursday night, his wedding bell." Well said, scribes!

"Mr. and Mrs. McLarnin left after the ceremony. Jimmy admitted plans might include several more fights. They will make their home in California."

The McLarnin Wedding

Pictures of Jim and Lillian sailing for Hawaii were carried by papers around the world with the headline, "Goodbye, America. Goodbye, Barney". My copy comes from the Oregon Daily Journal, Portland. How the stature of boxing has changed! When the welterweight champ got married, that was big news across the country. Underneath the picture, it said that McLarnin hopes the farewell to Ross is temporary, as he wants to fight for the championship again. Jimmy and his bride are pictured starting for Honolulu from Vancouver, B.C. Jimmy is wearing a sporty white suit with tie and dark shirt, and Lillian is wearing a suit with gloves and a little hat on the side of her head. They both are all smiles. Jimmy is waving.

"It was a lovely trip, and we had a great time in Hawaii," said Jim, smiling, and then started to laugh, "I've got to tell you. Pop found that we were booked at the Royal Hawaiian Hotel – classy, expensive. He decided that we would get better value at the second best hotel, so he telegrammed and cancelled our reservations. He wasn't going to have me throwing my money around just because I was on my honeymoon. Oh, he loved Lil. He thought my marrying a hometown girl was just what a man should do. He had been sending girls away who had come to my camp to see me.

I put my new car on the boat and drove it off in Honolulu with Lil, and we drove up to the Royal Hawaiian, to find that Pop had changed our reservations." Then Jim laughed and punched Billy Varga, who had been sitting in Jim's front room chuckling, even though he had heard the story many times before. I suspect that it is famous in the McLarnin family, so typical of Pop. It must have been embarrassing for young Jim, who wanted to show his bride the very best.

It was all so long ago, when I was five, and my dad was 45, Jimmy was 27 and sailed with his sweet Lillian to Hawaii. The world was golden for us all.

In the Society Section of *The Province*, that July 11, 1935, there was the usual type of write up on the Cupit-McLarnin wedding. "Lovely Wedding unites Popular Couple". The bride wore imported silk net and satin wedding gown. Attendant in yellow chiffon. At the home of the McLarnins, 1466 William Street, Mr and Mrs. Cupit's only daughter Lillian was united in holy matrimony with the well-known Mr. James McLarnin by the Rev. W. A. Galloway. The wedding took place under a decorated arch in the garden. The couple stood under a white wedding bell. Wedding music was by Mr. Ernest Cupit. The bride looked lovely in a gown fashioned on princess lines. "She looked like a princess, too," said Jim huskily as I read it to him after those 40 years. It continues, "fullness falling into a graceful train. Veil hand embroidered, tulle cap trimmed with seed pearls held in place by orange blossoms. Shower bouquet of Ophelia roses and white sweet peas." As usual, the groom seems something of a footnote, and this is one time that Jimmy McLarnin did not take top billing on the card. "Groom attended by Mr. Charles Foster, his manager in his professional work". At no time in this write up was it mentioned that the groom, Mr. James McLarnin, made his money by beating the hell out of the toughest men in the world. This reticence seems amusing. "Miss Florence Fleming sang 'Because'. Couple received guests at a buffet supper. The three tiered wedding cake was embedded in pink tulle. Miss Florence Davies and Miss Althea McLellan presided at the urn. For travelling, the bride wore a beige crepe dress with hat and accessories to match, and a brown squirrel coat, a gift of the groom. They will travel to Honolulu via Seattle and San Francisco."

Jimmy, as he sailed on the Pacific, was a different man from the 95 pound seasick boy who had gone down that way when he and Pop set out to prove that 16-year-old Jimmy could lick any hardened professional in the world. Jimmy's glasses were misted up after my going over the wedding with him, but he reflected on that trip. "It's all magic," he said. "Jesus loves me." It would seem that way, Jim, it really would!

By an odd coincidence, I came across Jimmy's wedding certificate. A tennis friend of mine, Dr. Don McKinnon, who worked for the Surrey School board, had an uncle who had been the minister at Lillian and Jimmy's wedding. Don dug out an old book and gave me the document. It said that a wedding in that day might cost you $20. James Joseph McLarnin, 1466 William St., age 27, United Church, Methodist, occupation athlete (not the deadliest puncher in pro boxing – although the whole town was bursting with pride, and the newspapers plastered it all over the front page). Born Belfast, Ireland; father Samuel McLarnin, born Ireland; mother Mary Ferris; born Ireland. Lillian Grace Cupit, 1606 McLean Drive, born Vancouver, age 21, occupation teacher, father Henry Herbert Cupit, born Liverpool, England, (same as Pop Foster), mother Grace Renowden, born St.Ives, Cornwall, England. Witnesses Florence H. Davies, 1841 Commercial Drive, and Charles Foster, "Pop" written in, Los Angeles, California, for Pop was a citizen of the world, as many Britishers were in those days.

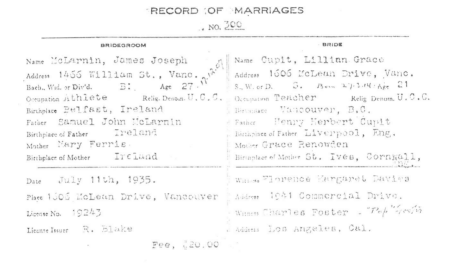

Record of Marriage

B: The Canzoneri Fights

"They were the Glory of their Days"
Ecclesiasticus.

So Jim took another year off boxing, to be with his bride. I broached the subject of their relationship, but Jim looked at me as he would if he had signed to meet me for fifteen rounds. I dropped the matter.

Jimmy insisted on returning to the ring. He was at an age when, in spite of what most sports writers say, athletes and boxers are usually at their best, late twenties and early thirties, and it has always been said that Irish fighters mature late. In his early thirties, Jim was losing his desire. Pop could see that. Jim retired near his peak, in his late twenties, before his best years. He had started boxing young. Now, he asked Pop to get him a good fight; maybe he wanted to show his new bride how good he was – she had never seen him fight.

Pop made an extraordinary match for a boxer on the comeback trail after a lay-off. He matched Jim with the most outstanding fighter of his time, outside of McLarnin – triple champion, Italian American Tony Canzoneri. Canzoneri was lightweight, featherweight, and junior welterweight champ. He had been beaten twice by Barney Ross, but the second was questionable. He was known affectionately as "The Little Paisan", and was a very popular fighter. He liked to trade punches. He could knock out any unwary boxer with a single punch. He fought a career studded with K.O.s. He became lightweight champ by K.O.ing Al Singer in 66 seconds.

When Jim was making his fortune, the world was plunged in the Great Depression. Every town in North America was full of fight clubs, in which hungry young men boxed for money. Each section of town would have its club. Competent, but not superior fighters were known as "good club fighters", and added an extra hundred dollars or so to their wages. Once a week, the local club needed six to ten pro fighters. Most men in those days had fought not only on the streets as kids, but also sparred in gyms as teenagers. Sometimes at the local boxing club one of the fighters would not show up. There would be an appeal for substitutes. Boxers at McLarnin's level became very good through this training ground. Around these clubs were also the great teachers of boxing, intelligent men who had been fighters, but who had been slightly short on ability or luck, and so burned with the joy of passing on their knowledge.

Any art form grows, matures, decays, and perhaps is reborn if conditions are right. The English drama has always been of a high order, and is still, but its great years were a mere twenty, between 1590 and 1610, when not only Shakespeare, but Marlowe and Jonson and many others wrote. The competition in those small but crowded theatres was intense. Boxing, I believe, was at its peak just before, during, and immediately after McLarnin's time. There are sociological reasons for this, and also the law of the survival of the fittest. It began on the streets in childhood. You can take a fine athlete and make him a good, competent boxer, but not a great fighter. Great boxers have to begin as "junk yard dogs" fighting in the streets for survival, and then small clubs for a few dollars for food money. Of course, they have to be natural athletes as well. Then they must meet a great teacher. McLarnin and Canzoneri both had that. When Canzoneri fought McLarnin, Tony was lightweight and junior welterweight champion, and one of the greatest of all time. When Barney Ross moved up to the welterweight division, Canzoneri fought the leading contender, Lou Ambers, another Italian American, and Tony won back his title. He was at the top of his form when he fought McLarnin. Pop tried again before the fight to persuade Jim to retire. Pop knew that Jim was no longer a hungry fighter, completely focused on winning fights. He had other things on his mind. But Jim wanted to continue. He felt that with every bout, his timing would improve and that he would eventually win back his crown. Why did Jim want to continue fighting? People who had seen Jim fight Ray Millar or Billy Petrolle in his two revenge fights could understand. McLarnin just could not accept being beaten by any fighter. He could not accept that decision of Dempsey's in the third Ross fight as being the last word in his fighting career. I say he was crazy to start boxing again, and I say he was right. The great French philosopher and scientist Blaise Pascal said that the heart has reasons that the mind cannot understand, and the peculiar thing is that the heart is often right. Jim had three bouts after he lost his title and they covered him with fistic glory. I wouldn't have wanted to end Jim's book on the sour note of that bad decision by a man that Jim idolized. That kind of bitter irony would make the biography modern.

The first McLarnin/Canzoneri fight was spectacular. Jim had few weaknesses as a boxer, and his jaw was not one of them. You could break your hands on McLarnin's jaw. However, a blow to the temple could sometimes stun him. The papers expected a great fight and they got it. But it was not as expected. It was the largest crowd to squeeze into Madison Square Garden in five years. The papers said it would be the most spectacular duel of small fighters in years. Not only were they both accepted masters of the boxing trade, but they were both knock-out punchers with dynamite in both hands. The bout drew over 16,000 fans.

As the fight started, Canzoneri looked nervous in his corner, while McLarnin looked relaxed. That was taken as a good sign for McLarnin. But it is not always a good sign to be relaxed in boxing. Jim's new bride, Lillian, waited, excited, at ringside. When the bell rang, Tony came out fast, but Jim met him with hard left jabs. Jim had come a long way from the right-hand puncher from Vancouver. "I developed a heavy left jab," Jim told me. "I could drop men with it. I would sometimes drop a heavyweight in training camp, just fooling around." Jim's jab improved over his entire career. In the movies of the third Ross fight, it is much better, for example, than it is in the Leonard fight. By this time it was awesome, and he gave Canzoneri a beating with it in round one. After a minute and a half, Canzoneri looked as if he were about to be knocked out, for he could not stop McLarnin's rapier of a jab. Gamblers noted this at ringside and odds began to change dramatically. It looked as if McLarnin would win in a breeze. Early in the round, Jim hit Tony with a dynamite left followed by a hard right, the old one two. The one is the set up and the two is the killer. Canzoneri staggered against the ropes as McLarnin drove him before him, using his powerful left and his six pound weight advantage. The bell was the only thing that saved Tony at the end of the round. The crowd buzzed at the ease with which McLarnin was handling the redoubtable Canzoneri. He almost had him out in round one, and not from one lucky punch, but simply because Tony did not seem to be able to stop the speed and power of McLarnin's left. Jim came out in round two, full of justifiable confidence. As they squared off, Canzoneri, suddenly and unexpectedly, caught McLarnin with a hard right, high on the side of Jim's head, on the temple. Jim dropped to one knee, but was up before a count. It was an odd punch that had come in high and overhand. Jim should have been able to move his head and slip the punch. Either Jim's confidence or his year's lay off kept him still. Jim boxed out the round, but he was in worse shape than anyone realised. His brain was dulled by the blow to the temple; and he was slowed for the rest of the fight. In round three, Tony made Jim miss three of the straight lefts that had been so deadly in round one. This time Tony blocked Jim's left, and rocked McLarnin with both hands to the jaw in succession. He moved Jim around with masterful footwork. In round four, however, Tony stood stock still and began to punch flat-footed. It was a mistake, for Jim's head had cleared somewhat, and Jim put enough lefts together, three hard ones in a row, although he missed a hard right, to win the round. It looked as though Jim might regain the initiative. Indeed, this may have been one of those rounds that persuaded Lillian that Jim was winning. "Yes," Jim said, smiling his ironic grin, "Lillian was the only one in the house who was convinced that Baby Face won. It was wonderful of her. But love is blind. The truth is that Canzoneri beat the hell out of me. Oh, I was a smart fellow. I invited my bride to see a fellow beat the living daylights out of me." In round five, Tony's hard left drew blood from Jim's nose. Tony had Jim backing up with half a dozen punches to the head. Canzoneri was continually beating Jim to the punch, something that Jim was supposed to be the master of. In the sixth, Canzoneri shifted his attack to the body, a wise move early in the fight, and when McLarnin came in, Tony stopped him with hard lefts to the body. In the 8th round, Jim's good lefts drove Tony back onto the ropes, and bloodied Tony's nose. "Yeah, it was a tough fight all around," Jim said as we read the old newspaper blow-by-blow of the fight. Jim won the round but it was the last round that he won, for that early punch to the temple began to catch up to him. In the 9th round, Canzoneri, despite pleadings in his corner, came out to punch with McLarnin, the heaviest hitter under the middleweight division in all boxing. I think Tony could tell that Jim was fading. You can tell things in a ring that can't be seen even from ringside. From the centre of a rugby scrum you can tell many things about the opposing scrum that can't be seen even by the sharpest observer on the touchline. You just feel it.

Tony rolled with Jim's heaviest punches, for Jim was not quite as fast as usual. Jim's timing was off, and this also made it easier for a fine boxer like Tony to do this. Then he punched back, staggering McLarnin. By the end of the round, Jim was groggy and almost helpless from punches to the head, with the ropes holding him up. Before the 10th round, Jim's handlers worked furiously to bring him around. Jim came out slowly and Tony met him and almost dropped him with lefts and rights to the head. Jim tried to reply with a hard right but missed and nearly fell. Tony attacked and Jim clinched and held on. He tried to counter but his punches were feeble. The bell sounded the end of the fight and Jim turned wearily to his corner. There was no victory somersault. He knew that he had been badly beaten. So did Pop. Lil was the only one who thought Jim won. There were no complaints. Jim gave Tony all the credit. "He's a great fighter, that Tony," said Jim, even as his handlers worked on his swollen jaw. "I guess I should quit." Jim was asked about his bad timing and ring rustiness. "This fighting once a year is no good," Jim replied. Yes, the fact was that Jim should either fight several fights a year as he used to, and as Barney Ross and Tony Canzoneri did, or else retire.

Pop thought he should retire. "I won't let him fight again," said Pop. "Jimmy's been fighting steady for 13 years. He's pretty well-heeled. He's married now. I am going to persuade him to quit for good this time." But even Pop did not know Jimmy's heart, the Irish Protestant's, "No Surrender". Jimmy wasn't going to quit no matter how much money he had, because pride and self-worth are more important than money. He was going to come back and beat Canzoneri and then beat Ross because he knew he could and should. He was going to fight Canzoneri again as soon as possible and he was going to whip him. That is the way McLarnin's mind worked, and that is what he did. "I was almost sorry for Tony," said Jim to me.

The media boys thought they had seen the last of McLarnin after that beating. Even the hometown paper, The Province, had an outline of Jimmy laid on the ground with "R.I.P. Jimmy" beside it. The write-up said, "McLarnin may end Ring career. Canzoneri hands Jimmy his worst defeat." They didn't understand McLarnin either, nor did they seem really to understand how he had been beaten. The papers suggested he fight Gordon Wallace, the Canadian welterweight champ. Fight him in Vancouver and let the hometown fans have a last look at their great hero before he retired, and make another nice little bundle of money for retirement. Besides, Jimmy had never tried for the Canadian title, for there was little money or prestige in it. Jim should have fought Wallace in Vancouver, but as a warm-up to the Canzoneri fight. Wallace did fight in Vancouver, but he was used as a warm-up for Ross's tough fights. Foster told the Vancouver press, "It has been Jim who has been eager to continue fighting." Everybody seemed to have ideas about what Jim should do, but Jim knew what he should do -- fight Canzoneri again. Pop wanted Jim to retire on his fortune. Vancouver wanted him to take a safe fight at home, and it is a pity that Vancouver never had a chance to see Jimmy after he had matured into a great fighter, but, as Jimmy said to me, "Their promoters offered me peanuts." They put 15,000 in the stands for a lacrosse game, and they should have been able to do the same with the famous McLarnin.

C: Jimmy wins the rematch again; this time it's Canzoneri.

A rematch was arranged for five months later in New York – just the right time to recover, yet not get rusty. As I read the papers of that summer, I was surprised at several things. Of course, the name Joe Louis caught my eye. The night McLarnin fought Canzoneri in the rematch, Joe Louis, the new sensational heavyweight contender, fought the tough contender for the heavyweight championship, Jorge Brescia, leading South American heavyweight. It was an eagerly anticipated match, for the winner would probably be fighting Jimmy Braddock for the heavyweight championship, but it was not as eagerly anticipated as the rematch between McLarnin and Canzoneri. So it was Jim and Tony who fought the final premier match of the night, as the headliners, and Louis and Brescia who fought the preliminary. After Joe won his match, his trainer Jack Blackburn brought him back to ringside to watch McLarnin's left, and learn.

Despite the hometown papers that had buried Jim's career, the betting favoured McLarnin. The wise boys of New York were right. McLarnin destroyed Canzoneri that night. The next morning the newspapers screamed, "Canzoneri Career Ended! McLarnin hammers Tony in Rematch, winning 9 out of ten rounds." One loses faith in sportswriters. Why should Tony's career be over? It was the first real beating he had ever taken. He was still in his twenties. He was outweighed by eight pounds that night and he had been beaten by the most feared puncher in boxing. McLarnin had figured Tony's style, but he was famous for doing just that. McLarnin's defeat of Canzoneri was complete, but Tony had many fights left in him as long as he stayed away from McLarnin.

It is said that after Jimmy won his championship, he lost his edge. That is mostly true. However, after he had lost to Canzoneri and Ross, two in a row, the only time in his career, and read about how he was finished at 27, he regained some of his old fire. Pop said Jim had a tendency to get complacent. Compared to Pop, that was certainly true. Pop was one who hoped for the best and prepared for the worst. Jim was more optimistic about life. He had come a long way. It took the sting of the double defeat to turn him back into something of the tiger he had been in his rise to the title. All of the newspaper reports said that Jim was in superb shape for the fight.

Perhaps this would be an appropriate time to give measurements, when he was at his peak. Even later in life, he maintained his physique with daily exercise and spare diet and, as he was in his boxing days, was never far out of shape. Here are the stats that came out when he was weighed in for the second Canzoneri fight. Jim weighed in at 146 pounds. He is listed at 5 foot 6 3/4 inches. His reach was 68 inches, which makes him long-armed for his weight and gave him a considerable reach advantage over other welterweights. His neck was 15 inches. His chest was 37 and 40 expanded. His thigh was 18, calf 14, ankle 8, forearms 12, biceps 14, waist 30, wrist 7, fist 11. He was wide of shoulder and long of arm, husky but slim of waist. He carried no weight in fat.

You may notice that he is small of hand and wrist. His small hands were broken at least five times because of his upper arm and shoulder strength. His secret was explosiveness, leverage and speed, plus timing and technique which Pop insisted he perfect. McLarnin was fast of hand and foot. No matter how powerful or tough a fighter is, he must be fast, at least of hand. Canadian heavyweight Willie de Witt, a silver medalist at the Olympics, had everything but hand speed, and couldn't last in the pros. Joe Louis, slow of foot, had great hand speed. McLarnin had never met a fighter whose hand and foot speed were faster than his, but Ross was as fast, and Canzoneri was close.

McLarnin was, however, the ultimate cerebral fighter. Like Gene Tunney or Ray Leonard, the movements of his last fight ran through his head like a movie. Jimmy and Pop planned in their training camp and chose their sparring partners who could fight somewhat like Canzoneri. So it was that on the night of October 8th in New York, McLarnin took Canzoneri to pieces as he never had been taken before or after. The papers shouted, "McLarnin, famous for his deadly right hand, did this one, with one of the most educated left hands of all time."

This was the way to handle Canzoneri, but the jabs had to be hard, for Tony kept coming. McLarnin's mastery in this fight was as great as Sugar Ray Leonard's in the second fight with Duran. The difference was that the great little Italian fighter fought by the code of pro boxers and he never stopped coming at McLarnin, no matter how badly he was hurt. There is a picture of Tony, with blood streaming down his face, moving towards McLarnin as Jim bunches the muscles of his back to hammer Tony as he comes in. Jim looked at it and said, "Poor Tony." You don't quit if you are a professional. It is madness, but it is superb. As the French observer said when he saw the suicidal charge of the English Light Brigade at Balaclava, "It is not war, but it is magnificent." It is the folly and the glory of man. The Old Guard was asked to surrender at the end of Waterloo when all was hopeless. Their commander, Cambronne replied, "Merde!" History books translate this as, "The Old Guard dies, but never surrenders." The Old Guard died. The term is immortalized now and one can avoid saying shit in French by saying, "the word of Cambronne."

The fight began as a slug fest. Both Tony and Jim came out fast in round one. McLarnin led with a heavy left jab and suddenly hooked a terrific left hook off that jab, which only a skilled boxer can do well, as the left foot positioning must be perfect, and balance and timing superb. The hook caught Tony on the eyebrow and split it wide open. Blood gushed down Tony's face. Tony fought nine more rounds half-blinded, and kept walking into McLarnin's heavy guns all the way. In that quintessential picture of professional fighting to which I referred earlier, there is pain and despair written on Tony's face as he moves in, but also determination, although he knew he could not but lose. Canzoneri, after that terrific blow, moved in and stood toe to toe with Jim while the two slugged, as the crowd of 12,000 rose to its feet and stood cheering. When the round ended, the crowd remained on its feet, clapping throughout the rest period. Tell me they make them like they used to. Round two began the same way, but suddenly, after the left jabs and hooks, McLarnin shifted his feet which moved him closer, and inside Tony's left as it came in, and caught Canzoneri on the chin with a terrific short right that travelled well under two feet. This is the most powerful type of punch a boxer can deliver. It is the way Marciano hit Walcott and knocked him out in round 13 of their first fight. That blow is probably the hardest punch struck by any human being, ever. From the force of that classic style punch of Jim's, down went Tony on the seat of his purple shorts, lifted right off his feet by that perfectly delivered classic blow. Tony knew what to do. He climbed back up and grabbed on to McLarnin, clinching until his head cleared, when they were separated by the ref. Back at each other they came, with Jim spearing Tony repeatedly with jolting lefts. McLarnin continued that pattern in round three. Jim's left jabs and hooks made Tony's head bob back repeatedly. At one point, Tony complained to the ref that Jim had back-handed him, an illegal move, but it was really a case of Tony being hit twice with the same hand at speed as one punches a light bag, and with the blood running down his face he couldn't see clearly. In his corner that round, he was told that he could not simply keep walking into McLarnin's punches or he might not be alive by round ten. Tony came out for round four with a changed style. He was on the move, on the balls of his feet, no longer standing flat-footed. He would punch and then immediately move left or right but not in any pattern.

Fans have seen an overgrown light-heavyweight, Michael Spinks, beat the heavy left-punching and well-conditioned heavyweight champ Larry Holmes doing just this. Spinks didn't do it very well. Indeed, he was slow and awkward at it and often simply bent sideways when he couldn't get his feet to work just right. Sports writers thought it was a new technique and couldn't understand it, but it completely stymied Holmes, who was used to big, slow heavyweights who could only move backwards or forwards, and not even backwards very well. It was a revelation when a champion's particular brand of incompetence is suddenly revealed.

McLarnin, however, was perfectly familiar with the "stick and move" strategy, and he had used it himself against hard punchers. Jim waited and struck Tony whenever he had the opportunity. This pattern continued in the 5th round which Tony managed to win with a flurry of punches at the finish. Between rounds, Foster told Jim that there was no need to let Canzoneri off the hook. "Press him." In the 6th, Jim moved aggressively after Tony with lefts at every opportunity, repeatedly catching him with punches to the face. The press wrote that Canzoneri's face seemed to be coming apart at the seams. He must have shed a bucket of blood. Only Tony's superb conditioning and reflex skill and fighting heart carried him through. Jim's fight was won by round seven. The writers spoke of Jim being "charitable" in rounds 7, 8, 9, and 10. He stood a distance away and maintained command with a variety of jabs and hooks.

"I was too strong for him, but he was a great little fighter." Jim received the unanimous decision, but Canzoneri received a great round of applause for his courageous stand. Tony could hardly see, and stumbled as he left the ring. At the finish, Jim went toward Tony's corner and shook his blood-soaked gloves at his gallant foe in token of his appreciation of a brave man. Boxers have a deep fellow feeling for each other, which you notice when they meet. They will throw a few imaginary punches at each other, fake, make a face, and then clinch, grin, and slap each other on the back. Jim then turned his traditional victory handspring, and went home. I doubt that any welterweight from any era could have beaten McLarnin by much that night, not Joe Walcott, Jack Britton, Ray Robinson or Ray Leonard.

Jim beats Tony Canzoneri

D: The Last Hurrah
The Final Victory – Jim's triumph over Lou Ambers, the man who beat Henry Armstong, the only Triple Champ

McLarnin had one more fight, his last, and one of his greatest. If he couldn't get another shot at Barney Ross, the next best thing was to fight and beat the lightweight champ, Lou Ambers, who had just beaten Tony Canzoneri, and the amazing Henry Armstrong, who was to destroy Barney Ross. Jim finished a winner, and at the top of his form. He never got old in the ring and didn't get beaten by a younger man as they say happens to all champions. Jim's career is simply not like that of most fighters. He finished not as deadly as he had been, but his mastery of ring strategy and general skills were never better than in his last fight. How many fighters can have that said about them? You have to go to Leonard or Gans or Pep or Wilde or Jack Johnson to match the mastery of McLarnin in his last two fights. There you have two Blacks, a Jew, an Italian, an Englishman, and an Irishman – the cultural mosaic that the politically correct multiculturalists talk about and actually miss. The joy of boxing is the mixture of these great races, each with its own genius, physical excellence, and emotion.

The lightweight division had a new champion, the Italian American, Lou Ambers – Lou Dambrozzia), named for his hometown, "The Herkimer Hurricane". He had challenged Canzoneri, lost, then beaten Tony to become lightweight champ, and defended it successfully against Canzoneri. Then he lost a decision to the amazing Henry Armstrong, but came back to beat Armstrong decisively, fighting a shrewd fight against that non-stop human buzz-saw, uppercutting Henry as he charged in and closing both of Armstrong's eyes by the final round. When Armstrong said he thought he won, Ambers remarked, "How can he say that? Henry didn't even see the last two rounds." Ambers was superbly conditioned and a constant puncher. He was managed by the cool, shrewd, well-connected Al Weill, who later managed Rocky Marciano. Ambers covered his opponent with a hail of leather. Unlike Jim, Lou loved to fight. Years later, he remarked to a scribe, "Lord, it was fun. What great times. God, how I loved to fight! I miss it."

Ambers didn't seem a brilliant fighter like Robinson or Ali. But one just couldn't beat him, not even Armstrong, who was considered, until he met Lou, unbeatable. Armstrong held the featherweight, lightweight, and welterweight championships all at one time. Armstrong annihilated Barney Ross and nobody else ever did. Many experts call him the greatest fighter of all. I don't, but he's close. Ambers, however, blinded him and beat him. Like Dempsey and Marciano, Armstrong fought in a constant battle rage – Dempsey, at 190 pounds, nearly killed lean, hard Jess Willard at 250 lbs. Armstrong paid for his constant offence, he was nearly blind when he retired to become a minister. The Vikings went into battle this way – BERSERK. Graziano said he liked Tony Zale, his famous rival, but in the ring he wanted to kill him, "No, I had to kill him."

So they matched Jim with the man who had beaten Armstrong in his last fight. The winner would be in line for a shot at Ross's title. The wise boys made Jim a 7 to 5 favourite because they knew that given a good referee, Jim could take any lightweight, welterweight or middleweight of his day. There was one caveat, that Jim would have to win early, because Lou was younger. The press was impressed by Jim's punching power but Lou had a well-connected manager and a superb trainer, Whitey Bimstein. These great trainers, Bimstein, Charley Goldman, Jack Blackburn, Eddie Futch, Angelo Dundee make the difference in a great fighter, but Foster was as good as any. They all see details others miss. There was a big drawing of Jim in The Province and a photo of "old" Jim, well-dressed in a light California suit. The press said that he was over 25 and so would tire early. One is constantly amused that writers thought that as Jim was 27, he must be out of shape. Generalizing on their own experience of sitting in the pub and exercising lightly if at all, they were out of shape. Correctly trained, your middle thirties should be your best years. The ancient Greeks expected their citizens to serve in the army, hand-to-hand fighting, from age 18 to 60. These Greeks trained daily all their lives. Some of the men who charged the Persians on the run at Marathon were in their fifties. The crack regiment, the "Silver Shields" of Phillip of Macedon, who went with Alexander to India and then fought after his death at the partition of his empire, were in their 60s and their officers were in their 70s. They fought hand-to-hand for their last battles. Fighting regularly had brought back Jim's reflexes. McLarnin gave Ambers a boxing lesson, slipping most of Lou's best punches almost contemptuously, had Lou almost out in round 6 and was hardly winded at the end of round 15. Everything forecasted about the fight was dead wrong. But the gamblers made money on the odds. The papers said, "Jim finds fountain of youth," and they ate crow. "After ten lopsided rounds, Ambers had a slashed eye and a heavy heart."

The pattern was set in round one. Lou came in aggressively but Jim kept him off with four hard lefts to the head while Lou missed his punches. Jim didn't have a single style that could be easily analysed. Jim often said you punch a boxer and box a puncher, but McLarnin was both. There is no single answer to such a fighter, especially if he has a good defence, as even the great Robinson didn't have. By round three, Jim seemed to be hitting Lou almost at will. When I sparred with Jim in his 70s, I could see that. Nobody had done that to Ambers for years. Eventually, Lou was knocked out by the wild and bizarre Lou Jenkins who loved to fight, drunk or sober. Jenkins was later a much-decorated Korean War hero and he said he enjoyed himself there also, drunk or sober. Jim said he couldn't understand it. "One good drink and I'd have trouble tying my shoes." Jim relied on fine timing, which alcohol destroys. Jenkins, Mickey Walker, and the great John L. Sullivan, however, liked a good stiff drink to warm them up. In the middle rounds, both boys had bloody noses, as both had landed hard punches. Lou sometimes roughed Jim across the ring. Lou was one tough Paisan. Round five was Ambers'. In round six, Lou pressed Jim, but Jim nailed him each time. He came in solidly so that Lou was dazed as he walked to his corner and looked as if he might be on the edge of going out. Under one eye, Ambers had a deep cut that his handlers worked on. There was a heated discussion in Lou's corner before round fifteen. He was told that he was far behind, so he came out punching. He threw two hard rights in a row and Jim caught him with an appalling right, just under Lou's heart. His face turned white, his breath stopped, and his jaw dropped open. He had been badly hurt. He didn't go down, but retreated, with his gloves high and elbows in tight to his body – as we were taught in college for ultimate defence. Jim stalked his wounded opponent, looking for a finishing blow. The final bell rang as Jim moved in for the kill in the final minute of his boxing career. The fighting career of Jimmy McLarnin, last of the great Irish born champions, B.C.'s only world champion boxer, and Canada's best, was over.

Jimmy's Last Fight, defeating Lou Ambers, Lightweight Champ

Jim's last two fights had been masterful, and his left, which he hadn't had to start with and of which he was so proud, had won them for him. Now it was ready for Barney Ross! "Lou made a gallant stand, but it was great victory for the Vancouver veteran," said the New York Times. "McLarnin in line for another fight with Ross." Jim had fought an intelligent fight against Ambers, taking no chances himself, keeping his chin tight behind his left shoulder. "Lou was a great fighter. He kept coming at me," said Jim to me. Jim's skills had gotten beyond his competitors, great as they were. Jim was now what Pop had dreamed for him. New York boxing fans held their breath in anticipation of what the perfected McLarnin could do now to Barney Ross, who had not looked that good beating Izzy Janazzio in his last defence. Unfortunately, the fourth fight was not to be. One suspects that McLarnin's new brilliance and return to his pre-championship form had not escaped Ross's managers. If they were going to take a chance on losing that lucrative welterweight championship with a guy like McLarnin, it was going to cost somebody a lot of money. When negotiations began, Pian and Winch demanded by far the largest percentage of the money, much more than Jim had taken as defending champion from Ross. This was despite the fact that McLarnin was still the better drawing card. McLarnin's non-title bouts with Canzoneri and Ambers were sell-outs. Foster would have taken the smaller purse, but not much smaller. The two camps continued to negotiate while papers reported and fans waited.

Pop began to get angry. "They want it all," he told Jim. "You'll be fighting for peanuts. We don't have to do that." Ross's side was not keen about fighting a rejuvenated McLarnin. They knew they were lucky to get out of those three fights with the edge. On Jim's side, Pop had checked the bank accounts and confirmed that Jim had about half a million dollars in the bank and Pop had over a quarter of a million. This was at the height of the Great Depression, when you could get a good breakfast for 50 cents, and a free smorgasbord lunch if you bought a ten cent beer.

"We don't have to listen to this stuff, Jim," said Pop. "Let's quit. We've got all the money we need. Why should you fight?" Does this sound like the greedy managers of popular fiction and film? "What do you say, Jim?"

"Well, O.K. but I'd still like to take that championship back. I know I can do it, Pop."

"What does it really matter, Jim? We've had it all," said Pop.

Pop had wanted to quit for a long time. Every time you step into a ring, you risk injury. Indeed, you do in any contact sport. These sports are wonderful and ridiculous. Now, Jim was getting used to the good life in California. Ross himself would have fought Joe Louis, but his managers were not keen. Asked how Jim was in the third fight, Barney said, "He was hell out there tonight!" After all that, Barney went on to fight the fearsome Japanese knights of Bushido in the South Pacific. That should be enough for any man.

So it was that the logical fight did not take place. It would have been like seeing Hector say goodbye to his son and go out to fight the terrible Achilles. "Blessed is the man who has seen such things before he goes into the hollow earth." My dad and I would have listened to it on the radio, but it never got beyond the planning stage.

So Jim retired to sunny California. Here, the famous fighter made business contacts and was welcome at Hollywood parties and sports reunions. He had a wide variety of friends, many of whom I enjoyed meeting. He often went to parties at Gables and Bogarts. Bogie asked him about tricks of boxing. He joined the expensive Lakeside golf club and played with his good pal, also from the Northwest, Bing Crosby. "Good old Bing," declared Jim, "he's sorely missed around here."

Jim's pal, Bing Crosby, in 1942

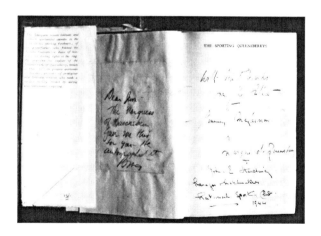

*Flyleaf of "The Sporting Queensberrys", given to Jimmy by
the Marquis of Queensberry; delivered by Bing Crosby*

He said he would have become a golf bum, for he loved it so much, so he went to work in a suit and tie as sales rep for the Dyer Plating Company. He taught a little boxing at boy's clubs, and did charitable work with boxers who had not had his talent or luck, and met once a week at the Golden State Boxing and Wrestling Club. He made a few investments and a bit of money in oil stocks and lost money in a machine parts business he bought after the war. During the war, he trained soldiers in the camp on Catalina Island. Gene Tunney interviewed him to head the combat training of the Marines, but was surprised to find that Jim was neither a Catholic nor a college graduate, for talking to Jim he had assumed both, and so withdrew his offer. Jim was disappointed and put off about Tunney.

Jim and Lil raised a family – Ellen, Jean, Nancy, and James – and sent them all to college. The old magician, Pop Foster, lived close by, in North Hollywood. Just like in the old fairy tales, Jim had kept the faith with the magician and had become the only kind of a fighter worth being – a champion of the world. "Everything that old man told me came true." They bought a big Spanish style house in Glendale. Jim was elected to the Boxing Hall of Fame and was given a fine ring from there. So an extremely happy end of one of the most remarkable careers in sports finished near Hollywood, where dreams come true: "and their young men shall dream dreams and their old men will see visions."

The McLarnin Family: Ellen, Jimmy, Lillian, Nancy, and Jean. James Junior was not yet born.

Chapter 31
Talking with Jim about his career and the famous Ross fights

And just so, Jim finished talking to me about his fighting career, ending with his splendid victory over the great, difficult, and resourceful Lou Ambers. What a way to finish, and to lead into his successful family and social life.

We sat in Jim's big front room in front of the tall fireplace. He sat forward to relate and relive the stories. One evening, after Jim and I had been sparring, he illustrated how he had beaten an awkward opponent, I think, Corbett. I tried to defend myself in textbook style. Being winded, I sat down at Jim's piano. He said, "We always had a piano. Lilian could play nicely." I began to play an old favourite one doesn't hear anymore, *When You were Sweet Sixteen*. Jim took it up, singing acceptably. "It was Pop's favourite song. Let's have it again. It reminded him of a girl from his youth." Jim and I sang it again, nearly in tears and laughing at ourselves for two sentimental Irish fools, and drank to Pop. Pop's spirit came down while we sang his song and listened, "I loved you as I never loved before... when you were sweet sixteen." Pop never married; his boxers were the boys he never had – especially Jimmy, his friend's son. I played *Annie Laurie* but Jim kept singing *Sweet Sixteen*. We poured ourselves a drink. "Well, I need one, now that Lil has gone. I'm glad you're here." So I had done something for my hero.

At breakfast next morning, we continued our conversation from the previous night. I asked, "Ambers was your last fight, Jim?"

"Well," said Jim, grinning, "I did have one fight after the Ambers fight. I was on the golf course with a gang when I was about 65 when one of them, a big guy who had done some boxing, about 185 pounds, a small heavy-weight, said, "You don't look much like a champ to me, and suddenly hit me full force on the side of the head as hard as he could and I went down on the grass. If it had been the asphalt, I wouldn't have gotten up. But I stood up, faked a right, and put all my 150 pounds into a left hook which broke his jaw. I chased him and threw my clubs at him until Crosby grabbed me. I had to go to the hospital, my hand was so cut. If you've been champ, some nut wants to say he put you down."

Jim and I alked about the greatest heavyweights: Dempsey, Louis, Corbett, Marciano, Ali.

We talked again of Barney Ross. Red Smith wrote in his obituary of Barney Ross that he was a "peaceful man who had fought ever since those two punks murdered his father in his store and finished his life like the champion he was." Barney's mom came to all his fights, wishing that his dad could be there. Jim's dad was at his famous Ross fights in Madison Square Garden in New York. Jim's dad lived to be 96 and so did Jim.

Barney was never stopped or knocked out, and only McLarnin put him down once. Just so, Jimmy was never knocked out and only stopped once, on cuts. Both men finished all fights on their feet.

Finale : Round Fifteen

Really true stories never end. They begin again. Open Melville's *Moby Dick*. Read the first page, "Call me Ishmael". Even Stevenson's *Treasure Island*, "I remember him as if it were yesterday" and there comes the old pirate with his sea chest and the treasure map to the Admiral Benbow Inn. Try Sam Putnam's translation of Cervantes' – now there's a great old wounded warrior and hero of the Christian victory over the Moslem fleet at Lepanto – *Don Quixote*. "In a village of La Mancha, the name of which I have no desire to recall, there lived not so long ago, one of those gentlemen who always have a lance in the rack, an ancient buckler, a skinny nag, and a greyhound for the chase," -- and you, and "the knight of the sorrowful countenance", and good Sancho Panza, set off again on the incredible quest and the impossible dream. We have participated in their dreams and deeds and they have become part of ours, and our world and our souls have been enlarged.

As I talked to Jim, I set off again on that perilous quest and impossible dream, with the young hero and the old magician to beat the world and its greatest champions. Charles "Pop" Foster, the archetypal magician, with a squint and a limp, and arcane knowledge suddenly appears and says, "Come with me, be brave and have faith, and I will give you riches and the championship of the world."

In his 80s, Jim still looked amazed when he reflected. Jim said again, "Everything that old man told me came true." For me, they set off again in quest of the impossible dream, an old half blind man, and a boy not 5 feet tall. It was impossible and they were mad.

So the summer of Jimmy McLarnin came to an end for me. I woke up the next morning and I could hear Jim on his bench in his back yard, whistling for some of the birds who were his friends, and about whom he liked to tell me – what a gentle and fearsome man. He had been up since 5 or so, "I never got over my training," he says, grinning. What a constitution he was born with. Monica made breakfast and I could see that Jim was going to miss having "family" in his big house. I suggested one for the road. "Now is the hour," said Jim and poured a stiff vodka into our orange juice.

We raised our glasses and I said, "Here's to the times when I was a boy, and McLarnin ruled the world."

"I'll drink to that," said Jim.

Jim helped us leave, carrying Monica's luggage out, as he had carried it in. "Come again and stay a while," Jim said as he stood beside the car.

"Phone us when you and Billy get in the mood. If you're up visiting your family, come over for dinner."

"Keep that left up, champ, and your fanny off the canvas," said Jim. Then I backed down Jim's long narrow driveway slowly, which Jim did at speed, and onto the shaded street. I shouted goodbye.

As we drove away, I looked back and could see Jim standing in his long driveway, looking wistfully up into the sky. Our weeks of talk had called back those ghosts from the past. To me, he looked like the hero Roland as he stands alone in the pass of Roncevalles through the Pyrannes after all the Franks have fallen to the Saracen ambush, and he winds his horn to call back the great king Charlemange for vengeance on the infidel. I wish we could have blown back Pop from the realms of air and darkness. But we had called back the ghosts to that incomparable paladin from the golden age of boxers, and the old champion stood alone, looking up into the blue California sky, looking for Pop and Lil, and Sam and Mary McLarnin, hearing Jimmy Walker and those tumultuous crowds, and seeing the flashing fists of a hundred hard and skilful warriors that he had fought, and fifteen of them champions, yes champions, of the world: LaBarba, Villa, Taylor, Fields, Kaplan, Mandell, Singer, Fuller, Leonard, Thompson, Brouillard, Corbett, Barney Ross, Canzoneri, and Ambers, and beaten them all. Now they are all dead. There was no one left to tell, in person, of their greatness but McLarnin, the toughest of them. Jim stood alone in his driveway like Ishmael from *Moby Dick*, "And I only am escaped alone to tell thee."

What battles he had told me of! Farewell, great warrior! Ave atque vale. Farewell, hero of my father and my childhood and thousands of other men of those days. Farewell, peerless champion without fear and beyond reproach, "bon chevalier, sans puer et sans reproche".

Jimmy McLarnin spent his last years close to his children in Washington State. He died at age 96 and is interred at the Forest Lawn Cemetery, close to his home in Glendale, California.

There is the story of our hero for my father and the men and boys of his generation whose lives were made larger by Jimmy's fearsome battles and for all the guys down in East Vancouver and Los Angeles who remember Jim's glory. But, truly, the story should be more for all our grandchildren, that they may know that all heroes and magicians are not just in storybooks. These are not merely old forgotten far off things and battles long ago. They are the stuff of the legends of our country and our humanity, and our grandchildren must know that once upon a time, not so long ago, there lived by the shores of this Pacific Ocean, yes, right here – giants! They did great deeds. Let us set off again on that fearsome quest with our indomitable champions, Foster and McLarnin, for their deeds are beyond the telling, yes, far beyond my telling of them. But in the next world, I will introduce him to my wonderful father, Ernie Corry, to whom I owe my introduction, while listening to the fights, to my hero, Jimmy McLarnin.

Tanto nomini
Nullum par Eloqium
"Such names are beyond my ability to praise"

More stories, more sparring. Jimmy and Des, Victoria, 1991

A fine old man reflects on his illustrious career

Record of Jimmy McLarnin

1908 – December 19, born Inchacore, Ireland. Weight 112 to 150 lbs. Height 5 feet 7 and a half inches. Manager Charles "Pop" Foster.

"Really I had well over 100 fights. They're not all recorded. None of my fights in Nanaimo, for instance, are recorded." McLarnin.

1923 – Vancouver, George Ainsworth w 4, Young Frye w 4, Red Peterson w 4, Ainsworth w 4, Mickey Gill w 4, Hector McDonald w 4, Young Wallace w 4, Peterson w 4, Wallace w 4, Mickey Gill w 6.

1924 – Frankie Sands, Oakland w 4, Eddie Collins KO 3, Joe Conde, San Francisco, KO 3, Sands w 4, Sammy Lee, Oakland, w 4, Jimmy Griffiths TKO 2, Frankie Grandetta w 4, Johnny Lightener w 4, Joe Dillon w 4, J. Griffiths, Sacramento w 4, Abe Gorden KO 2, Benny Diaz, Vernon w 4, Frankie Dolan w 4, Young Nationalista w 4, Fidel LaBarba w 4, Labarba d 4, Memphis, Pal Moore d 4

1925 – La Barba, Vernon, w 10, Teddy Silva w 10, Young Farrell, L.A., w 6, Eddie Rammies, San Francisco, w 6, Bud Taylor, Vernon, L 10, July 4, Pancho Villa, flyweight champ , Oakland, w 10, Mickey Gill, w 10, Jackie Fields L.A. KO 2, Dec 8, Vernon, Bud Taylor, bantamweight champ wf 2.

1926 – Tayor L 10, Joey Sangor, L.A., KO 3, Johnny Farr L10, Sammy Glick w 10, Doc Snell, Hollywood, L 10

1927 – Tommy Cello, San Fran, d 10, Cello, L.A., w 10, Freeman Black, San Diego KO 2, Johnny Lamar, Hollywood, w 10, Lope Tonorio, w 10, Charlie McBride, San Diego, KO 2, Don "Terror" Long, KO 3, Oct 18, Louis "Kid" Kaplan, featherweight champ, Chicago, KO 8, Billy Wallace, Detroit, w 10

1928 – Sid Terris, New York, Madison Square, KO 1; May 21 New York for lightweight championship, Sammy Mandell, L 15, Phil McGraw N.Y. KO 1, Packey O' Gattey, Detroit w 3, Stanislaus Loayza, KO 4, Nov 30, Ray Miller, TKOed by 8

1929 – Joe Glick, NY, w 10, Glick KO 2, Mar 22 Ray Miller NY w 10, Sgt. Sammy Baker KO 1, Nov 4, Sammy Mandell, lightweight champ, Chicago, W 10, Ruby Goldstein, NY, KO 2

1930 – Mar 1, Sammy Mandell, lightweight champ, Chicago, w10, Mar 28, Yg Jack Thompson NY w 10, Sept 11 Al Singer NY KO 3, Nov 21 Billy Petrolle NY L 10.

1931 – May 27, Petrolle NY w 10, Aug 20, Petrolle NY w 10.

1932 – Aug 4 Lou Brouillard, middleweight champ, NY, L 10, Oct 7 Benny Leonard NY TKO 6, Dec 16, Sammy Fuller, junior welterweight champ, KO 8.

1933 – May 29 Young Corbett III, LA, (McLarnin won world welterweight championship) KO 1.

1934 – May 28 Barney Ross, Long Island City L 15 (McLarnin lost welterweight title), Sept 17 Barney Ross, LIC, w 15, (McLarnin regained welterweight championship).

1935 – May 28, Barney Ross, L 15 (McLarnin lost welterweight championship).

1936 – May 8, Tony Canzoneri, NY, L 10, Oct 5, Canzoneri, NY, w 10, Nov 20, Lou Ambers, NY, w 10

Summary:

Fights – 77
Knock-outs – 20
Won by Decision – 42
Won on a Foul – 1
Draw – 2
Lost by Decision – 10
Lost on a Foul – 0
Technical Knock-outs – 1

About the Author

Des Corry has had a lifelong involvement in academics and athletics. As a small boy, he shared his dad's love of boxing by listening to McLarnin's fights on the radio. In his teens, he swam for the Victoria Swim Club. At Victoria College, he played basketball for the Vikes. While earning his B.A. at UBC, he boxed for his fraternity. During the 36 years he taught English, he played basketball, rugby, and lacrosse, coached basketball and wrestling, and attained an M.A. at Western Washington University. Most important, he has sparred with a boxer and a gentleman, Jimmy McLarnin.

CPSIA information can be obtained at www.ICGtesting.com
Printed in the USA
LVOW08s0000230714

395361LV00001B/47/P

9 781460 242438